# How to Read a Talmudic Story

By Jeffrey L. Rubenstein

ALSO BY JEFFREY L. RUBENSTEIN

*The History of Sukkot in the Second Temple and Rabbinic Periods* (Scholars Press, 1995)

*Talmudic Stories: Narrative Art, Composition, and Culture* (Johns Hopkins University Press, 1999)

*Rabbinic Stories* (Paulist Press, 2002)

*The Culture of the Babylonian Talmud* (Johns Hopkins University Press, 2003)

*Stories of the Babylonian Talmud* (Johns Hopkins University Press, 2010)

*The Land of Truth: Talmud Tales, Timeless Teachings* (Jewish Publication Society and University of Nebraska Press, 2018)

# HOW TO READ A TALMUDIC STORY

By Jeffrey L. Rubenstein

HADAR PRESS
New York

Hadar Press is supported in part by the Levine Library
in memory of Rabbi Jonathan D. Levine, *z"l*, a lover of Jewish books.



FIRST EDITION

Library of Congress Control Number: 2025935377



Designed by Rachel Jackson | binahdesign.com

Cover design by Dov Abramson, Studio Dov Abramson, Jerusalem
Cover art by David Goldstein

*In memory of my mother, Dr. Denise Rubenstein*

לזכר נשמת אמי מורתי דינה בת שרגא וחיה זירה

# Contents

# ACKNOWLEDGMENTS

I WOULD LIKE TO thank the many people who have contributed to this book.

New York University, where I have taught for over 30 years, continues to be a wonderful scholarly environment and academic home. I thank the administration, including President Linda G. Mills, Provost Gigi Dopico, Dean Antonio Merlo, and Dean Una Chaudhuri, for their constant support. I am also grateful to my colleagues in the Department of Hebrew and Judaic Studies for creating such a stimulating intellectual space and for their encouragement and collegiality.

My thanks to Dr. Robert Eisen, Mr. Larry Solomon, Mr. Hanokh Messner, Dr. Barry Holtz, Rabbi Kenneth Berger, and Rabbi Yitzchak Blau for reading through chapters and drafts, for providing helpful suggestions and comments, and for calling attention to errors.

I am grateful to Rabbi Shai Held, who first suggested that I approach Hadar Press about publishing this book, and to all of the leadership and staff of the Hadar Institute who have helped make it a reality. My deep thanks to Elisheva Urbas, who painstakingly and thoughtfully edited the book, and who is responsible not only for polishing the prose but also for her many suggestions regarding the content, and for always prodding me to think more deeply about values and spiritual meaning. The book is far better due to her efforts. Thanks also to Michelle Kwitkin for the excellent copyediting, to Rachel Jackson for creating the interior design, to Dov Abramson of Studio Dov Abramson for the cover design, and to David Goldstein for the beautiful calligraphy.

I thank my extended family for all their devotion and support over the years. I am especially grateful to my wife, Dr. Mishaela Rubin, and children, Ayelet, Maya, Adam, and Noah, for their good humor, excellent company, relentless curiosity, laughter and jokes, dedication to learning Torah, unwavering love, and always reminding me what really matters in life.

This book is dedicated to my mother, Dr. Denise Rubenstein, who passed away on January 10, 2024. Born in Pretoria, South Africa, my mother studied English literature before entering medical school in 1953 at the University of Witwatersrand, Johannesburg, one of eight women in a class of 100. She practiced pediatrics and dermatology in South Africa and Chicago for over three decades. One of my fondest memories is my mother reading Dickens and other classics to me every afternoon on our living room couch when I was young, and I believe her passion for literature was crucial to the development of my academic interests. She was a devoted sister, daughter, wife, mother, and grandmother. May her memory be for a blessing. יהא זכרה ברוך.

Jeffrey L. Rubenstein
OCTOBER 1, 2024 · 28 ELUL 5784

# INTRODUCTION

**תלמוד בבלי, כתובות סז ע״ב**

[A] מר עוקבא הוה עניא בשיבבותיה דהוה רגיל כל יומא דשדי ליה ארבעה זוזי בצינורא דדשא.

[B] יום אחד אמר: איזיל איחזי מאן קעביד בי ההוא טיבותא. ההוא יומא נגהא ליה למר עוקבא לבי מדרשא אתיא דביתהו בהדיה. כיון דחזיוה דקא מצלי ליה לדשא נפק בתרייהו.

[C] רהוט מקמיה עיילי להוא אתונא דהוה גרופה נורא. הוה קא מיקליין כרעיה דמר עוקבא. אמרה ליה דביתהו: שקול כרעיך אותיב אכרעאי. חלש דעתיה. אמרה ליה: אנא שכיחנא בגויה דביתא ומקרבא אהנייתי.

**Talmud Bavli, Ketubot 67b**

[A] Mar Ukba—there was a poor man in his neighborhood into whose door-socket he used to place four *zuz* every day.

[B] One day [the poor man] thought, "I will go and see who does me this kindness." On that day [it happened] that Mar Ukba was late at the house of study and his wife was coming home with him. As soon as [the poor man] saw them moving the door he went out after them.

[C] They ran away from him and entered into an oven from which the fire had just been swept. Mar Ukba's feet were burning. His wife said to him, "Raise your feet and put them on top of my feet." He became distressed. She said to him, "I am usually at home and my benefactions are direct."

This talmudic story is not at all easy to understand. The story is extremely terse, even frustratingly so, providing only the minimum information necessary for the plot, and requires the audience to fill in narrative gaps. We learn that the rabbinic sage, Mar Ukba, supported a poor man with a charitable gift each day.[1] We don't know the exact value of the *zuz*, which fluctuated during the talmudic era, but a daily donation of four *zuz* would have amounted to a very generous sum over the course of a year. Mar Ukba placed the coins in the door-socket, rather than give them to the poor man directly, because he wished to keep his identity hidden. The story does not explain why the rabbi values anonymity so highly, but the audience would readily understand that he wishes to spare the recipient the embarrassment involved in taking a hand-out. Many talmudic sources warn against shaming others, even equating it with bloodshed, and considering it among the most severe transgressions. Mar Ukba's tactic has evidently succeeded—the poor man has yet to discover the identity of his benefactor. However, this man does not seem concerned about the shame he might experience at such an encounter and resolves to go out of his way to learn the source of the donations [B]. He may have remained at home throughout the day rather than departed for work or to the market, waiting and listening for a sound at the door, or set up a chair directly inside the doorway to "ambush" his patron.

On that very day Mar Ukba happened to stay later than usual learning Torah in the house of study, which apparently prompted his wife to retrieve him and escort him home. For that reason the rabbi was accompanied by his wife when he made his way to the recipient's house for the daily charity deposit—evidently he dropped off the money on his way home. The door and socket, into which the bolt slides to secure the lock, are important symbols of separation, representing the divide between Mar Ukba and the poor man, a barrier that the rabbi believes must not be breached.[2] Thresholds are liminal spaces, between and betwixt two domains, and in literature often function as sites of transitions or danger. Unbeknownst to Mar Ukba, the peril he fears lurks on the other side of the threshold, just

1 On this story, see Admiel Kosman, "A Talmudic Detective," "Woman's Spiritual Place," and "On the Use of the Protagonist's Name"; Jennifer Nadler, "Mar Ukba in the Fiery Furnace"; and Moshe Simon-Shoshan, "A Doorway of Their Own," 97–106.

2 Some interpreters understand the socket to be the hole in the ground at the threshold in which the hinge of the door rotates; see Rashi, Ketubot 67b, *s.v. tzinora*.

behind the closed door, ready to cross over and issue forth, threatening to disrupt the delicate balance.

Upon perceiving the door swing as the mysterious giver places the money in the socket, the poor man moves to exit his house in order to see who provides the alms. Mar Ukba, confronting the very situation he had endeavored to avoid, turns on his heels and flees in a desperate effort to remain anonymous, with his wife dutifully following along [c]. They jump into an oven to hide—ovens in talmudic times were large and pyramid-shaped, made of clay, stationed outside in the yard, with a large aperture at the top or on one side. Alas, this oven had just been used and although the ashes had been swept out, the bottom of the oven was still hot, or perhaps a few fiery embers remained there. Mar Ukba's feet naturally begin to burn, but his wife's feet unnaturally and surprisingly do not, and she bids her husband place his feet upon hers to protect them from the scorching floor. Her miraculous invulnerability to this harm is a sign of, and reward for, her outstanding piety. But her immunity to harm distresses Mar Ukba, who suddenly realizes that she ranks above him on the holiness scale, despite his charitable exertions, pursued each and every day, and in what he believes to be the optimal, anonymous, way. The wife explains that her superiority in this respect is because she generally stays at home throughout the day and gives charity directly to beggars who come to her door. These personal encounters with the needy, where she undoubtedly offers compassionate and encouraging words together with alms, are apparently acts of even greater virtue than those of her husband.

What does this storyteller wish to teach his audience? Certainly Mar Ukba's practice serves as an exemplary model of piety. The rabbi provides constant, ongoing support that a needy individual can count on, clearly a superior type of charity to a one-time donation that simply tides the recipient over until those funds are exhausted. Mar Ukba's method of giving also comports with the high rabbinic value of preserving the dignity of others. As with many talmudic stories, the rabbinic protagonist serves as role model for correct legal observance or ethical behavior. Yet the end of the story complicates this understanding, for it turns out that Mar Ukba's wife is the true hero(ine) of the tale. The unnamed wife merits the supernatural protection that saves Mar Ukba, despite her giving alms in the conventional manner when indigents knock on her door. Should we infer that Mar Ukba's noble aspiration for anonymity is not as necessary as he believes? Or that to avoid shaming others in general is of critical importance, but other considerations take precedence in the context of charitable donations? Sympathy and emotional support, kind words from another human being, may be of even more value to those in desperate circumstances than material aid. Or perhaps the storyteller teaches that Mar Ukba, while having his heart in the right place, took the ideal of anonymous giving to an extreme: if a poor man wishes to know the source of the largesse and does not worry about the potential embarrassment, then why should the donor concern himself with this problem? Some poor, after all, may find it meaningful to thank their benefactors personally, to tell them how important the funds are to their survival, perhaps offering tokens of gratitude like a thank you note.[3] The purpose of giving anonymously is to protect the dignity of the poor—it is not an end in and of itself—and this poor man clearly does not value that protection. The comic image of a rabbi fleeing a poor man's residence in a panic, clambering into an oven to hide, and nearly burning himself to death in the process may be intended as ridicule of Mar Ukba's exaggerated piety. Or again, should we understand that Mar Ukba's regular and methodical giving has become too routine, something to check off his list of daily duties, divorced from any emotional and personal connection with a suffering human being?

The story involves three houses—the house of study, the poor man's house, and Mar Ukba's house—and we might consider the significance of each and the relationship among them as we ponder these questions. Indeed, if the fact that Mar Ukba tarried in the house of study did not contribute something to the story's meaning, the storyteller need not have mentioned it at all. He could have told very much the same story without disclosing Mar Ukba's whereabouts before arriving at the poor man's house, or had him come from the market or elsewhere. The house of study is the domain of the rabbinic elite, where Mar Ukba and his colleagues immerse themselves in the study of Torah. It contrasts with both the house of the poor man and the rabbi's own house, which is in fact the domain of his wife: she occupies their private residence while Mar Ukba spends his days at the rabbinic school. At the house of study Mar Ukba has learned the rabbinic laws of charity and the ideal methods of giving, and for that reason he flees from the poor man's house. Yet the wife's charity is very much a function of the personal encounters that take place at her house,

---

3 The importance of this personal experience is emphasized by two references to sight: the poor man's interior monologue, "I will go and *see* who does me this kindness," and the narrator's acknowledgement that he "*saw* them moving the door."

that can only take place at one's house where the poor come knocking at the door. Are we to conclude that Mar Ukba's Torah-knowledge works better in theory than in practice, that the rabbinic teachings about charity stand in tension with the lived reality that those excluded from the study house spontaneously intuit? Or has Mar Ukba misunderstood these teachings and failed to apply them correctly?

Modern analogies are often tricky, but one might think about two types of charitable endeavors today in order to attain a perspective on the story. How would we compare an individual who writes checks and sends money to charitable causes with someone who volunteers in food pantries or walks the streets offering meals to the homeless? No doubt both are praiseworthy, but we might consider that direct involvement does more to shape character and help the giver become a more virtuous and generous person, especially if writing out checks becomes a matter of routine.

Together with its complex message, this story has several characteristics typical of talmudic stories. It includes a supernatural or miraculous element (from our point of view), namely the wife's immunity from burning, which provides a valuable clue as to where the storyteller's sympathies lie. The ending involves a reversal of expectations, as the audience assumes that Mar Ukba's outstanding piety, together with his involvement in Torah study, should bestow the miraculous protection upon him, rather than upon his unnamed and otherwise unknown wife. The story begins with the sage's name to clarify from the outset who the story is about, but this produces an awkward syntax in the original Aramaic, replicated here in the translation. The story's extreme terseness leaves us wishing to know much more. For example, the storyteller tells us neither the name of the poor man nor of Mar Ukba's wife, nor offers the slightest description of them or their surroundings. We don't know why he became poor, nor how long Mar Ukba has supported him in this way. That Mar Ukba stays late at the house of study serves to explain why his wife accompanied him home that day. But we naturally wonder: Did he often get lost in his studies such that she would go to escort him home at dinnertime, as I suggested above? Or was she out visiting her sister or shopping late in the afternoon and stopped by the house of study before returning home on the off chance her husband was still there? The wife's explanation, "My benefactions are direct" (מקרבא אהנייתי), in particular, deserves more elucidation. The Aramaic phrase is awkward, and can also be translated as, "My benefits are immediate." Does she mean that the quality of her charity surpasses that of her husband because she provides food, which is of immediate benefit, rather than money? Or is it that she also expresses empathy and encouraging words, and this personal interaction, the emotional support, is more important to the recipients than the economic assistance? Finally, the name Mar Ukba may be symbolic, and relate to the themes of the story. "Ukba" shares the same triliteral Hebrew root with the words for "heel," ע-ק-ב/*a-k-b*, as in the patriarch Jacob/Yaakov's name (see Genesis 25:26), and for "footsteps," alluding to the role that feet play in the story.

~

This book is about how to read a talmudic story. The Babylonian Talmud ("the Bavli," edited ca. 700 CE), the great compendium of Jewish tradition, though celebrated for its law and legal discussions (*halakhah*), also contains a great deal of non-legal material (*aggadah*), including prayers, sayings, biblical interpretations, historical memories, poems, and more. In many respects the Talmud should be considered less a legal textbook than an anthology of traditions that includes diverse sources of varied genres. The Talmud is also a vast treasury of many hundreds of stories. Still more stories can be found in other compilations that together with the Talmud comprise the world of rabbinic literature, compiled by the rabbis in late antiquity (200–700 CE). These compilations include the Mishnah, the earliest rabbinic collection of law (edited ca. 200 CE); the Talmud Yerushalmi or Jerusalem Talmud, the Babylonian Talmud's complement from the Land of Israel (edited ca. 400 CE); and many works of midrash or rabbinic biblical interpretation (200–700 CE). (In this book, "Talmud" refers to the Babylonian Talmud.)

Talmudic stories provide a wonderful entry into the world of rabbinic Judaism and to the ideas, values, struggles, beliefs, and hopes of the talmudic rabbis. In the wake of the destruction of the Jerusalem Temple in 70 CE, the rabbis adapted the Judaism of the previous eras to the new reality, creating the essential form of Judaism that continues to the present day. The rabbis did not leave us historical writings, theological treatises, autobiographical diaries, or ethical works. They fashioned a detailed, elaborate, wide-ranging system of law, *halakhah*, by which to organize our lives, and they told stories—stories to justify and ground that legal project; stories to grapple with tensions and problems; stories to explain their origins, background, and goals; stories to address recurring challenges of religious life. Through stories the rabbis tell us about who they are, what they believe, how to live life, and how to fit into the larger society.

The rabbinic religious imagination is expressed—and internalized—through stories, which provide a means to connect to matters of morality, justice, and spirituality, to issues of ultimate concern. Reading and absorbing stories enriches our ordinary experiences with depth and significance too. Rabbinic stories encourage us to rethink our relationships with ourselves, with our families, with others, and with the wider world. They provide novel frameworks to structure and deepen our commitments and responsibilities. Those wishing to understand rabbinic Judaism and to access its traditions, beliefs, concepts, and ideas will benefit tremendously from learning its stories and how to read them.

Talmudic stories typically take the form of brief biographical anecdotes recounting an episode of the lives and deeds of a rabbi or of several rabbis—the same rabbis whose legal traditions are found throughout the Talmud. These stories serve as legal precedents, relating how a certain rabbi behaved on Shabbat, formulated a prayer, carried out business, or observed another aspect of Jewish law. Some stories deal with the rabbis' quest to learn Torah, the difficulties in mastering the great quantity of tradition, and their interactions with fellow students, colleagues, and teachers in rabbinic schools and academies. Other stories engage issues related to the rabbis' relationships with their wives, families, government officials, aristocrats, and other figures they encountered. A number of stories deal with historical figures such as Alexander the Great, Roman emperors, and Persian kings. However, since most of these stories involve the interaction of that important non-Jewish figure with a leading rabbi, they can also be classified as biographical anecdotes.[4]

Although talmudic stories tell of biographical events, they are not biographical sources in our contemporary sense of "biography," but closer to what we would call fiction. That is, while the stories appear to be reports of events that happened (such as Mar Ukba giving charity), they should be understood as didactic fiction—noting that our literary genres such as "fiction," "biography," and "history" did not exist in the same way in antiquity. The rabbis were not interested in the events of the past out of a dispassionate commitment to the objective historical truth. Nor, for that matter, were just about any premodern peoples. Our contemporary ideas

---

4 These stories are sometimes called "sage stories" to distinguish them from rabbinic retellings of biblical narratives. Stories of this second type are called "exegetical narratives" because they derive in part from rabbinic biblical interpretation. They require separate discussion and are not treated in this book.

about biography and history as faithful records of what actually happened, or as the most accurate reconstructions that we can achieve on the basis of limited evidence, are modern notions. Many talmudic stories have a historical or biographical kernel, but to identify the precise contours of that kernel and to separate it from the non-historical embellishments is generally not possible. In any case, such an approach misses the point of the rabbinic storytellers, just as asking whether the cherry tree that George Washington confessed to his father that he had cut down was a black cherry tree or a fire cherry tree, and whether it happened at age twelve or sixteen. The rabbis told stories to model behaviors, transmit messages, teach values, and grapple with tensions they faced in the different dimensions of their lives. They reworked and revised stories they had received from earlier generations for their own purposes, changing the plots and characters where they deemed it necessary to do so. They sought to communicate truths through the stories they told, but these truths were not historical-biographical reports of past events, but truths about values, beliefs, practices, religious commitments, and how one ought to live life. The storytellers endeavored to portray the sages they featured in their stories as role models, generally positive but occasionally negative, as we learn as much from their failures and mistakes as from their great deeds and successes.

Because so many of the tools that the sages used to produce talmudic stories are what we could call literary methods, the most productive method for studying these stories is close reading based on literary analysis. This method combines analysis of the narrative art—the structure, figurative language, metaphors, wordplay, repetitions, irony, and other literary features—with attention to the content, namely the main themes and motifs. What meanings did the storytellers wish to convey to their audience and how did they convey them? As with other types of imaginative and artistic literature, the goal is not to get behind the text to a putative historical reality (what street did Mar Ukba actually live on? or even, did these events actually take place as described?), but to understand the text and the narrative world as constructed by the storytellers. Only in this way can the complex messages and nuanced perspectives of talmudic stories be appreciated.

This type of literary analysis is commonly applied to poetry, short stories, novels, and other genres of fiction, and should be familiar to students of literature. We all have some experience reading and interpreting stories, poems, and other texts. For this reason talmudic stories are relatively accessible to readers who have limited familiarity with rabbinic literature. Yet talmudic stories, as a component of the Talmud and integrated within the flow of rabbinic discourse, share some specific features with talmudic legal passages and rabbinic literature more broadly. Talmudic stories frequently include biblical verses, which are sometimes used to construct lines of the characters' dialogue, in many cases accompanied by formal midrashic interpretations. The context of talmudic stories is also important, as many stories should be understood in relation to the legal discussions with which they are juxtaposed. Some talmudic stories appear in a series of stories or in a larger literary unit, and these contexts too can be crucial to their interpretation. And like any particular corpus of literature, the Talmud contains specific symbols, literary conventions, technical terms, allusions, and locutions, which also appear in its stories and must be appreciated to comprehend the stories' meanings. These particular characteristics render some aspects of talmudic stories difficult to fully understand and appreciate for those not familiar with the Talmud and rabbinic literature. Even for those with more extensive background but who have not been exposed to contemporary modes of Talmud study, literary analysis is an alternative approach that has the potential to add new dimensions to their understanding of the text. In this respect talmudic stories are no different from the tragedies of Sophocles, dramas of Shakespeare, novels of Jane Austen, or poetry of William Blake. Anyone can read these literary texts, understand them at a certain level, appreciate some aspects of their art, and gain some insight as to their meanings. At the same time, the more we know about the genres of those works and about the world and concerns of the people who wrote them and encountered them in their own times and places, the more we can appreciate them in all their complexity and nuance. Talmudic stories offer us a window into the rabbinic religious imagination, and provide a rich source of meaning for those of us reading Torah as part of our engagement with Jewish tradition.

The Talmud is a form of oral literature, and many of the literary aspects of talmudic stories share features that characterize oral literature the world over. The Talmud, together with the Mishnah and midrashic texts, comprise the "Oral Torah" (תורה שבעל פה/*torah she-be'al peh*) that complements the Bible, "the Written Torah" (תורה שבכתב/*torah she-bikhtav*). These rabbinic texts were learned, taught, and transmitted orally until well into the Middle Ages, when they were written down and, with the advent of the printing press in the late fifteenth and sixteenth centuries, printed. Now we encounter the stories in written form, as readers learning how to make sense of a literary text (hence the title: "How to Read a Talmudic Story"). But it is always important to remember that the original audience were "listeners" who heard the story recited by a storyteller or fellow sage and then committed it to memory themselves. Oral stories are extremely terse to facilitate memorization, with no elaborate descriptions or digressions from the main plot. They often have clearly defined structures and verbal repetitions, which also make them easier to commit to memory. Talmudic stories, like much oral literature, make copious use of wordplays and figurative language that registers on an audience listening attentively to the sounds articulated by a storyteller. Many of these features also characterize folktales, which also originally were transmitted orally, so talmudic stories and folklore have much in common.

The goal of this book is to provide a guide for the process of reading and studying a talmudic story by spelling out the steps involved in a comprehensive analysis. That analysis, in turn, should enable us to appreciate the beauty and complexity of the stories and to discover spiritual insights and religious values. Each chapter highlights an important literary characteristic of talmudic stories, explains how it contributes to our understanding of the story, and provides examples of how it is applied in analyses of several stories. The book is divided into two parts.

Part 1 focuses on the narrative art of talmudic stories. Chapter 1 explores the structures of talmudic stories and discusses how appreciating their structure is a key to discovering their meaning. Tripartite structures are particularly common, but many other structures are also found. Repetition of words, phrases, and lines of dialogue are the main building blocks of these structures. To understand and analyze the story we start by identifying and assessing these structural elements. Chapter 2 discusses characterization, focusing in particular on the symbolic names of protagonists and other characters. Symbolic names often connect to the themes of the story and contribute to the message in various ways. They are an extremely economical method of characterization, as they point directly to the salient characteristic(s) that the storyteller wishes to emphasize. Chapter 3 treats biblical quotations that are featured in Talmud stories. (All biblical translations are taken from the NJPS[5] translation,

5 *The Holy Scriptures: The New JPS Translation according to the Traditional Hebrew Text* (Philadelphia: Jewish Publication Society, 1985).

unless otherwise noted, with minor changes as needed by the context.) Many stories employ verses or parts of verses to construct the dialogue placed in the mouths of characters. In still other stories the storytellers quote biblical verses to provide general perspective on the story's themes and conflicts. In some cases the verses are accompanied by midrashic interpretations, typically to advance an argument or to apply the verse to the story. Chapter 4 turns to wordplay and punning as a literary technique that adds interest and entertainment to the story, and that also helps focus attention on its main themes. Rhyme, alliteration, homonyms, and other such resemblances between words invite the audience to make connections among narrative elements. This aspect of the narrative art of the story is difficult to appreciate when working exclusively with translations, as most wordplay is a function of the original language. Yet it is so prominent in talmudic stories, as in much oral literature, that it is worth digging into the underlying language to see how this phenomenon adds to the texts and their messages. Throughout these chapters I also discuss other aspects of the narrative art of talmudic stories, including irony, allusion, interior monologue, and literary conventions, presenting them where relevant, in conjunction with structure, wordplay, and so forth.

Part 2 turns to the contexts of talmudic stories and the different possible relationships between the stories and their larger literary contexts. Talmudic stories appear juxtaposed to other talmudic passages, both literary and legal. Chapter 5 examines the contexts in which stories appear and the impact of this context on their meanings. Many stories directly engage the Mishnah, as the Talmud is first and foremost a commentary to the Mishnah, and every talmudic passage is contextualized with a given paragraph of Mishnah. Talmudic commentary, however, frequently proceeds in an associative manner; succeeding passages may be linked to a law, idea, verse, rabbi's name, or to some other element of the preceding discussion. Stories may likewise be introduced on the basis of association with disparate elements of the proximate talmudic passages. In many cases these relationships of the story to its textual or legal context are crucial to appreciating the story's message. Chapter 6 continues the discussion of context by focusing on "story-cycles," groups of three or more stories that follow each other in succession. These groupings invite the audience to compare and contrast the individual stories, and the implications of the connections and differences can function as a quasi-philosophical way of addressing larger theological and cultural issues. Chapter 7 presents comparative study as a method of gaining insight into the story's meaning. Very often, different versions of the same basic story appear in the different rabbinic compilations. Studying the differences among the versions helps us identify the different messages and purposes of the respective storytellers, and provides a productive method with which to analyze a story. The volume's conclusion draws on all the modes of analysis presented throughout the book to analyze a rich and complex talmudic story, and in so doing offers a larger picture of how these narratives enrich our experience of the religious imagination of the rabbis.

This book is intended to offer readers a pathway into the realm of rabbinic stories, appreciation for their literary artistry, and guidance on how to study stories on their own. I draw here on the books, articles, and publications of many other scholars who have contributed to the academic study of talmudic stories. While I offer some original readings and also present some of my own analyses from earlier scholarly writings, I have borrowed liberally from the best scholarship in the field. Readers interested in diving deeper into those scholarly works, including the broader historical background, comprehensive discussions of all parallel rabbinic passages, and details about textual variants in the manuscripts of the Talmud, can find references in the footnotes, with fuller citations of those sources in the bibliography. Note also that some of the rabbinic texts I present follow the readings found in talmudic manuscripts rather than the standard printing, as the standard printing (also known as the "Vilna printing" or "Vilna Talmud") sometimes has mistakes and omissions. Throughout, my hope is that readers will attain a better understanding of the beauty, spiritual depth, and moral complexity of talmudic stories, as well as the way they work as literary texts.

For readers not familiar with the main works of rabbinic literature, an appendix at the end of the volume provides a guide to these texts with short introductions, definitions, and orientation.

# PART 1

# Narrative Art

# CHAPTER 1
## Structure and Repetition

THE FIRST AND most important step for understanding a talmudic story is to analyze its structure, as the structure enables us to perceive the relationship among the story's parts. In this respect, analysis of talmudic stories is no different from studying any literary work, including novels, poems, short stories, and even prose essays. A novel, for example, may consist of three main parts, such as the protagonist's childhood, college years, and adulthood; or may have two halves, which take place in two cities; or may recount four major events, say three weddings and a funeral. Because talmudic stories were originally oral literature, their structural divisions are particularly important and often extremely prominent. Structures functioned partly as mnemonic aids; audiences attended to structures as they heard stories and then reflected on their meaning. Folktales and children's stories, the oral literature with which we are most familiar today, frequently exhibit such clearly defined structures. Thus the story of "Goldilocks and the Three Bears" uses tripartite structures with repeated phrases to describe the action: "She tried the first bowl of porridge but it was too hot; she tried the second bowl but it was too cold; she tried the third bowl and it was just right, so she ate it all up...She tried the first bed but it was too hard...too soft...just right, so she lay down and went to sleep." Having heard such stories just once or twice, the audience can remember them, repeat them, and more easily assess their lessons.

An awareness of the structure is particularly useful in discerning relationships among parts of a story in a nonlinear way. When we read or hear a story we usually process it in a linear, or sequential, manner: the first section, then the second section, followed by the third section, and so forth. This is obviously how narration generally proceeds, and how we encounter sentences on a written page or hear language from a storyteller. But in many cases, parts of a literary work are also related to the sections that do not immediately precede or follow them: the beginning of a novel may have connections to the final chapter, and the third stanza or a poem may relate more to the sixth stanza than to the second or fourth. These relationships are harder to detect because we must overcome our natural propensity toward linear interpretation. Dividing a story into discrete sections and identifying each part's important features and repeated phrases helps the audience more easily draw connections among the parts that do not follow each other directly.

Some scholars argue that literary structures are essentially objective properties and believe that there is a single correct way of delineating a story's structure. There have even been efforts, especially among some proponents of the theory known as "structuralism," to connect the structures of literary texts to the very structures of human thought and the way the brain processes information. In my opinion, however, structures are subjective and are more profitably considered strategies of both the storytellers and their audiences to remember and make sense of a text. Stories generally can be divided up in different ways, and often these different structures will emphasize different aspects of a story and lead to different interpretations. Of course some structural divisions are more persuasive than others, just as some interpretations of a poem or story are more compelling than others. Likewise, some structures are more helpful than others in analyzing a story and decoding its meanings. But in theory stories can be divided in many ways based on different criteria.

Certain aspects and features of a story are especially useful in discerning a story's structure and the relationship among its parts. For example, the structure of talmudic stories is often created by repetition of phrases or sentences, either verbatim or with minor variations, as repetition is an aid to memorization and helps the audience absorb the story more easily. So repeated language, especially repeated sequences of dialogue, typically correlates with substantive divisions. So, too, a change of location or character generally signals a new part of the story. Longer stories also often contain highly structured sub-units, which help the audience perceive the dynamic of each individual part, and also contribute to the overall structure of the story.

## Tripartite Structures

Tripartite structures, like the familiar one of "Goldilocks and the Three Bears" mentioned above, are often found in rabbinic stories. Both entire stories and sub-units within stories frequently can be divided into three parts. The most basic type of tripartite structure involves threefold repetition of dialogue or action. This story about Hillel provides a good example:[1]

**תלמוד בבלי, שבת ל ע״ב-לא ע״א**

[A1] תנו רבנן: לעולם יהא אדם ענוותן כהלל ואל יהא קפדן כשמאי.

[A2] מעשה בשני בני אדם שהמרו זה את זה. אמרו: כל מי שילך ויקניט את הלל יטול ארבע מאות זוז. אמר אחד מהם: אני אקניטנו. אותו היום ערב שבת היה והלל חפף את ראשו.

[B1] (a) הלך **ועבר על פתח ביתו**, אמר: מי כאן הלל, מי כאן הלל? נתעטף ויצא לקראתו. אמר לו: בני, מה אתה מבקש?

(b) אמר **לו**: שאלה יש לי לשאול. אמר לו: שאל בני, שאל.

(c) [אמר לו:] מפני מה **ראשיהן של בבליים סגלגלות**? אמר לו: בני, שאלה גדולה שאלת. מפני **שאין להם חיות פקחות**.

[B2] (a) הלך **והמתין שעה אחת, חזר ואמר**: מי כאן הלל, מי כאן הלל? נתעטף ויצא לקראתו. אמר לו: בני, מה אתה מבקש?

(b) אמר לו: שאלה יש לי לשאול. אמר לו: שאל בני, שאל.

(c) [אמר לו:] מפני מה **עיניהן של תרמודיין תרוטות**? אמר לו: בני, שאלה גדולה שאלת. מפני **שדרין בין החולות**.

---

1 For studies of this story, see A. A. Halevi, *Gates of Aggadah*, 195–97; Louis Rieser, *The Hillel Narratives*, 31–38; Amram Tropper, "On Condition That"; Joseph Telushkin, *Hillel*, 61–65. Parallels to the story appear in Avot D'Rabbi Natan, Version A, chapter 15 and Version B, chapter 29.

[B3] (a) הלך **והמתין שעה אחת. חזר ואמר**: מי כאן הלל, מי כאן הלל? נתעטף ויצא לקראתו. אמר לו: בני, מה אתה מבקש?

(b) אמר לו: שאלה יש לי לשאול. אמר לו: שאל בני, שאל.

(c) [אמר לו:] מפני מה **רגליהם של אפרקיים רחבות**? אמר לו: בני, שאלה גדולה שאלת. מפני **שדרין בין בצעי המים**.

[C1] אמר לו: שאלות הרבה יש לי לשאול, ומתירא אני שמא תכעוס. נתעטף וישב לפניו. אמר לו: כל שאלות שיש לך לשאול שאל. אמר לו: אתה הוא הלל שקורין אותך "נשיא ישראל"? אמר לו: הן. אמר לו: אם אתה הוא, לא ירבו כמותך בישראל. אמר לו: בני, מפני מה? אמר לו: מפני שאבדתי על ידך ארבע מאות זוז.

[C2] אמר לו: הוי זהיר ברוחך. כדי הוא הלל שתאבד על ידו ארבע מאות זוז וארבע מאות זוז, והלל לא יקפיד.

**Talmud Bavli, Shabbat 30b–31a**

[A1] Our sages taught: One should always be a gentle person like Hillel and never be an impatient person like Shammai.

[A2] Once two people made a wager with each other. They said, "Whoever goes and angers Hillel will get 400 *zuz*." One of them said, "I will anger him." That day was Shabbat eve and Hillel was washing his head.

[B1] (a) He went and **passed by the entrance to his house** and said, "Who here is Hillel? Who here is Hillel?" He (Hillel) covered himself and went out to greet him. He said to him, "My son, what do you want?"

(b) He said to him, "I have a question to ask." He said, "Ask, my son, ask."

(c) [He said to him,] "Why are **the heads of Babylonians round**?" He said to him, "My son, you ask an important question. Because they **have no skilled midwives**."

[B2] (a) He went and **waited one hour. He returned and said**, "Who here is Hillel? Who here is Hillel?" He covered himself and went out to greet him. He said to him, "My son, what do you want?"

(b) He said to him, "I have a question to ask." He said, "Ask, my son, ask."

(c) [He said to him,] "Why are **the eyes of the Tadmorians slanted?**"[2] He said to him, "My son. You ask an important question. Because they **dwell among the deserts.**"

[B3] (a) He went and **waited one hour. He returned and said,** "Who here is Hillel? Who here is Hillel?" He covered himself and went out to greet him. He said to him, "My son, what do you want?"

(b) He said, "I have a question to ask." He said, "Ask, my son, ask."

(c) [He said to him,] "Why are **the feet of Africans wide**?" He said to him, "My son. You ask an important question. Because they **dwell among ponds of water.**"

[C1] He said to him, "I have many questions to ask, but I am afraid lest you get angry." He (Hillel) covered himself and sat before him. He said to him, "Ask all the questions that you want to ask." He said to him, "Are you Hillel who is called the Patriarch (*nasi*) of Israel?" He said to him, "Yes." He said to him, "If it is you, may there not be many like you in Israel." He said to him, "Why, my son?" He said, "Because I lost 400 *zuz* on your account."

[C2] He (Hillel) said to him, "Be careful about your disposition. It is worth your losing four hundred *zuz* on Hillel's account, and yet another 400 *zuz*, and Hillel not become angry."

If we focus on repeated language as a structuring device, we immediately see (or hear, if listening) three sequences of dialogue repeated three times, almost word for word. These three repetitions are all in the central section of the story that is labeled [B1], [B2], [B3]. The few minor differences between those repetitions, set in bold, provide the necessary contrasts that

2 Tadmor is the Hebrew name for Palmyra, a city in central Syria. In the third century CE Palmyra became an important power and conquered parts of the Roman province of Palestine, Egypt and Persia.

move the action along. (Without these variations the storyteller would simply be repeating the same sentences.) Thus the first time the man approaches, the storyteller states, "He went and passed by the entrance to his house," whereas the second and third times the storyteller relates, "He went and waited one hour. He returned." Even here the storyteller repeats the same language for the second and third attempts to provoke Hillel. The only other differences appear in the questions and answers themselves, and even these share a common pattern. The questions concern a distinguishing physical feature of a particular people and take the form: "Why are the body parts **x** (heads, eyes, feet), of ethnicity **y** (Babylonians, Tadmorians, Africans) so oddly shaped in form **z** (round, slanty, wide)?" The answers, too, are very similar: a brief retort beginning "Because they…" Again, the second and third units have even more in common and point to a geographic feature, both stating "Because they dwell among…"

Each of the three encounters involves three dialogical exchanges, for a total of three questions and responses, between Hillel and his interlocutor. Within each section here they are labeled: (a), (b), (c). These three subsections do not feature repeated language and are accordingly a less prominent structural feature, though they share the question-and-answer form. Thus one way of analyzing all of section [B] is in terms of a nested tripartite structure of three encounters, each involving three questions and their responses. Someone who hears this story just once will certainly pick up on the three encounters, and probably on the fact that each encounter involves three exchanges, and in all likelihood will be able to remember the story almost verbatim. In any case, the exact words are less important than the basic plot, so even if the audience substitutes some variation in the dialogue when retelling the tale, very little is lost.

These three interchanges are bracketed by a beginning, [A1]–[A2], and an ending, [C1]–[C2]. The beginning sets the stage with a general exhortation to the audience identifying Hillel's praiseworthy quality, followed by the exposition that leads to the ensuing interactions, the test of Hillel's "gentleness." That the first section contrasts Hillel with Shammai, who is not otherwise mentioned in this story, indicates that this section is not part of the story proper. This story is in fact followed by several other stories that feature both Hillel and Shammai; the talmudic editors added this frame as a general introduction to the whole group of stories. In the final section the bettor concedes defeat, and Hillel admonishes him for his shenanigans, articulating the lesson about the importance of good character. Thus the basic three-part structure of beginning, middle, end, common to many tales, has been enhanced by the tripartite middle unit with its verbatim repetitions: [B1], [B2], [B3]. To see how simple it is to memorize a story when conscious of underlying structural units, try reading the story aloud once or twice, and then close the book and retell it yourself.

Let me emphasize that even in a story that seems as powerfully formally structured as this one, we can imagine other ways that we might analyze some elements of the story's construction. For example, one could consider the section containing the man's admission [C1] as part of the previous section and include it there [B3], as it seems to follow immediately after this third failure to provoke Hillel. Or one could count it as a fourth dialogue and label it [B4]. These alternative possibilities focus less on repeated wording as a structuring device than on other factors. I think they are less useful in appreciating the movement and plot of the story, but they are certainly acceptable, and a reader wanting to teach or emphasize certain elements might choose them for those reasons.

The threefold repetition, apart from its mnemonic function, enhances the message by emphasizing Hillel's great forbearance in the face of blatant provocation. Even one such question, at the eve of Shabbat when everyone busily prepares for the holy day, is inappropriate enough that Hillel's gentle response testifies to his exemplary character. But perhaps one could argue that Hillel's patience was nothing out of the ordinary—because he should have allowed for the possibility that this fellow was innocent of malicious intent, that he forgot it was the eve of Shabbat, or that he was psychologically unsound. The audience knows this is not the case because the omniscient narrator informs us of the bet, but Hillel does not. After the man returns a second and third time, and certainly after his confession at the end, there can be absolutely no doubt that he is a provocateur and rogue, and consequently that Hillel displays unfathomable tolerance.

Scholars have debated whether the questions themselves are provocative or only the timing inappropriate. Because we don't entirely understand the cultural context of the rabbis, it is hard to be sure what such questions would have meant to them. In classical culture, inquiries into the particular physical appearance and character traits of different tribes and peoples were areas of philosophical debate, and questions like these were not unprecedented. In my opinion, however, the questions should be taken as silly or irrelevant, and not merely inopportunely timed. The storyteller intends to heighten the aggravation Hillel deserves to feel by having the rogue pose the most inane questions at the worst possible time, and in doing so magnifies the heroism of Hillel's response. Even if the questions could be considered serious in some possible context (imagine a conversation around the dinner table about different peoples and their disparate features), why should they be asked of a rabbinic sage at his home? But either way, the story beautifully illustrates and offers both the talmudic audience and contemporary readers a lesson from Hillel's incredible patience, even when confronted by deliberate provocation.

Let us look at a second example:[3]

**תלמוד בבלי, עבודה זרה יא ע"א**

[A] אונקלוס בר קלונימוס איגייר.

[B1] **שדר קיסר גונדא דרומאי אבתריה.** משכינהו בקראי. **איגיור.**

[B2] **הדר שדר גונדא דרומאי אחרינא אבתריה. אמר להו: לא תימרו ליה ולא מידי.** כי הוו שקלו ואזלו, אמר להו: אימא לכו מילתא בעלמא. ניפיורא נקט נורא קמי פיפיורא, פיפיורא לדוכסא, דוכסא להגמונא, הגמונא לקומא, קומא מי נקט נורא מקמי אינשי? אמרי ליה: לא. אמר להו: הקדוש ברוך הוא נקט נורא קמי ישראל, דכתיב: וה' הולך לפניהם יומם בעמוד ענן לנחתם הדרך ולילה בעמוד אש להאיר להם (שמות יג:כא). **איגיור.**

[B3] **הדר שדר גונדא אחרינא אבתריה. אמר להו: לא תשתעו מידי בהדיה.** כי נקטי ליה ואזלי, חזא מזוזתא דמנחא אפתחא. אותיב ידיה עלה ואמר להו: מאי האי? אמרו ליה: אימא לן את. אמר להו: מנהגו של עולם, מלך בשר ודם יושב מבפנים ועבדיו משמרים אותו מבחוץ. ואילו הקדוש ברוך הוא עבדיו מבפנים והוא משמרן מבחוץ, שנאמר: ה' ישמר צאתך ובואך (תהלים קכא:ח). **איגיור.**

[C] תו לא שדר בתריה.

**Talmud Bavli, Avodah Zarah 11a**

[A] Onkelos b. Kalonimos converted [to Judaism].

[B1] **The emperor sent a company of Roman [soldiers] after him.** He captivated them with scriptural verses. **They converted.**

3 On this story see Alyssa M. Gray, "The Power Conferred" and Jeffrey L. Rubenstein, "The Story-Cycles of the Bavli," 267–76.

[B2] **He (the emperor) again sent another company of Roman [soldiers] after him. He said to them, "Don't say anything at all to him."** When they were taking him away and going forth, he said to them, "Let me say something to you. A torch-bearer carries the torch before the overseer, the overseer for the commander, the commander for the general, the general for the magistrate. But does the magistrate carry a torch before anyone?" They said to him, "No." He said to them, "The Holy One, blessed be He, carries a torch before Israel, as it says, *YHVH went before them in a pillar of cloud by day, to guide them along the way, and in a pillar of cloud by night to give them light (Exodus 13:21).*" **They converted.**

[B3] **He (the emperor) again sent another company after him. He said to them, "Don't speak at all with him."** While they were carrying him out, he saw a *mezuzah* upon the doorway. He placed his hand upon it and said to them, "What is this?" They said to him, "You tell us." He said to them, "It is the way of the world that a human king sits inside and his servants guard him outside. But the Holy One, blessed be He, guards Israel from outside, as it says, *YHVH will guard your going and coming (Psalm 121:8).*" **They converted.**

[C] He (the emperor) did not send [soldiers] after him again.

This story easily divides into a tripartite structure. In the beginning Onkelos converts to Judaism, in the middle the Roman emperor attempts to arrest Onkelos, and in the end the emperor abandons his efforts. As in the Hillel story above, the middle section consists of its own tripartite division, [B1]–[B3]. In each of these three subsections, the emperor dispatches soldiers, they fail to arrest Onkelos, and they convert to Judaism instead. Each of these three parts of the middle unit begin and end with verbal repetition: "The emperor sent….the emperor again sent… the emperor again sent," and "they converted…they converted…they converted." The second and third parts of the middle unit also feature a common pattern: the emperor warns the soldiers not to speak with Onkelos but as they drag him out Onkelos manages to get in a question, the soldiers make a brief reply ("No" / "You tell us"), and he responds with a lesson and scriptural prooftext.

The three encounters exhibit more variation than those of the Hillel story, but they still allow for easy memorization. Indeed, such variations are often an important dimension of the storyteller's lessons. In this case, the Jewish scriptures themselves [B1], theological teachings based on scripture [B2], and ritual objects [B3] all point to the spiritual beauty and superiority of Judaism. The audience is to understand that the advantages of Judaism and God's love of Israel are not single but manifest in multiple ways. While the storyteller offers three, he invites the audience to think of others.

We do not know much about Onkelos b. Kalonimos, though he is evidently a member of the Roman elite with some connection to the government or imperial family, as his conversion to Judaism provokes the emperor to order his arrest.[4] When the soldiers arrive, however, a stunning reversal occurs, and those directed to apprehend the convert join him instead. Onkelos "captivates them" with scripture, apparently teaching them the beautiful morals, beliefs, and wisdom of the Bible. The emperor's second attempt has a similar result despite his warning the troops not to converse: this time Onkelos offers a brilliant parable contrasting the greatness of the Jewish God with the inferiority of Roman officials—including the very military officers the soldiers serve. Whereas the Master of the Universe provides illumination and leads out God's "soldiers," the Roman officials—the emperor included—behave in the opposite way. The soldiers immediately absorb the lesson of the advantages of serving God rather than the emperor, and they convert. The emperor's third attempt likewise fails. Despite the warning against engaging in any discussion whatsoever, the soldiers cannot resist taking the bait and inquiring about the *mezuzah*. Again, the teaching of the reversal of "the ways of the world" precipitates a narrative reversal. When the soldiers learn that the divine king guards Israel (that is, God's subjects), whereas the terrestrial king (=Roman emperor) requires his subjects to guard him, they throw in their lot with the convert they were sent to arrest.

Parables involving a Roman emperor, high official, or army are common in rabbinic literature. In this case they are extremely pointed, in that the first parable invokes the Roman army and the second features the king—

---

4 See below, pp. 108–109, for another story about this character.

perfectly mirroring the characters of the Roman soldiers and the emperor involved in the story. Onkelos's Roman audience within the story knows its own world and quickly understands its limitations, in contrast to the Jewish God and people. But of course the story's real audience is the Jewish students of Talmud outside of the story, and they too know the inferiority of the Roman religion—the emperor was considered a god and had his own cult—in contrast to their own.

This story can be classified as a "fantasy of reversal," in which the subjugated people imagine triumphing over their more powerful oppressors. In contrast to the typical fantasy of a violent military victory in which an army, perhaps aided by supernatural beings, destroys the persecutors, this story imagines a theological-spiritual conquest, in keeping with the biblical vision: "Not by might, nor by power, but by My spirit—said YHVH of Hosts" (Zechariah 4:6). This and other such stories undoubtedly provided spiritual sustenance to Jews throughout the generations as they struggled to maintain their faith against powerful regimes that claimed to rule by the grace of God. Traditional Jews have always believed that the true measure of God's love is not the size of an army or earthly power, but rather the covenantal relationship that the Jewish people share with God. But there is certainly an enjoyable vindication in imagining that the covenantal relationship persuades outsiders and enemies to rethink their worldview.

## TRIPARTITE STRUCTURES AND SPECTRUMS OF RESPONSES

Talmudic stories are very rich in dialogue. Indeed, a preference for dialogue over narration is one distinctive characteristic of rabbinic stories. In many stories the tripartite structural unit consists of three dialogical sequences that set forth a spectrum of responses to a given question.

The opening anecdote of a long story about the sage R. Shimon bar Yoḥai relates:[5]

---

5 For additional literature on this story, see: Jeffrey L. Rubenstein, "Torah and the Mundane Life: The Education of R. Shimon bar Yohai (Shabbat 33b–34a)," in *Talmudic Stories*, 105–38, and the literature cited there; Charlotte Elisheva Fonrobert, "Plato in Rabbi Shimeon Bar Yohai's Cave," with further references in the footnotes; and Michal Bar-Asher Siegal, *Early Christian Monastic Literature*, 133–69 and the notes there.

**תלמוד בבלי, שבת לג ע״ב**

[I] דיתבי רבי יהודה ורבי יוסי ורבי שמעון ויתיב יהודה בן גרים גבייהו.

[A] פתח ר׳ יהודה ואמר, כמה נאים מעשיהן של אומה זו:

[1] תקנו שווקים

[2] תקנו גשרים

[3] תקנו מרחצאות.

[B] ר׳ יוסי שתק.

[C] נענה רשב״י ואמר, כל מה שתקנו לא תקנו אלא לצורך עצמן:

[1'] תקנו שווקין להושיב בהן זונות

[2'] מרחצאות לעדן בהן עצמן

[3'] גשרים ליטול מהן מכס.

[II] הלך יהודה בן גרים וסיפר דבריהם, ונשמעו למלכות.

[A'] אמרו: יהודה שעילה יתעלה

[B'] יוסי ששתק יגלה לציפורי

[C'] שמעון שגינה יהרג.

**Talmud Bavli, Shabbat 33b**

[I] R. Yehudah and R. Yose and R. Shimon [bar Yoḥai] were sitting, and Yehudah b. Gerim was sitting beside them.

[A] R. Yehudah opened and said, "How pleasant are the acts of 'this nation' (=Rome):

[1] They established markets.

[2] They established bath-houses.

[3] They established bridges."

[B] R. Yose was silent.

[C] R. Shimon bar Yoḥai answered and said, "Everything they established, they established only for their own needs:

[1'] They established markets—to place prostitutes there,

[2'] bath-houses to pamper themselves,

[3'] bridges to take tolls."

[II] Yehudah b. Gerim went and retold their words, and it became known to the government.

[A'] They (=the Romans) said: "Yehudah who extolled—let him be extolled.

[B'] Yose who was silent—let him be exiled to Sepphoris.

[C'] Shimon who disparaged—let him be killed."

Three rabbis sit in discussion and advance three disparate perspectives on the Roman Empire. R. Yehudah praises three Roman contributions to civilization: markets (an asset to commerce), bath-houses (a benefit for hygiene and leisure), and bridges (which facilitate travel). R. Shimon bar Yoḥai denigrates these same features: markets house prostitutes and thus facilitate vice, bath-houses cater to decadence and self-indulgence, and bridges provide opportunities for tolls and taxation. R. Yose's silence suggests a middle position of neutrality between these two opposing views. The Romans respond to the three perspectives with three judicial (perhaps extra-judicial) sentences: praise, exile, and death. (R. Yose's silence apparently was not enough for the Romans to respond in kind, by ignoring him, since his lack of disagreement implies partial assent.) The story thus contains two sets of neatly matched tripartite units: the three rabbis' actions labeled [A, B, C] versus the Romans' three responses to them [A', B', C'], and the three positive views of Roman culture [1, 2, 3] versus the negative reframings of the same institutions [1', 2', 3'].

These tripartite units are packaged in an overall two-part structure: rabbis' pronouncements [I] and Roman responses [II]. A character named Yehudah b. Gerim appears in both parts: he hears (or overhears) the rabbis' words in the first part, and in the second part he repeats them, such that they become known to the Roman authorities. Here, too, an audience conscious of the structure can memorize this part of the story with minimal effort.

This story contains a few additional verbal repetitions, including "they established...they established...they established" within R. Yehudah's pronouncement [A], and the Roman formulaic dictates: Rabbi **x** (Yehudah, Yose, Shimon) who **y** (extolled, kept silent, disparaged), let him be z (extolled, exiled, killed) [A', B', C']. However, the repetitions are not as pronounced as in the Hillel story discussed above, and they do not contribute to the main tripartite structure.

The three rabbis' opinions—positive, neutral, and negative—cover the spectrum of possible attitudes to Rome with maximum economy. Of course, many more perspectives that fall closer to one or the other of these poles are possible, as are more complex and nuanced assessments. Storytellers recounting the story to a live audience would be able, if they so desired, to embellish the details, perhaps elaborating on these three perspectives and offering others as well.

In this story, the main tripartite structure derives from the three different rabbis articulating three different perspectives. So the function of the threefold structure is different here from those we saw above, serving to present a range of perspectives rather than reinforce a single, repeated lesson. Put differently: because the second and third parts of the Hillel story consist mainly of repetition, the story would work, albeit not as effectively, without the tripartite unit. We appreciate Hillel's character from his first response, and the second and third iterations amplify his greatness. Similarly, the story of Onkelos would convey its meaning, although much less successfully, with only one or two companies of Roman troops converting. In contrast, this story requires the tripartite unit to set forth the spectrum of three different opinions.

## TRIPARTITE STRUCTURES AND ALTERNATIVE POSSIBILITIES

In many cases the tripartite structure presents three alternative possibilities. The following unit is part of a long story of the sages' efforts to remove Rabban Gamaliel from his position as Head of the Academy and stage a kind of coup:[6]

---

6 For studies of this story, see Robert Goldenberg, "The Deposition of Rabban Gamaliel II"; Devora Steinmetz, "Must the Patriarch Know 'Uqtzin?"; Hayyim Shapira, "The Deposition of Rabban Gamaliel"; Jeffrey L. Rubenstein, *Stories of the Babylonian Talmud*, 77–90; Geoffrey Herman, "Insurrection in the Academy."

**תלמוד בבלי, ברכות כז ע״ב–כח ע״א**

[I] [A] אמרי: עד כמה נצעריה וניזיל?

[1] בר״ה אשתקד צעריה.

[2] בבכורות במעשה דר׳ צדוק צעריה.

[3] הכא נמי צעריה.

[B] תא ונעבריה. מאן נוקים ליה?

[1] נוקמיה לרבי יהושע? בעל מעשה הוא.

[2] נוקמיה לר׳ עקיבא? דילמא עניש ליה, דלית ליה זכות אבות.

[3] אלא נוקמיה לר׳ אלעזר בן עזריה, דהוא חכם, והוא עשיר, והוא עשירי לעזרא.

[a] הוא חכם – דאי מקשי ליה מפרק ליה.

[b] והוא עשיר – דאי אית ליה לפלוחי לבי קיסר אף הוא אזל ופלח.

[c] והוא עשירי לעזרא – דאית ליה זכות אבות ולא מצי עניש ליה.

[C] אתו ואמרו ליה: ניחא ליה למר דליהוי ריש מתיבתא?

[II] אמר להו: איזיל ואימליך באינשי ביתי. אזל ואמליך בדביתהו.

[A] אמרה ליה: דלמא מפייסי ליה ומעברין לך?

[A'] אמר לה: גמירי, מעלין בקדש ואין מורידין (משנה מנחות יא:ז).

[B] אמרה ליה: דלמא עניש לך.

[B'] אמר לה: לשתמש אינש יומא חדא בכסא דמוקרא ולמחר ליתבר.

[C] אמרה ליה: לית לך חיורתא.

[C'] ההוא יומא בר תמני סרי שני הוה. אתרחיש ליה ניסא ואהדרו ליה תמני סרי דרי חיורתא.

**Talmud Bavli, Berakhot 27b–28a**

[I] [A] They (=the rabbis of the academy) said: "How long will he (Rabban Gamaliel) go on distressing him (R. Yehoshua)?

[1] He distressed him last year on Rosh Hashanah.

[2] He distressed him in [the matter of] the firstling, in the incident involving R. Tzadok.

[3] Now he distressed him again.

[B] Come, let us depose him. Who will we raise up [in his place]?

[1] Let us raise up R. Yehoshua? He is involved in the matter.[7]

[2] Let us raise up R. Akiva? Perhaps he (Rabban Gamaliel) will harm him, since he has no ancestral merit.

[3] Rather let us raise up R. Eleazar b. Azariah, for he is wise, and he is wealthy, and he is tenth [in descent] from Ezra.

[a] He is wise—so that if anyone asks a difficult question, he will be able to solve it.

[b] He is wealthy—so that if he has to pay honor to the emperor, he can pay honor.

[c] And he is tenth in descent from Ezra—that he has ancestral merit and he (Rabban Gamaliel) will not be able to harm him."[8]

[C] They said to him, "Would our Master (=you, R. Eleazar b. Azariah) consent to be the Head of the Academy?"

---

7 That is, the rabbis are deposing Rabban Gamaliel due to his harsh treatment of R. Yehoshua. Therefore, R. Yehoshua is an "interested party."

8 The merit of his illustrious ancestors will protect him. But R. Akiva has no illustrious ancestors, hence no such merit to ward off evil.

[II] He (R. Eleazar b. Azariah) said to them, "Let me go and consult with the members of my household." He went and consulted with his wife.

[A] She said to him, "Perhaps they will reconcile with him and depose you?"

[A'] He said to her, "There is a tradition: *One raises the level of holiness but does not diminish it (Mishnah Menaḥot 11:7).*"[9]

[B] She said to him, "Perhaps he (Rabban Gamaliel) will harm you?"

[B'] He said, "Let a man use a valuable cup for one day even if it breaks on the morrow."

[C] She said to him, "You have no white hair."

[C'] That day he was eighteen years old. A miracle happened for him and he was crowned with eighteen rows of white hair.

The thought process of the rabbis of the academy unfolds in three parts in section [I]: [A] the crisis, Rabban Gamaliel's verbal abuse of his colleague R. Yehoshua; [B] the sages' response, to depose him and appoint a replacement; [C] the execution of the plan, offering the office to another sage, R. Eleazar b. Azariah.

The first part of this section [I.A.1–3] recounts three occasions of abusive behavior, alluding to two stories found elsewhere in the Talmud Bavli.[10] Yet the story can be understood perfectly even without knowledge of those episodes. The audience gleans from these mentions that Rabban Gamaliel has acted in similar fashion in the past, and for that reason the other rabbis are very upset. The pattern of inappropriate behavior is emphasized by the verbal repetition "he distressed...he distressed...he distressed." This was

9 R. Eleazar applies this principle of Temple law—that once an object or sacrifice takes on a certain level of holiness it cannot be reduced to a less holy state—to his situation. Once he has been promoted to the position of Head of the Academy he will not be demoted.

10 This allusion to other stories is rare. Most talmudic stories are self-contained and make no reference to other narrative traditions.

no isolated incident but continues a pattern of high-handed and abusive conduct.

The second unit [I.B.1–3] uses another tripartite scheme to explore the different possible replacements, again with the verbal repetition: "let us raise up….let us raise up….let us raise up." Problems with the first two suggestions lead to the third, which, like Goldilocks's third bowl of porridge, is just right. The rightness is explained by delineating three important qualifications [I.3]: wisdom, wealth, and "ancestral merit," that is, esteemed lineage. The story assumes that Rabban Gamaliel may curse or otherwise harm his rival through supernatural means, but that R. Eleazar b. Azariah's ancestral merit confers protection. Of course the storyteller could have had the rebellious rabbis contemplate appointing other contemporary sages as well, but he brings only three possibilities.

Similarly, R. Eleazar b. Azariah's consultation with his wife [II] explores three possible objections to accepting the appointment. She suggests that he may be deposed, that he may be harmed by Rabban Gamaliel, and that he is too young: lacking white hair, a mark of older age, he may not be treated with respect by his seniors [A, B, C]. Each objection is parried [A', B', C']. First, quoting a mishnah, R. Eleazar b. Azariah responds that once promoted, he cannot be demoted. Second, he suggests that the prestige of serving as Head of the Academy is worth any harm he might experience. The wife's third objection is countered by divine intervention that miraculously bestows on the rabbi the white hair marking old age. (Here is a good example of the miraculous tendencies of rabbinic stories, as mentioned in the introduction.) Thus the story features tripartite units to explore both the possible replacements for Rabban Gamaliel and the possible problems with R. Eleazar b. Azariah accepting the office.

In this example the rabbis' decision to select R. Eleazar b. Azariah is told entirely in dialogue [I.B.1–3]. The exchange between R. Elazar b. Azariah and his wife, however, exhibits a variation: the third section culminates not with a verbal response but with an event—in this case the supernatural aging. This structure is particularly common: the third utterance by one character is followed not by a response but by an action or event. Here is another example:[11]

11 On this story, see Jay Rovner, "Rav Assi Had This Old Mother," 113–19; Admiel Kosman, "'Internal Homeland' and 'External Homeland'"; Yonatan Feintuch, "The

**תלמוד בבלי, קידושין לא ע"ב**

רב אסי הוה ליה ההיא אמא זקינה.

[A] אמרה ליה: בעינא תכשיטין.

[A'] עבד לה.

[B] בעינא גברא.

[B'] נייעין לך.

[C] בעינא גברא דשפיר כותך.

[C'] שבקה ואזל לארעא דישראל.

**Talmud Bavli, Kiddushin 31b**

Rav Assi—he had this elderly mother.

[A] She said to him: "I want jewels."

[A'] He got them for her.

[B] [She said to him:] "I want a husband."

[B'] [He said to her:] "I will look into it for you."

[C] [She said to him:] "I want a husband who is as handsome as you."

[C'] He left her and went to the Land of Israel.

Rav Assi's mother has apparently been widowed and turns to her son for support. (Babylonian rabbis generally have the title "Rav," whereas those from the Land of Israel are designated "Rabbi." Both honorary titles mean "master.") She first asks him for jewels, which he procures for her, as a dutiful son honoring his parent's request. He agrees to try to find her a new husband too. But when she stipulates the new husband be "as handsome as you," Rav Assi flees. He seems to realize there will be a never-ending cycle of increasingly difficult demands, placing him in the impossible situation of potentially dishonoring his mother by failing to satisfy her desires.

---

Aggada about R. Assi and His Mother"; and Jeffrey L. Rubenstein, *Land of Truth*, 21–32.

(There may also be Freudian overtones to her third request—another reason to avoid the situation entirely.) The verbal repetition "I want…I want…I want" emphasizes the oppressive and incessant quality of her requests. The storyteller wants us to understand that these three requests are not the only things she has asked of her son, but rather that she has made increasing and unreasonable requests over the course of weeks or months, to the point where her son can no longer endure it. The unit ends not with a verbal response but with an action, Rav Assi's departure.

The short story may have a comic element in the mother's inappropriate third request, which immediately puts the son to flight. But there is a serious, even tragic, dimension too, which many of us experience in contemporary times, in part due to longer lifespans. How do we adequately honor aging parents, who make difficult requests or demands on our time and resources, sometimes due to loneliness or illness or other factors not completely in their control? Where do we draw the line between their needs and ours? Even when we have the purest of intentions and aspire to honor our parents to the utmost, we can be driven to despair by such situations. The rabbis were as aware of these challenges as we are; indeed, one rabbinic tradition identifies honoring parents as the most difficult *mitzvah*. The story does not provide a simple answer to this situation, but rather an opportunity for the audience to reflect on the different aspects of the predicament.

## Two-Part Structures

While tripartite structures are particularly common, many stories are also found with more straightforward two-part structures. Almost by definition, two-part structures offer a contrast between two different situations, approaches to an issue, or points of view. The following story reports an encounter between a "Roman matron," a stock character who features in many rabbinic stories representing an elite or aristocratic Roman woman, and a rabbi.[12]

---

12 On this story, see Avigdor Shinan, "'Difficult as the Parting of the Red Sea,'" Menachem Fisch, "Bossy Matrons and Forced Marriages," and Tal Ilan, "Matrona

**מדרש ויקרא רבה ח:א**

[A1] מטרונה שאלה את רבי יוסי בר חלפותא: לכמה ימים ברא הקדוש ברוך הוא את עולמו? אמר לה: לששת ימים, דכתיב: כי ששת ימים עשה ה' את השמים ואת הארץ (שמות לא:יז).

[A2] אמרה לו: מיכן ואילך מה יושב ועושה? אמר לה: יושב ומזויג זיווגים: בתו שלפלוני לפלוני, אשתו שלפלוני לפלוני, ממונו שלפלוני לפלוני.

[A3] אמרה לו: כמה עבדים וכמה שפחות יש לי ולשעה **קלה** אני מזווגתן. אמר לה: אם **קלה** היא בעיניך קשה היא לפני המקום כקריעת ים סוף, דכתיב: א-להים מושיב יחידים ביתה מוציא אסירים בכושרות אך סוררים שכנו צחיחה (תהלים סח:ז). הלך לו ר' יוסי בן חלפותא לביתו.

[B1] מה עשתה? שלחה והביאה אלף עבדים ואלף שפחות והעמידה אותן שורות שורות. אמרה להן: פלוני יסב פלניתא, ופלנית יסב פלן.

[B2] מן צפרא אתו לגבה. דין פריע ראשיה. דין סמי עייניה. ודין תבירא ידיה. ודין תבירא רגליה. דין אמר: לית אנא בעי הדא. ודא אמרה: לית אנא בעי הדין.

[B3] שלחה לו ואמרה לו: יפה תורתכם נאה ומשובחת. אמר לה: לא כך אמרתי ליך, אם **קלה** היא בעיניך קשה לפני המקום כקריעת ים סוף, דכתיב: א-להים מושיב יחידים ביתה מוציא אסירים בכושרות (תהלים סח:ז)?

**Midrash Vayikra Rabbah 8:1**[13]

[A1] A Roman matron questioned R. Yose b. Ḥalfuta: "In how many days did God create His world?" He said to her, "In six days, as is written, *For in six days YHVH made heaven and earth (Exodus 31:17).*"

[A2] She said to him, "Since then, what does He sit and do?" He said to her, "He sits and arranges marriages: So-and-so's daughter is for So-and-so, the wife of So-and-so [who died] is for So-and-so, the estate of So-and-so is for So-and-so."

[A3] She said to him, "How many male and female slaves do I have, and in a **brief** (*kalah*) moment I can marry them off!" He said to her, "Although it is an **easy** (*kalah*) thing in your eyes, it is as difficult

---

and Rabbi Jose," 34–37. There is a close parallel to this story in Bereishit Rabbah 68:4. In some versions the rabbi's name appears as R. Yose b. Ḥalafta.

13 *Midrash Vayikra Rabbah*, ed. M. Margulies (reprint: New York, 1993), 164–66.

before the Omnipresent as the parting of the Sea of Reeds, as is written, *God restores the lonely to their homes, sets free the imprisoned, safe and sound while the rebellious must live in a parched land (Psalm 68:7).*" R. Yose b. Ḥalfuta went home.

[B1] What did she do? She sent [word] and they brought one thousand male slaves and one thousand female slaves and she lined them up in rows. She said to them, "So-and-so will marry So-and-so, and So-and-so will marry So-and-so."

[B2] In the morning they came to her. This one's head was disheveled. That one's eye was blinded. This one's hand was broken. That one's leg was broken. This one said, "I don't want her." That one said, "I don't want him."

[B3] She sent word to him (R. Yose b. Ḥalfuta) and said to him, "Your Torah is fine, beautiful and praiseworthy." He said to her, "Did I not say to you that 'Although it is an **easy** (*kalah*) thing in your eyes, it is as difficult before the Omnipresent as the parting of the Sea of Reeds, as is written, *God restores the lonely to their homes, sets free the imprisoned, safe and sound (Psalm 68:7)*?'"

With even a cursory reading (or hearing), the audience discerns two main episodes, dividing the story into two halves. The first episode involves a conversation between the Roman matron and R. Yose b. Ḥalfuta [A]; the second consists of her matchmaking experiment, which precipitates a shift in perspective [B]. In the first episode the matron expresses surprise and skepticism toward R. Yose's b. Ḥalfuta's words; in the second she acknowledges their truth with belief and understanding. The key didactic point emerges from the contrast between God's efforts in arranging marriages, described in the first half, with the matron's disastrous attempts in the second half. The structural divisions thus derive primarily from the temporal sequence and content, rather than from verbal repetition (as we saw in the three questions put to Hillel) or parallel form (as in the statements of three rabbis about Rome). However, we should note that R. Yose b. Ḥalfuta repeats his characterization of the difficulty of making marriages, "Although it is an easy thing…" (at [A3] and [B3]), which reinforces the two-part structure—especially since these words come near the conclusion of each half of the story. The narrator adds the datum "R. Yose b. Ḥalfuta went home" to mark the end of the first half, to signal to the audience that this encounter has concluded. So too he adds the rhetorical question "What did she do?" to signal the beginning of the next part. The two-part structure fits the didactic interests of the story: the transition from lack of understanding to understanding, from innocence to awareness, from a superficial view of the nature of things to a deeper, spiritual, rabbinic insight.

The story combines serious theological inquiry with humor. To a Roman or Greek, what the Jewish God does with His time might have been a serious question. Pagan gods lived busy lives full of conflict and competition, romance and sex, creative endeavors, eating and drinking, carousing and merrymaking—much like human beings—and they meddled amply in human affairs, to boot. Some gods also had specific tasks to occupy their time, like the sun god Helios who drove his chariot across the heavens each day. Romans would have understood that creating the world engaged the God of the Jews, even if the Greek and Roman creation myths proceeded along different lines. But if that task required only six days, there would be a lot of empty hours to fill. Yet this question may have perplexed a Jew, or even a rabbi, just as much. Rabbinic sources often project potentially troubling or subversive theological questions onto outsiders and "others" to render them less threatening.[14] What exactly does God do, day in and day out, up in heaven with the angelic retinue?

Surprisingly, R. Yose b. Ḥalfuta responds that God is occupied by figuring out who should marry whom and facilitating these couplings. This answer astonishes the Roman matron, and presumably the audience too: not only does it seem like a mundane and tiresome job, below God's dignity as it were, but also easy and straightforward. If creating the universe, an endeavor that required awesome power and prodigious intelligence, required less than a week of God's time, should not the trivial matter of pairing off men and women take even less? What sense does it make that God spends the years and centuries since creation in matrimonial organization? The matron will prove to R. Yose b. Ḥalfuta how simply and speedily nuptials can be arranged by an ordinary human being, thereby providing empirical evidence to reject his claim.

The rabbi, however, has a source of truth that is superior to experience—the truth of scripture. And as a rabbi, he holds the key to understanding that truth: rabbinic interpretation or midrash. This is a fundamental move in

14 See Christine Hayes, "The 'Other' in Rabbinic Literature."

talmudic stories (and chapter 3 takes up this phenomenon in more detail). R. Yose quotes a verse, Psalm 68:7, and uses it to suggest how epically challenging the project of matchmaking really is. The first half of the verse says א-להים מושיב יחידים ביתה, "God restores the lonely to their homes." In his reading, the "lonely" are those without spouses, and God "restores" or "settles" them in their homes, namely the dwellings they establish when they marry. The Hebrew word יחידים/*yeḥidim*, translated here as "lonely," can also mean "singles," while the word ביתה/*baytah*, "home," can also mean "wife," so the verse can also be rendered as "God settles single [men] with their wives." The preceding verse, Psalm 68:6, speaks of God as "the father of orphans, the champion of widows," which connects nicely to this family theme. However, the end of Psalm 68:7 and the next verse shift the focus from family life to the exodus from Egypt: "While the rebellious must live in a parched land. O God, when You went at the head of Your army, when You march through the desert" (Psalm 68:7–8). Why does the psalmist move from God helping people find their partners to saving the Israelites from the Egyptians? To teach us, R. Yose suggests, that these are equally great deeds, equally difficult, and equally a testimony to God's power. Here is the source of, and proof for, the rabbi's lesson: arranging a marriage is "as difficult before God as parting the Sea of Reeds."

Unimpressed and unconvinced by this answer, the Roman matron returns home to conduct an empirical test of the rabbi's claim, while the rabbi, too, returns "home" to his own wife. The matron assembles 1000 each of male and female slaves and quickly pairs them off in the ancient version of shotgun marriage. Echoing the rabbi's description of God's marital pronouncements [A2], she too summarily dictates which male and female slaves are to marry each other [B1]—and as she speaks her words are fulfilled, much like God's pronouncements in the biblical creation account. The aftermath, however, is quite different. The storyteller thus employs the motif of *imitatio dei*, the "imitation of God," in an exaggerated and perverse way. This theological principle teaches that humans should be God-like by "walking in God's ways" to seek holiness. According to the classic talmudic source: "Just as God clothes the naked, so you should clothe the naked. Just as God visits the sick, so you should visit the sick. Just as God comforted the bereaved, so you should also comfort the bereaved. Just as God buried the dead, so you should bury the dead."[15] Yet

15 Sotah 14a and parallels.

there is an important line between imitating God and impersonating or playing God, and this matron has clearly crossed it.

The storyteller's artful use of language contributes to this point through a fine wordplay based on the Hebrew word קלה/*kalah*, which means both "brief," when used of time, and "easy," when used of an action: the matron states that in a *kalah*/brief time she can arrange the marriages, to which the rabbi responds that it should not be considered so *kalah*/easy. One way to render the wordplay in English might be: "'She said...in a **small** (קלה) moment I can marry them off!' He said to her, 'Although it is a **small** (קלה) thing in your eyes...'" That which the matron considers easy to do, requiring but a brief amount of time, for God is very difficult (like splitting the sea), and requires a great amount of time—all God's time since the six days of creation! The wordplay contrasts her (mis)judgment about how challenging this endeavor is with God's true assessment, underscoring that her efforts to be God-like are doomed to failure.

The storyteller now introduces a comedic element: the next morning the unhappy husbands and wives, bruised and battered, complain about their assigned mates [B2]. They have not spent their wedding nights in newlywed bliss but in frustration and disappointment. The naive Roman matron is the main target of the humor, but its scope is far wider, as the audience will surely appreciate the difficulty of maintaining a happy marriage. They may even chuckle sympathetically at her simplistic view, perhaps recalling when they too thought marriage was a straightforward affair before experience taught them otherwise—even for a couple very much in love initially, never mind the random matches of the story. Moreover, given that the marriages of many audience members probably were arranged by their fathers, as was the norm in antiquity, they may have felt they knew something of the experiences of these slaves—even if their fathers tried harder than the Roman matron to find a fitting partner, and even if they believed that God worked behind the scenes to make a propitious match.

At this point the matron sends word to the rabbi, acknowledging the truth and wisdom of his Torah, which represents Judaism—in contrast to her Roman worldview [B3]. The storyteller concludes, as we have noted, with a repetition of the lesson, both for the matron and for the audience. Those who have had trouble finding the man or woman of their dreams, as well as those who still search desperately for their soulmate, will certainly appreciate this insight. Although the main didactic point concerns the challenge of finding the right partner—so difficult even for God—the sense that God plays a role in the process may tap into the feeling that marital love is mysterious, even miraculous: so special that it must contain something of the Divine. To this day traditional Judaism has a concept of one's *bashert,* the partner that one is divinely destined to marry, and there are similar notions in other religions. The story offers a concrete and vivid picture of just how these heavenly unions originate.

From a broader perspective, the story reflects Judaism's belief that God is known through relationships and that God actively seeks to enter into loving relationships with humans, as evidenced by the covenants made with the biblical patriarchs and then with the entire people of Israel. R. Yose's image of the Holy One as immersed in the intimate relationships of God's creations reflects this relational aspect of God, emphasizing a personal connection where love and commitment are foundational—a very different divine orientation from the one the matron expects from her gods. The love that humans experience and express in marital relationships is considered a reflection of this divine love, mirroring God's compassion, faithfulness, and desire for deep connections with God's creations. This understanding fosters a sense of mutual care and responsibility, where the love of one's spouse—and all other humans too, if to a lesser extent—becomes a way of experiencing and sharing in God's love.[16]

## TWO-PART STRUCTURES: ACTION AND REACTION

Two-part stories often consist of a character's action, narrated in the first half, and the ensuing reaction or consequence, recounted in the second half. Yet delineating even these simple structures helps us more clearly appreciate the relationships among the stories' parts. Here is a brief story of about fifty words in the original Hebrew:[17]

---

16 For more on this idea, see Shai Held, *Judaism Is About Love.*

17 On this story, see Jeffrey L. Rubenstein, *Land of Truth,* xi–xiv, and Yonatan Feintuch, "The Talmudic Chassid and the Stone-Clearer."

**תלמוד בבלי, בבא קמא נ ע״ב**

מעשה באדם אחד שהיה מסקל מרשותו לרה״ר. ומצאו חסיד אחד, אמר לו: ריקה מפני מה אתה מסקל מרשות שאינה שלך לרשות שלך? לגלג עליו. לימים נצרך למכור שדהו. והיה מהלך באותו רה״ר ונכשל באותן אבנים. אמר: יפה אמר לי אותו חסיד, מפני מה אתה מסקל מרשות שאינה שלך לרשות שלך?

**Talmud Bavli, Bava Kama 50b**

Once a man was removing stones from his field [and putting them] into the public domain. A certain *ḥasid* (pious or holy man) found him and said, "Scoundrel! Why do you remove stones from a domain that does not belong to you [and put them] into your domain?" The man laughed at him. After some time that man was in need and he sold his field. He was walking in that very place and he stumbled on those very stones. He said, "That *ḥasid* spoke well to me [when he said], 'Why do you remove stones from a domain that does not belong to you [and put them] into your domain?'"

The story tells of events that take place during two discrete times in the protagonist's life: the first, when he owns a field, the second, when he has sold his field. So we might divide the story into two halves along these temporal lines. Despite the extreme brevity, the storyteller repeats the holy man's words, "Why do you remove stones from a domain that does not belong to you [and put them] into your domain?" That those words are first spoken near the beginning of the story by the *ḥasid* and the second time at the end by the protagonist also suggests the story be divided into two corresponding parts.

Here is a table showing how we can align the two halves of the story and compare them to each other.

| First half | Second half |
|---|---|
| | לימים נצרך למכור שדהו. |
| מעשה באדם אחד שהיה מסקל מרשותו לרה״ר. ומצאו חסיד אחד. | והיה מהלך באותו רה״ר ונכשל באותן אבנים. |
| אמר לו: ריקה, **מפני מה אתה מסקל מרשות שאינה שלך לרשות שלך?** | אמר: יפה אמר לי אותו חסיד, **מפני מה אתה מסקל מרשות שאינה שלך לרשות שלך?** |
| לגלג עליו. | |

| | |
|---|---|
| | After some time that man was in need and he sold his field. |
| Once a man was removing stones from his field [and putting them] into the public domain. | He was walking in that very place and he stumbled on those very stones. |
| A certain *ḥasid* found him and said, "Scoundrel! **Why do you remove stones from a domain that does not belong to you [and put them] into your domain?"** | He said, "That *ḥasid* spoke well to me [when he said], '**Why do you remove stones from a domain that does not belong to you [and put them] into your domain?**'" |
| The man laughed at him. | |

In the first half of the story the man does not understand the *ḥasid*'s words. He believes he is tossing stones **out** of the field that he owns—clearing his field in order to plant crops or vegetables, or simply to enjoy a smooth backyard without annoying obstacles—**into** a domain that does not belong to him, the adjacent street or public thoroughfare. He even laughs at the *ḥasid,* thinking the words nonsensical and perhaps judging the man crazy. In the second half the protagonist encounters those same stones, this time stumbling upon them where they lie in the street. At this point he quotes those same words, now appreciating their truth, and presumably realizing that the *ḥasid* was wise after all. The ironic reversal precipitates this shift in perspective. Seeking to avoid a situation, stumbling on stones in his (apparent) domain, the protagonist ends up bringing it about, stumbling on stones in his (true) domain. Measure for measure, his actions in the first half boomerang upon him in the second. The story thus moves the (anti)hero, and with him the audience, from ignorance in the first half of the story to understanding in the second.

While the storyteller essentially spells out his didactic point by quoting the *ḥasid*'s words, he imparts it more effectively through the turn of events. We typically think of possessions as our own, as belonging to us, and this is especially true of our real estate, which, unlike money or valuables, cannot be pocketed by thieves, carted off, or easily taken away. (Thus the term "real" in real estate derives from the Latin *res,* "thing," and distinguishes "real property," which is fixed and immovable, from personal possessions or "movables.") Yet in truth all material wealth is ephemeral. Even land can be confiscated legitimately or illegitimately by the government, overrun by an army, or seized by strongmen. Financial reversals may force us to sell our landed property, even a patrimony that has been in the family for generations. Paradoxically, the only wealth that cannot be taken away is that which we share with all others: the public domain—in this story, the public roadway, but in our own world, public parks, beaches, forests, nature preserves, and libraries. As in many talmudic stories, the storyteller here moves his audience from a superficial view of reality to a deeper, more insightful, rabbinic view. I do not think delineating the structure is absolutely essential to appreciating the dynamics and meaning of the story in this case, but by so neatly demonstrating the inverted parallel between the two situations, it certainly helps.

Several other narrative devices enhance the story. First, the word used here for removing stones from a field, מסקל/*mesakkel,* comes from the root used in biblical and rabbinic sources to mean the capital punishment of stoning, itself a powerful and fearful image.[18] The double entendre and

**18** The image of throwing stones also recalls Jesus's saying, "Let he who is without sin, throw the first stone" (John 8:7).

imagery contribute to our understanding of the protagonist's offense: not only did he create a hazard for others, who might have hurt themselves on the stones that he threw into the public thoroughfare, but he ended up "stoning" himself. His "stoning" (=removing stones) turned into a stoning (=hurting himself with stones). Second, the word for "stumble," נכשל/*nikhshal,* derives from the same root as the word for "stumbling block," מכשול/*mikhshol,* of Leviticus 19:14: "Do not put a stumbling block before the blind." The protagonist was spiritually blind, or metaphorically blind to the consequences of his actions, and literally stumbled on the stones he threw. Finally, the holy man calls the man a "scoundrel," ריקא/*reika,* which might be related etymologically to the word for "empty," ריק/*reik.*[19] Perhaps he alludes to the man's attempts to empty his field of stones, or to the fact that he is empty or devoid of understanding.

The storyteller does not inform us why the man had to sell his field. This is a good example of a narrative gap, an element of the story omitted by the storyteller and left to the audience to fill. All literature has gaps, as even the most dedicated author cannot possibly include all aspects of the characters, settings, backgrounds, and other details of the narrative world. In addition, some of the audience's pleasure in reading or hearing stories comes from filling gaps as part of the interpretive process. Perhaps we are to understand the unfortunate turn of events as punishment for laughing at (mocking?) the *ḥasid*'s words; in this reading, the man lost his wealth as divine punishment for his sin, or at least in order to teach him a lesson. On the other hand, the loss of his field (and house?) may have resulted from sheer bad luck, from the vicissitudes of life beyond his, or anyone's, control, and not due to any fault or offense. Or again, it may have resulted from similar behavior of this sort, disregard of the public good, and a selfish focus on his own situation. The way we choose to fill the gap clearly makes a difference to the didactic force of the story, offering a secondary message to complement the main lesson about the ephemeral nature of material possessions.

## Seven-Part Structures

Seven-part structures are less common, but since seven is a special number in Jewish tradition, some stories are structured accordingly. Among them

---

19 On the meaning and other uses of this term, see Michal Bar-Asher Siegal, *Jewish-Christian Dialogues,* 43–65.

is the tale of the martyrdom of the mother and her seven sons. These events are generally associated with the persecutions that precipitated the Hasmonean (Maccabean) revolt of 167–166 BCE leading up to the festival of Hanukkah. The talmudic story, however, is not presented as a historical account, as we will presently see:[20]

**תלמוד בבלי, גטין נז ע״ב**

[A] כי עליך הורגנו כל היום נחשבנו כצאן טבחה (תהלים מד:כג). רב יהודה אמר: זו אשה ושבעה בניה.

[B1] אתיוהו קמא לקמיה דקיסר. אמרו ליה: פלח לעבודה זרה. אמר להו: כתוב בתורה: אנכי ה׳ א־להיך (שמות כ:א). אפקוהו וקטלוהו.

[B2] אתיוהו לאידך לקמיה דקיסר. אמרו ליה: פלח לעבודה זרה. אמר להו: כתוב בתורה: לא יהיה לך אלהים אחרים על פני (שמות כ:ג). אפקוהו וקטלוהו.

[B3] אתיוהו לאידך. אמרו ליה: פלח לעבודה זרה. אמר להו: כתוב בתורה: זובח לאלהים יחרם (שמות כב:יט). אפקוהו וקטלוהו.

[B4] אתיוהו לאידך. אמרו ליה: פלח לעבודה זרה. אמר להו: כתוב בתורה: לא תשתחוה לאל אחר (שמות לד:יד). אפקוהו וקטלוהו.

[B5] אתיוהו לאידך. אמרו ליה: פלח לעבודה זרה. אמר להו: כתוב בתורה: שמע ישראל ה׳ א־להינו ה׳ אחד (דברים ו:ד). אפקוהו וקטלוהו.

[B6] אתיוהו לאידך. אמרו ליה: פלח לעבודה זרה. אמר להו: כתוב בתורה: וידעת היום והשבות אל לבבך כי ה׳ הוא הא־להים בשמים ממעל ועל הארץ מתחת אין עוד (דברים ד:לט). אפקוהו וקטלוהו.

[B7] (a) אתיוהו לאידך. אמרו ליה: פלח לעבודה זרה. אמר להו: כתוב בתורה: את ה׳ האמרת וגו׳ וה׳ האמירך היום (דברים כו:יז–יח). כבר נשבענו להקדוש ברוך הוא שאין אנו מעבירין אותו באל אחר ואף הוא נשבע לנו שאין מעביר אותנו באומה אחרת.

(b) א״ל קיסר: אישדי לך גושפנקא. וגחין ושקליה כי היכי דלימרו קביל עליה הרמנא דמלכא. א״ל: חבל עלך קיסר חבל עלך קיסר. על כבוד עצמך כך, על כבוד הקב״ה על אחת כמה וכמה. אפקוהו למיקטליה.

[C] אמרה להו אימיה: יהבוהו ניהלי ואינשקיה פורתא. אמרה לו: בניי לכו ואמרו לאברהם אביכם אתה עקדת מזבח אחד ואני עקדתי שבעה מזבחות. אף היא עלתה לגג ונפלה ומתה. יצתה בת קול ואמרה: אם הבנים שמחה (תהלים קיג:ט).

---

20 On this story, see Robert Doran, "The Martyr." There is a parallel version of this story in Eikhah Rabbah 1:16.

**Talmud Bavli, Gittin 57b**

[A] *It is for Your sake that we are slain all day long, that we are regarded as sheep to be slaughtered (Psalm 44:23).* Rav Yehudah said, "This [verse] refers to the woman and her seven sons."

[B1] They brought out the first one before the emperor. They said to him, "Bow down to the idol." He said to them, "It is written in the Torah, *I am YHVH your God (Exodus 20:1).*" They took him out and killed him.

[B2] They brought out the next one before the emperor. They said to him, "Bow down to the idol." He said to them, "It is written in the Torah, *You shall have no other gods besides me (Exodus 20:3).*" They took him out and killed him.

[B3] They brought out the next one. They said to him, "Bow down to the idol." He said to them, "It is written in the Torah, *Whoever sacrifices to a god other than YHVH alone shall be proscribed (Exodus 22:19).*" They took him out and killed him.

[B4] They brought out the next one. They said to him, "Bow down to the idol." He said to them, "It is written in the Torah, *You must not worship any other god (Exodus 34:14).*" They took him out and killed him.

[B5] They brought out the next one. They said to him, "Bow down to the idol." He said to them, *"It is written in the Torah, Hear O Israel! YHVH our God, YHVH is one (Deuteronomy 6:4).*" They took him out and killed him.

[B6] They brought out the next one. They said to him, "Bow down to the idol." He said to them, "*Know therefore this day and keep in mind that YHVH alone is God in heaven above and on earth below; there is no other (Deuteronomy 4:39).*" They took him out and killed him.

[B7] (a) They brought out the next one. They said to him, "Bow down to the idol." He said to them, "It is written in the Torah, *You have affirmed this day that YHVH is your God, that you will observe His laws and commandments and rules, and that you will obey Him. And YHVH has affirmed this day that you are, as He promised you, His treasured people (Deuteronomy 26:17–18).* We have sworn to the Holy One, blessed be He that we will not exchange Him for another god. And He has sworn to us that He will not exchange us for another people."

(b) The emperor said to him, "Let me throw my seal before you. Bend down and pick it up such that they will say that you accepted the authority of the king." He said to him, "Shame on you, O emperor. Shame on you, O emperor. If [you have] such [concern] for your own honor, for the honor of the Holy One, Blessed be He, how much the more so!" They took him out to kill him.

[c] His mother said to them, "Give him to me that I might kiss him." She said to him, "My sons. Go and tell Abraham our father: You bound [a sacrifice] on one altar. I bound [sacrifices] on seven altars." She then went up to the roof and cast herself off and died. A heavenly voice went forth and said, "*[He sets the childless woman among her household as] a happy mother of children (Psalm 113:9).*"

This story has a brief introduction, in which Rav Yehudah presents the account to follow as an exemplification of a biblical verse [A], and a conclusion detailing the mother's parting words and suicide [C]. The main story recounts the martyrdom of seven brothers who each in turn refuse to worship an idol and profess their monotheism [B]. So one way to conceptualize this story is to focus on that tripartite structure. But I do not think that is the most powerful or relevant way to understand how this story is put together. Because the heart of the story consists of the recounting of the fate of the seven brothers, the seven-part structure stands out. The introduction is in fact not part of the story proper, and what I call the conclusion could be seen as a continuation of the death of the seventh son and included with the previous section. An alternative structure along those lines would consist of seven parts alone. Or we could understand the story as tripartite with a seven-part middle section. What is clear, however, is that in all of these possibilities, the seven-part unit explicitly marked by mention of the "seven sons" at the outset captures the audience's attention.

The deaths of the first six brothers are recounted with the standard structuring device of verbatim repetition, which renders the narration formulaic and repetitive, almost tedious from our perspective today. Each brother is commanded to bow down, refuses by quoting a biblical verse, and is led out and killed (again, an internal tripartite structure). The only variation is the biblical verse articulated by each brother (and that the first two are "brought out before the emperor" whereas the others are just "brought out").[21] This pattern provides an array of disparate injunctions against worshipping other gods, including some of the most celebrated biblical passages, two from the Ten Commandments and one from the Shema [B1, B2, B5]. Diverse admonitions against betraying one's faith, scattered over the course of the many chapters of the Torah, are collected and concentrated here in a relentless series of defiant acts. The structure with its repetitive elements accordingly functions to emphasize to the audience the import of the monotheistic precept and its centrality within the biblical and rabbinic worldviews. The resoluteness of the oppressor, even to the point of murdering one Jewish brother after another after another, must be countered by the faithful with equal resoluteness. Again and again and again the incredible cruelty and shocking suffering impact the audience, together with the incredible fortitude of the brothers. A briefer story with two or three sections would not have the same effect.

By placing the verses in the mouths of the martyrs, the storyteller also gives the biblical verses a "real-life" setting, which translates what appear to be matters of theology or intellectual propositions into action. What do "I am YHVH your God" and "Hear O Israel, YHVH our God, YHVH is one" entail? How does one realize these precepts? The story's answer: through accepting death rather than acknowledging a false god. The Torah, in fact, nowhere makes explicit the idea of martyrdom, that Jews must die rather than compromise monotheism or violate biblical law (and if so, which laws?). The narrativization of these passages, however, effectively communicates to the audience the rabbinic understanding

---

21 However, most manuscripts omit "before the emperor" even for the first two brothers. In addition, the storyteller begins "they brought out the first one" and then shifts to "they brought out the next one" for the following six.

of these texts: that one must submit to death if necessary, rather than worship other gods.

The pattern of the first six sections changes in the seventh, though it, too, begins with the same command to bow down and concludes with the same report of execution [B7]. In this last section, though, the brother not only quotes a biblical passage but glosses it with his own explanation. This is necessary because the Hebrew word translated as "affirmed" (האמרת/*he'emarta*) is difficult—the NJPS translation adds a note "exact meaning of Hebrew uncertain." The brother interprets the reciprocal action in terms of swearing an oath: Israel and God each swear eternal loyalty to the other. The victim will die before capitulating to the oppressor because Jews not only have been *commanded* against idolatry, as per the other biblical verses, but have *sworn* to obey this and the other commandments. This passage, as opposed to the previous verses, also recognizes God as an active partner in the relationship, who swears a divine oath of loyalty in response to Israel's faithfulness. This reassures the audience that God has not abandoned the Jewish people and "exchanged" them for the oppressors. Notwithstanding appearances, the emperor's power to persecute does not indicate that he has divine support, nor does the Jews' suffering imply their loss of divine favor. On the contrary, the continuation of the biblical passage, which the audience would have in mind, hints at an eventual reward for obedience: "*...His treasured people who shall observe all His commandments, and that He will set you, in fame and renown and glory, high above all the nations that He has made; and that you shall be, as He promised, a holy people to YHVH your God (Deuteronomy 26:18–19).*" The audience is to understand that the recompense envisaged in the verse's larger context, though obviously not taking place in this world, will materialize in the next, as soon becomes clear from the proclamation of the heavenly voice. Indeed, even in the face of this abject suffering the martyrs should take heart that the covenant between God and the Jewish people remains in force, and consequently that, despite their deaths, they will ultimately enjoy the blessings promised to those who uphold that covenant.

The major variation in the seventh section features the emperor trying to save face through a ruse [B7](b). Failing to beat the brothers into submission despite repeated attempts, he essentially concedes defeat, now seeking a show of phony obedience in place of real acceptance of his authority. If the brother bends down to pick up the emperor's seal, which presumably has the emperor's image engraved upon it, he will not only be following an order but will appear to bow to the emperor as well. But the seventh brother denies him even this feigned token of compliance. His explanation to the emperor articulates with utmost brevity the rabbinic theology underlying the obligation of martyrdom. The brothers' rejection of the emperor's demands devolves from the exact reason he wishes them to accept his authority: disobedience is dishonor, and when faced with the choice of disobeying either an earthly king or the divine King of kings, logic demands that they obey the higher authority. If the emperor's honor is so important that he requires a sham display rather than the dishonor entailed in public defiance, then he (and the audience) should understand why the brothers cannot capitulate. Our English term "martyrdom" derives from the Greek for witness (*martur*), based on the notion that accepting death bears witness to the truth of the victim's belief. The rabbinic term, however, is קידוש השם/*kiddush hashem*, "sanctification of the (=God's) Name" or "sanctification of the Name in public," which has a slightly different sense. The victim's refusal to violate a commandment sanctifies and honors God by demonstrating that God is the ultimate value and in turn causing others to regard God with reverence. The issue is not only whether Jews technically violate a commandment or not, but the impact of their actions on all parties involved, including the persecutors themselves and public witnesses, both Jewish and gentile.

The final scene shifts the focus to the mother, whose kisses intensify the emotional and tragic dimensions of the tale. Up to this point, the story has played out as a test of wills between males, culminating in violent death. As the gender dynamics shift, the theological focus gives way to the emotional impact of human loss. What can be more heartrending than a mother kissing her son goodbye for the last time before watching him be murdered? And this after beholding the deaths of six other sons? She invokes Abraham, aptly calling him "our father," in this context not only indicating his status as patriarch of the nation, but also underscoring his relationship to his son Isaac. Her message to him is both ironic and tragic, as her far greater suffering stems not from the seven sons versus the single son she mentions, but in the unmentioned conclusion of their respective ordeals: her sons were sacrificed, whereas Isaac was saved. If Abraham's greatness derives from his willingness to give up his son out of his faith and love of God, how much greater that this mother in fact experienced the loss from which Abraham was spared!

The mother's suicide may seem surprising in light of the negative view of suicide that is typically found in rabbinic legal sources. However, suicides are sometimes found in rabbinic stories, as opposed to halakhic sources, and her extreme distress certainly can be understood. More importantly, her death precipitates the heavenly voice that quotes from Psalm 113:9, *He sets the childless woman among her household as a happy mother of children.* The audience thereby understands that the mother is reunited with her children in heaven, receiving everlasting bliss ("a happy mother") as reward for her tremendous piety. Though momentarily "childless," both she and her sons enjoy eternal life in the world to come in return for their willingness to give up "temporary life" in this world. This expectation of otherworldly recompense for this-worldly death is fundamental to the rabbinic martyrdom ethic.

## Structures of Oral versus Written Literature

The verbal patterns and repetitions that provide key elements of the structures of rabbinic stories facilitate memorization, which is crucial in oral settings but less necessary with written texts. To illustrate the contrast between the styles of narratives as they appear in relation to written versus oral modes of transmission, we can look briefly at a different version of this same tale of the seven martyred brothers.

This version is found in the Second Book of Maccabees, a text included in a collection of scriptures known as the Apocrypha of the Catholic Bible, but not included in the Jewish Bible. It is likely that this account, written in Greek around 150 BCE, hundreds of years before the Talmud, was the source of the talmudic story. The author provides an account of the background and the events that culminated in the Hasmonean revolt, the course of the battles, the Jewish triumph, and the celebration victory that would become the festival of Hanukkah. Chapter 7 tells the story of the persecution of a mother and her seven sons:

> [7.1]It happened also that seven brothers and their mother were arrested and were being compelled by the king, under torture with whips and cords, to partake of unlawful swine's flesh.
>
> [2]One of them, acting as their spokesman, said, "What do you intend to ask and learn from us? For we are ready to die rather than transgress the laws of our fathers." [3]The king fell into a rage, and gave orders that pans and cauldrons be heated. [4]These were

heated immediately, and he commanded that the tongue of their
spokesman be cut out and that they scalp him and cut off his
hands and feet, while the rest of the brothers and the mother
looked on. 5When he was utterly helpless, the king ordered them
to take him to the fire, still breathing, and to fry him in a pan.
The smoke from the pan spread widely, but the brothers and
their mother encouraged one another to die nobly, saying, 6"The
Lord God is watching over us and in truth has compassion on
us, as Moses declared in his song which bore witness against the
people to their faces, when he said, 'And he will have compassion
on his servants.'"

7After the first brother had died in this way, they brought forward
the second for their sport. They tore off the skin of his head with
the hair, and asked him, "Will you eat rather than have your
body punished limb by limb?" 8He replied in the language of his
fathers, and said to them, "No." Therefore he in turn underwent
tortures as the first brother had done. 9And when he was at his
last breath, he said, "You accursed wretch, you dismiss us from
this present life, but the King of the universe will raise us up to an
everlasting renewal of life, because we have died for his laws."

10After him, the third was the victim of their sport. When it was
demanded, he quickly put out his tongue and courageously
stretched forth his hands, 11and said nobly, "I got these from
heaven, and because of his laws I disdain them, and from him I
hope to get them back again." 12As a result the king himself and
those with him were astonished at the young man's spirit, for he
regarded his sufferings as nothing.

13When he too had died, they maltreated and tortured the fourth
in the same way. 14And when he was near death, he said, "One
cannot but choose to die at the hands of men and to cherish the
hope that God gives of being raised again by him. But for you
there will be no resurrection to life!"

15Next they brought forward the fifth and maltreated him. 16But
he looked at the king, and said, "Because you have authority
among men, mortal though you are, you do what you please.
But do not think that God has forsaken our people. 17Keep

on, and see how his mighty power will torture you and your
descendants!"

[18]After him they brought forward the sixth. And when he was
about to die, he said, "Do not deceive yourself in vain. For we
are suffering these things on our own account, because of our
sins against our own God. Therefore astounding things have
happened. [19]But do not think that you will go unpunished for
having tried to fight against God!"

[20]The mother was especially admirable and worthy of honorable
memory. Though she saw her seven sons perish within a single
day, she bore it with good courage because of her hope in the
Lord. [21]She encouraged each of them in the language of their
fathers. Filled with a noble spirit, she fired her woman's reasoning
with a man's courage, and said to them, [22]"I do not know how you
came into being in my womb. It was not I who gave you life and
breath, nor I who set in order the elements within each of you.
[23]Therefore the Creator of the world, who shaped the beginning
of man and devised the origin of all things, will in his mercy give
life and breath back to you again, since you now forget yourselves
for the sake of his laws."

[24]Antiochus felt that he was being treated with contempt, and
he was suspicious of her reproachful tone. The youngest brother
being still alive, Antiochus not only appealed to him in words,
but promised with oaths that he would make him rich and
enviable if he would turn from the ways of his fathers, and that
he would take him for his friend and entrust him with public
affairs. [25]Since the young man would not listen to him at all, the
king called the mother to him and urged her to advise the youth
to save himself. [26]After much urging on his part, she undertook to
persuade her son. [27]But, leaning close to him, she spoke in their
native tongue as follows, deriding the cruel tyrant: "My son, have
pity on me. I carried you nine months in my womb, and nursed
you for three years, and have reared you and brought you up to
this point in your life, and have taken care of you. [28]I beseech you,
my child, to look at the heaven and the earth and see everything
that is in them, and recognize that God did not make them out
of things that existed. Thus also mankind comes into being. [29]Do

> not fear this butcher, but prove worthy of your brothers. Accept death, so that in God's mercy I may get you back again with your brothers." 30While she was still speaking, the young man said, "What are you waiting for? I will not obey the king's command, but I obey the command of the law that was given to our fathers through Moses. 31But you, who have contrived all sorts of evil against the Hebrews, will certainly not escape the hands of God. 32For we are suffering because of our own sins. 33And if our living Lord is angry for a little while, to rebuke and discipline us, he will again be reconciled with his own servants. 34But you, unholy wretch, you most defiled of all men, do not be elated in vain and puffed up by uncertain hopes, when you raise your hand against the children of heaven. 35You have not yet escaped the judgment of the almighty, all-seeing God. 36For our brothers after enduring a brief suffering have drunk of everflowing life under God's covenant; but you, by the judgment of God, will receive just punishment for your arrogance. 37I, like my brothers, give up body and life for the laws of our fathers, appealing to God to show mercy soon to our nation and by afflictions and plagues to make you confess that he alone is God, 38and through me and my brothers to bring to an end the wrath of the Almighty which has justly fallen on our whole nation." 39The king fell into a rage, and handled him worse than the others, being exasperated at his scorn. 39So he died in his integrity, putting his whole trust in the Lord. 40Last of all, the mother died, after her sons.[22]

The reader is immediately struck by the length and detail of this account compared to the brevity of the talmudic story. Writing allows the author to expatiate on the outstanding personal qualities of the characters, the type and variety of the tortures, the speeches each brother makes before his death, and the theological underpinnings of their choice of martyrdom. This version is indisputably more descriptive, vivid, and moving: one cannot but be impressed by the courage of the brothers and mother, feel the defiance of their powerful words, and experience outrage at the horrible suffering. The basic plot itself differs only slightly from the rabbinic version: the brothers are commanded to eat pig rather than bow

---

**22** Translation from Daniel R. Schwartz, "2 Maccabees."

to an idol; the king is named—Antiochus—and he appeals to the mother to instruct the seventh son to save himself, but she instead encourages him to refuse; how the mother dies is not explained, presumably by murder not suicide; the king does not propose a deception, but offers riches instead; and no heavenly voice concludes the story.[23]

However, the written and oral modes of transmission make the similarities in plot between the two versions pale in comparison to the substantially different form. Most importantly, the version of 2 Maccabees has no prominent structural divisions, verbal repetitions, or repeated phrases. The one major structural element devolves from the fact that there are seven brothers, hence seven sub-units, as each brother in turn is tortured and killed. The author, however, narrates these deaths in very different ways and puts diverse speeches in their mouths: he does not want to bore his reader any more than a modern author who varies their prose to keep the reader interested. He even narrates the entrance of each brother with different wording, rather than emphasizing the repeated events with the same formulaic wording as the talmudic story does. Rather than exploit the potential of the seven-part structure, he undermines it. While the author of 2 Maccabees minimizes repetition so as to engage and entertain his reader, the talmudic storyteller does the opposite, maximizing repetition so as to allow his audience to follow and memorize the story. And he succeeds: one can memorize the talmudic story fairly easily. To memorize this account from 2 Maccabees would require a great deal more time and effort, and many readers might never be able to commit the long text to memory.

The differences between these two accounts also help us appreciate the difference between historical writing and the didactic-fictional genre of rabbinic stories. The rabbinic storyteller does not actually connect the tale to the Hasmonean persecutions, nor to any specific historical event for that matter. He presents it as the exemplification of a biblical verse: "*It is for Your sake that we are slain all day long, that we are regarded as sheep to be slaughtered (Psalm 44:23)*...This [verse] refers to the mother and her seven sons" [A]. In other words, when the psalmist formulated this verse, he had in mind the future episode of this mother and her seven sons, and

---

23 The previous chapter of 2 Maccabees recounts a ruse similar to that of the talmudic story, in which the persecutors propose the victim substitute kosher meat while pretending to obey the persecutor's demand to eat swine flesh, but he refuses. This may be the source of that episode in the rabbinic story.

other similar events too. This scripture, understood as a type of prophecy, comes true in this story. Exactly when the story took place, the identity of the king, and the circumstances that precipitated the persecution—all these are beyond the storyteller's purview. The story takes place almost out of time and space, or within its own internal time and space. For this reason the story is not historical but paradigmatic. It relates not to a real episode, but to a time and event within the story's narrative world. The story functions as a paradigmatic example of persecutions of Jews by real kings in other historical times. For the rabbis, we could fairly say, this story was *also* about the Roman and Persian persecutions in antiquity, as well as about the Inquisition in fifteenth-century Spain, or about the Holocaust. And indeed, the story has been an inspiration and example for generations of Jews who have faced persecution and the prospect of martyrdom until the present day.

Historians sometimes claim that this story testifies to the rabbis' memories of the persecutions before the Hasmonean revolt—in other words, that the story is (more or less) historical. Because the rabbinic story resembles that of 2 Maccabees (which, as we noted, may have been its ultimate source), scholars tend to harmonize the two, and presume that the rabbinic story also must be about the events of 167–166 BCE. But that approach is misguided. Nothing in the rabbinic story itself points to that historical setting, and it actually distorts the story's function and message to construe it in that way.

By contrast, the account of 2 Maccabees *is* historical. The author claims these events happened in a specific place and time (corresponding to 167–166 BCE), ordered by a particular infamous king, Antiochus IV. The author sets the story within a wider swath of historical time: it occurred after the chain of events narrated in the previous chapters, and resulted directly from what transpired previously. The following chapters in turn relate how other Jews reacted to these persecutions, namely that Judas Maccabeus and his brothers began the revolt. The author's manner of writing history may not align with modern standards, which require presentation of evidence, acknowledgment of sources, a dispassionate perspective, and so forth. It may not be completely accurate and may involve exaggeration, embellishment, and perhaps even some outright fabrication, as was the norm in the historical writings of both Greeks and Romans. We might consider it bad history, though such an assessment would be anachronistic and unfair; we do not consider Greek medicine or science "bad" because their methods do not conform to contemporary criteria and because they get many things wrong. Yet even bad history is history: its project is fundamentally to relate historical events. The rabbinic story, on the other hand, is neither set in any larger temporal sequence, nor presented in a causal chain of events. It is not history but rather a narrative paradigm—not a report of events that happened in a particular time and place, but a story that provides a conceptual framework to make sense of similar affairs in many other times and places.

## Chiastic Structures

Verbal repetitions and other such features typically make it fairly easy for us to identify two-part, three-part, and even seven-part structures. Chiastic structures, to which we now turn, are more difficult to delineate. The terms "chiastic" and "chiasm" come from the Greek letter *xi*, which corresponds to our letter X. In a chiastic structure the first part of the story corresponds to the last part, the second part to the second-to-last part, and so forth. A graphic diagram of the story, with the correspondences illustrated on the horizontal the axis, therefore resembles the letter X:

First part [A] [A'] Last part

Second part [B] [B'] Second-to-last part

Third part [C] [C'] Third-to-last part

[D]

Fourth part / center

Third-to-last part [C'] [C] Third part

Second-to-last part [B'] [B] Second part

Last part [A'] [A] First part

As readers or listeners, we typically process a literary text in a linear manner—in this diagram, reading down the left vertical axis. We start with the beginning or first part, and proceed to the second part, then the third, and so forth, until the end. We naturally interpret the elements of the story accordingly, relating what happens, say, in the third part of the story to what preceded it directly in the second part; and ordinarily these subsequent parts indeed result from the earlier parts as the plot unfolds in a causal sequence. In chiastic structures, by contrast, the first part connects with the last part, the second part to the second-to-last part, and so forth until the middle (reading across the horizontal rows of the diagram). A chiastic structure invites the audience to discern relationships among the different parts of the story in a non-linear manner, so as to uncover other meanings.

Discerning a chiastic structure enables the audience to encounter a story in a less linear way, similar to how we encounter a painting or statue or other work of visual art. When we look at a painting, our eyes can move from one part to another in any order, and easily go back and forth between the sides and the middle or between the top and bottom. We visualize the parts, in other words, in relation to the whole and to the other parts in various ways. By identifying different relationships among parts of a story, relationships other than the linear sequence of beginning to end, we can understand the story in new ways.

Chiastic structures can be found in stories from many different cultures, as well as in other texts such as lists and laws. Some scholars believe chiastic structures devolve from deep structures in the human brain that can order and process information in this way. Whether or not that is true, however, I believe it useful to understand chiastic structures as a strategy employed by storytellers to communicate meanings to their audience, an alternative to the typical linear progression. It is also possible that chiastic structures are particularly suited for certain messages or for stories that address specific kinds of issues.

To illustrate this phenomenon let us analyze the talmudic story of "Yosef the Shabbat-honorer," found in Shabbat 119a, and subsequently told and retold in different variations throughout the Middle Ages and until the present day. The story's clearly defined structure has been identified and analyzed in excellent studies by leading scholars:[24]

**תלמוד בבלי, שבת קיט ע"א**

יוסף מוקיר שבי – הוה ההוא נכרי בשבבותיה דהוה נפישי נכסיה
טובא. אמרי ליה כלדאי: כולהו נכסי יוסף מוקר שבי אכיל להו. אזל

---

24 This analysis is based on Norman Cohen, "Structural Analysis of a Talmudic Story" and Yonah Frankel, "Chiasmus in Talmudic-Aggadic Narrative." See too Reuven Kiperwasser, "What Is Hidden in the Small Box?" 85–94 and Hillel I. Newman, "Closing the Circle," 123–27.

זבנינהו לכולהו ניכסי. זבן בהו מרגניתא אותבה בסייניה. בהדי דקא
עבר מברא, אפרחיה זיקא, שדייה במיא, בלעיה כוורא. אסקוה.
אייתוה אפניא דמעלי שבתא. אמרי: מאן זבין כי השתא? אמרי להו:
זילו אמטיוהו לגבי יוסף מוקר שבי דרגיל דזבין. אמטיוה ניהליה.
זבניה. קרעיה .אשכח ביה מרגניתא. זבניה בתליסר עיליתא דדינרי
דדהבא. פגע ביה ההוא סבא. אמר: מאן דיזיף שבתא, פרעיה שבתא.

**Talmud Bavli, Shabbat 119a**

Yosef the Shabbat-honorer—a certain gentile lived in his neighborhood and he (the gentile) had many possessions. Astrologers[25] said to him: "Yosef the Shabbat-honorer will consume them." He (the gentile) went and sold all his possessions. He bought a pearl, and placed it in his turban. [Once,] when he crossed a bridge, the wind blew it, it tossed it into the water, and a fish swallowed it. They (fishermen) raised it (the fish) up. They brought it [to market] on the eve of Shabbat. They said, "Who will be buying now?" They (others) said to them, "Go and take it to Yosef the Shabbat-honorer who regularly buys." They brought it to him. He bought it. He cut it. He found the pearl inside it. He sold it for thirteen vessels of gold coins. A certain old man came upon him. He said, "Whoever lends to Shabbat, Shabbat pays him back."

Before proceeding to discuss the structure, we should be sure to understand the basic plot. Astrologers tell an unnamed gentile that he will lose his wealth and a Jew known as "Yosef the Shabbat-honorer" will come to possess it. They have seen his destiny in the configuration of the stars or movement of the planets, and know his future by means of their ability to read these signs, what today we would call his horoscope. The gentile takes this information seriously and attempts to avoid the prediction. He sells his possessions and buys a valuable pearl that he places in his turban, apparently the standard headdress at that time, perhaps fixing the gem into a secret pouch to keep it safe. Presumably he thinks that were he to do nothing, thieves could carry off his valuables and furnishings when he leaves his house or that a flood could wash his possessions downstream.

---

25 Literally "Chaldeans." Chaldea, a region in Mesopotamia, was considered the origin of astrology, and in the Talmud "Chaldeans" is a technical term for astrologers.

He may worry that if he placed silver or gems in his pockets skilled pickpockets could steal them from his pants or coat. By placing the pearl in a turban, on the other hand, he believes he could no sooner lose it than lose his head. Alas, one day when he is crossing a bridge, a strong wind blows the turban off his head and into a river. The pearl becomes dislodged by the fall or due to the water, a fish swallows it, and fishermen in turn catch that fish. It is late on a Friday afternoon when they bring the fish to market and shoppers are scarce, as most people have already made their purchases for Shabbat and are now busy cooking and cleaning. When the fishermen ask around as to who may be interested in a very fine and fresh fish, some of the market folk suggest taking it to Yosef the Shabbat-honorer. As this nickname implies, Yosef loves Shabbat so much that although he has already made his purchases—he probably begins to prepare for Shabbat on Tuesday or Wednesday, and not just on Thursday afternoon and Friday morning like most folk—he will buy this fish, too, in order to enhance his Shabbat experience, happy to serve an additional dish or to be able to invite a few more guests. While preparing to cook the fish he cuts it open and finds the valuable pearl, which he sells for a great sum of money. An "old man," a type of rabbinic figure or mouthpiece of Jewish wisdom, explains to Yosef—and really to the audience—why he enjoyed this fortune, articulating a common saying found elsewhere in rabbinic literature too. "Lending to Shabbat," that is, spending money on food and other purchases so as to make Shabbat a special day, will be rewarded, just as a loan is paid back by the borrower. One should not bemoan the high expenses incurred when procuring fine food, flowers, candles, even new clothing to enhance the Shabbat experience, as ultimately these outlays will be remunerated.

What is the storyteller's message? At first glance the lesson seems to concern the reward for keeping Shabbat. The old man's concluding pronouncement, which can be seen as the moral of the story, spells this out explicitly, and the protagonist's nickname, "Shabbat-honorer," points to the same theme. We could also generalize from Shabbat to the commandments more broadly, and understand the message in terms of a reward for observing all of the *mitzvot* without concern for their expense. Yet, while the importance of Shabbat and the commandments must be part of the lesson, it does not do justice to the entirety of the story, which is more complex. Were the storyteller only interested in promoting Shabbat observance among his audience, he could have told a much simpler story. For example: "Once there was a pious man called Yosef the Shabbat-honorer who always prepared for Shabbat meticulously, and even spent a large amount of his weekly wages on fine and costly food. One day he bought an expensive fish to serve to his guests. When he cut open the fish he found a valuable pearl inside, which he sold for a great deal of money. An old man came upon him and said, 'Whoever lends to Shabbat, Shabbat pays him back.'"

The talmudic story, however, has a second theme, that of astrology, which in fact is the focus of the first half of the story before Yosef appears on the scene. What is the storyteller's attitude to, and didactic interest in, astrology? A moment's reflection allows us to realize that he clearly believes in astrology and the wisdom of the astrologers. They reveal to the gentile that he will lose his possessions to Yosef the Shabbat-honorer and their prediction comes true. Nor should this be surprising. Astrology in antiquity and throughout the Middle Ages was believed to be a science. Today we distinguish astronomy from astrology and consider the former an arena of science and truth, the latter a pseudo-science practiced by fortunetellers and charlatans. (The fact that so many people today take an interest in their horoscopes and that newspapers publish columns on astrology suggests that this distinction, even in our scientific age, remains somewhat blurry.) For the ancients, however, astrology and astronomy were one and the same, and belief in the power of stars and planets to reveal and influence fates was almost universal. A rabbi could no more dismiss astrology outright than we today would reject the efficacy of modern medicine, whatever our belief in the power of therapeutic prayers and divine healing. In theory, if a storyteller were interested in rejecting astrology and exposing its deceptiveness, he could tell a story in which the astrologers' forecast fails to materialize such that they look like fools. In practice, it would be very difficult to do so given the worldview of the times and the expectations of his audience. We do find a few stories in rabbinic literature that evince a more nuanced perspective toward astrology, though not a full-blown rejection of its cogency, and I will discuss three such stories in chapter 6 (pp. 182–190). Our storyteller, in any event, relates that the future foretold by astrologers comes to fruition despite considerable efforts to prevent it.

With these preliminary observations in mind, we turn to the structure to help us understand the storyteller's message. As noted, the story has two distinct themes that feature in its two halves: the first centered on the unnamed gentile and astrology, the second on Yosef and Shabbat. Shifts in the acting character are often useful ways to identify different units of the structure, and here the shift from the gentile and his efforts to avoid the prediction to Yosef and his efforts to enhance Shabbat help distinguish the two halves. We might also observe that both halves feature wise men who offer the characters wisdom, the astrologers and the "old man." In addition, both protagonists possess the same pearl for a limited period of time: the gentile buys the pearl and then loses it, while Yosef finds the pearl and then sells it.

Dividing the story into smaller sections with an eye to these connections between the elements in the two halves of the story yields a structure something like this:

[A] יוסף מוקיר שבי – הוה **ההוא נכרי** בשבבותיה דהוה נפישי נכסיה טובא.
אמרי ליה כלדאי: כולהו נכסי יוסף מוקר שבי אכיל להו.

[B] אזל **זבנינהו** לכולהו ניכסי. זבן בהו מרגניתא אותבה בסייניה.

[C] בהדי דקא עבר מברא, אפרחיה זיקא, שדייה במיא, בלעיה כוורא.

[D] אסקוה. אייתוה אפניא דמעלי שבתא. אמרי: **מאן** זבין כי השתא?

[D'] אמרי להו: זילו אמטיוהו לגבי יוסף מוקר שבי דרגיל דזבין. אמטיוה ניהליה.

[C'] זבניה. קרעיה .אשכח ביה מרגניתא.

[B'] **זבניה** בתליסר עיליתא דדינרי דדהבא.

[A'] פגע ביה **ההוא סבא**. אמר: **מאן** דיזיף שבתא, פרעיה שבתא.

[A] Yosef the Shabbat-honorer—**a certain gentile** lived in his neighborhood, and he (the gentile) had many possessions. Astrologers said to him: "All your possessions—Yosef the Shabbat-honorer will consume them."

[B] He (the gentile) went and **sold** all his possessions. He bought a pearl, and placed it in his turban.

[C] [Once,] when he crossed a bridge, the wind blew it (*afraḥeih*), it tossed it (*shadyeih*) into the water, and a fish swallowed it (*bela'eih*).

[D] They (fishermen) raised it (the fish) up. They brought it [to market] on the eve of Shabbat. They said, "**Who** will be buying now?"

[D'] They (others) said to them, "Go and take it to Yosef the Shabbat-honorer who regularly buys." They brought it to him.

[c'] He bought it (*zevaneih*). He cut it (*kera'eih*). He found (*ashkaḥ beih*) the pearl inside it.

[b'] He **sold** it for thirteen vessels of gold coins.

[a'] **A certain old man** came upon him. He said, "**Who**ever lends to Shabbat, Shabbat pays him back."

This breakdown allows us to explore the correspondences between the individual parts of the story more clearly and to move beyond the linear reading that progresses from beginning to end. In the first part astrologers—gentile sages—tell the gentile that Yosef the Shabbat-honorer will get his wealth, while in the last part the old man—a Jewish sage—tells Yosef why he became wealthy. These parts, labeled [a] and [a'], contrast secular/scientific knowledge with rabbinic/spiritual knowledge.

In the second and second-to-last parts, labeled [b] and [b'], the gentile sells his wealth and buys the pearl, whereas Yosef sells the pearl and acquires wealth. These sections manifest an ironic reversal reminiscent of the one we saw in the story of the man throwing stones from his field to the common domain: in seeking to avoid a situation, the gentile ends up bringing it about. The pearl he buys in an effort to prevent Yosef from possessing his wealth is ultimately translated into wealth by Yosef.

In the third and third-to-last parts, the gentile loses the pearl, which is swallowed by a fish, and Yosef finds the pearl in the belly of the fish. The correspondence between these parts is enhanced by the cadences of the Aramaic, in that each contains three rhyming phrases, five of them simply verbal forms with an attached pronoun. In [c], the words are אפרחיה/*afraḥeih*, "blew it," שדייה /*shadyeih*, "tossed it," and בלעיה/*bela'eih*, "swallowed it"; in [c'], the words are זבניה/*zevaneih*, "bought it," קרעיה/*kera'eih*, "cut it," and אשכח ביה/*ashkaḥ beih*, "found in it." Even in the translation one can notice that the pearl is the object of three verbs (blew, tossed, and swallowed), while Yosef is the subject of three verbs (bought, cut, and found).

In the middle sections, the fishermen look for a buyer, finding none [d], until they learn that Yosef will always be ready to purchase even so close to Shabbat [d']. The center of the story focuses attention on Shabbat, emphasizing Yosef's exceptional piety in contrast to ordinary folk, who, having already spent their allotted funds, will not be interested in additional outlays.

The chiastic structure can be illustrated as follows, with each section summarized for its main idea:

[A] Gentile is told that Yosef the Shabbat-honorer will consume his wealth.

[B] Gentile sells his wealth and buys a pearl.

[C] Pearl goes from gentile to fish (three rhyming phrases).

[D] Others won't buy on Shabbat eve.

[D'] Yosef will buy on Shabbat eve.

[C'] Pearl goes from fish to Yosef (three rhyming phrases).

[B'] Yosef sells the pearl and gets wealth.

[A'] Old man tells Yosef the Shabbat-honorer why he became wealthy.

We are now in a position to appreciate the storyteller's message. He juxtaposes two belief systems, two worldviews: astrology versus Judaism, secular "science" versus Jewish theology, gentile knowledge versus Jewish tradition. He believes in both, much as today a religious individual must recognize the laws of nature. He assures his audience that though astrology is true, at least on one level, the system of *mitzvot* with the promise of reward and punishment is also true, or even more true. It may look as if Yosef became wealthy due to the influence of the celestial bodies—it may appear as if the astrologers can foretell the future—but the true driving force of reality is observance of Jewish traditions and fealty to its underlying theology. In fact, we should hesitate to spell out the storyteller's method of reconciling astrology and Jewish observance too precisely, because the two worldviews resist harmonization and stand in tension with one another, if not outright contradiction. The storyteller means to grapple with this tension, not to provide a facile resolution of it. In his telling the two systems stand in an exquisite tension such that both are true: one can eat one's astrological cake (or fish) and have the rewards for fulfilling Shabbat, too. However we explain this paradox, the story effectively moves the audience from a superficial view of the nature of things to a deeper, spiritual, rabbinic perspective—as many talmudic stories strive to do.

In this respect, the story is surprisingly relevant to contemporary times. Living a traditional life and embracing traditional Jewish (or Christian or Islamic, for that matter) theology today pose challenges to those who also hold a modern worldview. Belief in divine providence, revelation, and reward and punishment stands in tension with belief in the laws of nature, which, almost by definition, reject the supernatural. The same can be said for ideas such as evolution, which stand in tension with belief in divine creation. These worldviews or belief systems are not necessarily incompatible: many of us today seek out the best of modern medicine while also saying prayers for health that beseech God to heal illness. But dispassionate examination of the assumptions and underpinnings of the two systems, the traditional and the scientific, will inevitably reveal tensions and points of conflict between them. Long ago our storyteller grappled with similar tensions and insisted that one can hold on to both worldviews.

The chiastic structure is one of many elements of the literary artistry of the story that contribute to its power and beauty, including dramatic irony as well as the three rhyming phrases in the corresponding parts. The storyteller playfully employs the verb "consume" (אכיל/*akheil*, literally "eat") in the astrologers' prediction that the gentile will lose his possessions to Yosef [A]. More idiomatic would have been using the verb "acquire," "possess," or "inherit"; "consume/eat" is somewhat awkward, in both the original Aramaic and the English translation, but effectively alludes to the fish, which Yosef prepares to consume. The storyteller also echoes the reference to the "certain gentile" (ההוא נכרי/*hahu nokhri*) in the first section with "a certain old man" (ההוא סבא/*hahu sava*) in the final section, which helps the audience appreciate the correspondence between these sections. Section [D] ends with a question, "**Who** (מאן/*man*) will be buying now?" and the saying that concludes the story opens with the same word, though used not as an interrogative but as a relative pronoun: "**Who**[ever] lends to Shabbat, Shabbat pays him back." Thus the two halves of the story, the first focused on the gentile and astrology, the second on Yosef and Shabbat, each conclude with parallel language, providing an additional structural division. Finally, the Aramaic word for "lend," יזיף/*yazeif*, clearly echoes the name "Yosef" (יוסף). In theory the protagonist could have been "Moshe the Shabbat-honorer" or "David the Shabbat-honorer," but the storyteller wished to create a pun involving a word in the old man's aphorism. The story in fact begins with the word "Yosef," and by almost concluding with the punning word "lend," the storyteller creates a type of textual loop or envelope.

The density of these literary devices is testimony to the sophisticated narrative art of the storyteller, as well as evidence of the story's genre as didactic fiction. It is very difficult to employ irony, wordplay, and precise structural parallels when writing history or biography because the author is constrained by real historical events, which afford less freedom and flexibility to choose language and shape the contours of the plot.

Studying the structure of a rabbinic story—whether tripartite, two-part, seven-part, chiastic, or other types—is a crucial step in appreciating its meaning. As oral literature, rabbinic stories are formulated extremely economically and tersely, with few extraneous sections or even phrases. By identifying a structure, readers are often able to discern relationships among these sections that they might otherwise not notice.

# CHAPTER 2
## Symbolic Names and Characterization

THE BRIEF AND compact nature of oral literature requires that characterization be done in the most economical way possible. Novels and short stories routinely devote many pages to providing the audience an understanding of characters, supplying detailed accounts of formative events in their lives, and having an omniscient narrator explicitly recount their various personality traits. In talmudic stories, as in other genres of oral literature such as folktales, characterization is much more succinct, often contained within the character's name itself. These "symbolic" names convey the essence of the character in an extremely brief way, as no other description is necessary for the storyteller's purposes.

English language readers are most familiar with this kind of name in folktales and children's literature: Snow White and the Seven Dwarves (Sleepy, Grumpy, etc.), the Wicked Witch of the West, Sleeping Beauty, Little Red Riding Hood, The Big Friendly Giant, Tom Thumb, and Captain Hook. Yet we find them in a variety of modern literary novels and other texts as well. Henry Fielding's *Tom Jones* features Mr. Allworthy, a very worthy and virtuous man, who employs a tutor Mr. Thwackum, who regularly thrashes his students. In Thomas Mann's *Dr. Faustus*, the character Professor Schleppfuss, whose name literally means "drag foot," limps and drags his foot.

Symbolic names are also common in the Bible, and this background helps explain their prominence in rabbinic stories. In the Book of Genesis, the patriarchs receive symbolic names: God changes Abram's name to

Abraham (אברהם/*Avraham*) and explains "for I will make you the father (אב/*av*) of a multitude (המון/*hamon*) of nations" (17:5). Jacob (יעקב/*ya'akov*) "emerged holding on to the heel (עקב/*ekev*) of Esau, so they named him Jacob" (25:26). Later the supernatural being with which Jacob wrestles changes his name to Israel (ישראל/*yisrael*) and explains "for you have striven (שרית/*sarita*) with beings divine (א-להים/*elohim*) and human" (32:29). God tells Hagar to name her child Ishmael (ישמעאל/*yishmael*), which means "God hears" because "YHVH has heard (שמע/*shama*) your suffering" (16:11).[1] The Prophets feature even more spectacular examples of such names. A famous case is that of Naval/Nabal in 1 Samuel 25:25. After Naval rebuffs David's request for provisions in an insulting way, his wife Abigail seeks to appease David, who has 400 armed followers: "Please, my lord, pay no attention to that wretched fellow Naval. For he is just what is name says. His name means 'boor' (*naval*) and he is a boor."

Talmudic stories are also replete with such symbolically named characters:

- Ḥoni the Circle-Drawer (מעגל/*me'agel*), who draws a circle when his prayers for rain are not answered, stands within it, and tells God: "Master of the Universe! Your children turned to me, for I am like a member of the household before You. I swear by Your great name that I shall not move from here until You have mercy upon Your children" (Mishnah Ta'anit 3:9 and Ta'anit 23a).[2]
- Neḥunya Digger of Cisterns, whose daughter falls into a cistern and is ultimately saved by a supernatural figure (Bava Kama 50a–b).

---

1 Additional examples from the Book of Genesis: Adam's name derives from the earth from which he was created: "YHVH God formed man (אדם/*adam*) from the dust of the earth (אדמה/*adamah*)" (1:7), though in this case the biblical text does not explicate the origin of the name directly. Leah, Rachel, Bilhah, and Zilpah give their sons symbolic names (29:31–30:13, 30:18–24). For example, Leah "conceived again and bore a son, and declared, 'This is because God heard (שמע/*shama*) that I was unloved and has given me this one also,' so she named him Shimon (שמעון/*shimon*)" (29:33).

2 Some scholars explain the name as Ḥoni the Roller, related to a rolling device to spread plaster on roofs, apparently his profession. But this is not the explanation given in the story.

- Naḥum of Gamzu, who states "This (זו/*zu*) too (גם/*gam*) is for the good" when a terrible disaster befalls him, though all ultimately ends well (Ta'anit 21a).
- Nakdimon ben Gurion, Ben Kalba Savua, and Ben Tzitzit Ha-Keset, three rich men of Jerusalem. In this case the Talmud explains their names: "Nakdimon b. Gurion [was so called] because the sun cut through (*nakdah*) [the clouds] for him. Ben Kalba Savua [was so called] because whoever entered his house hungry as a dog (*kelev*) departed full (*save'a*). Ben Tzitzit Ha-Keset [was so called] because his fringes (*tzitzit*) dragged on pillows (*kesatot*)" (Gittin 56a).

The full story of the sun cutting through the clouds for Nakdimon appears elsewhere in the Talmud (Ta'anit 20a). Nakdimon borrows cisterns of water from a Roman official during a drought, agreeing to pay a large amount if he fails to return them full of water by a set date. At the last minute Nakdimon returns the water—but the Roman claims the sun has set and the deadline has been missed. Nakdimon prays and the sun breaks through the clouds. The story concludes: "Nakdimon was not his [real] name, but rather his name was Buni. Why was he named Nakdimon? Because the sun broke through (נקדה/*nakdah*) for his sake."[3] Thus the Talmud itself provides an etiology for his symbolic name.

We have already encountered an excellent talmudic example of a symbolic name, "Yosef the Shabbat-honorer," in the story discussed in the previous chapter (pp. 60–68). This name tells us everything we need to know about Yosef for the purposes of the story: Yosef was meticulous in observing Shabbat each week, and this information will prove crucial to the plot. Because Yosef is known to be such a Shabbat-honorer, fishermen bring him the fine fish they catch just before Shabbat, by which time most people have already made all their Shabbat purchases. Recall too that the name Yosef also plays on the concluding proverb, "He who lends (*yazeif*) to Shabbat, Shabbat pays him back." Thus both the name and the sobriquet connect to the themes of the story. Such names are also a marker of the fictional nature of talmudic stories: the correlation between name and

3 This is the reading in the manuscripts. The standard printed edition reads נקדרה/*nikderah*, "penetrated." See Rashi ad loc.

content is a function of the storyteller's art, which depends on the freedom to choose a name that matches the needs of the plot.

Another good example of this phenomenon appears in a talmudic story that features a character named Pantokaka, which derives from the Greek *pantos* (wholly, in all ways) and *kakos* (evil), thus "Mr. Completely-Evil" or "Mr. All-Immoral."[4] This story appears in the Yerushalmi, compiled when the Land of Israel was a province of the eastern Roman Empire, where Greek was the vernacular, and the audience could be expected to understand such basic Greek words. It is also possible "Mr. Completely-Evil" was a stock villain regularly used in folktales and familiar to the audience.

**תלמוד ירושלמי, תענית א:ד (סד ע"ב)**

[A] איתחמי לרבי אבהו. פנטקקה יצלי ואתי מיטרא. שלח רבי אבהו ואייתיתיה.

[B] אמר ליה: מה אומנך? אמר ליה: חמש עבירן ההוא גוברא עביד בכל יום. מוגר זנייתא. משפר תייטרון. מעיל מניהון לבני. מטפח ומרקד קדמיהון. ומקיש בבבולייא קדמיהון.

[B'] אמר ליה: ומה טיבו עבדת? אמר ליה: חד זמן הוה ההוא גברא משפר תייטרון אתת חדא איתא וקמת לה חורי עמודא בכייא. ואמרת לה: מה ליך? ואמרה לי: בעלה דהיא איתתא חביש, ואנא בעייא מיחמי מה מעבד ומפנינה. וזבנית ערסי ופרוס ערסי ויבית לה טימיתיה, ואמרית לה: הא ליך. פניי בעליך ולא תיחטיי.

[A'] אמר ליה: כדיי את מצלייא ומתענייא.

**Talmud Yerushalmi, Ta'anit 1:4 (64b)**

[A] It appeared to R. Abbahu [in a dream] that Pantokaka (=Mr. Completely-Evil) should pray so that rain would come down. R. Abbahu sent and had him brought before him.

[B] He said to him, "What is your profession?" He said, "I commit five sins every day: I engage prostitutes. I decorate the theater. I carry their (the prostitutes') garments to the baths. I clap and dance before them. And I clash the cymbals before them."

4 See Saul Lieberman, *Greek in Jewish Palestine*, 31 n. 18; Michael Sokoloff, *Dictionary of Jewish Palestinian Aramaic*, 437.

[B'] He said to him, "What good deed have you done?" He said to him, "One day when I was decorating the theater a certain woman entered and stood behind a column [posing as a prostitute] and wept. I said to her, 'What is the matter?' She said to me, 'My husband is incarcerated, and I want to see what I can do to free him.' I sold my bed and bedding and gave the money to her, and I said to her, 'This is for you. Free your husband and do not sin.'"[5]

[A'] He (R. Abbahu) said to him, "You are worthy to pray and to be answered."

The absence of the winter rains is a critical problem in the Land of Israel, which depends almost exclusively on rain for crops to grow, so that even minor droughts can quickly result in disaster. An entire tractate of Mishnah, Ta'anit (meaning "fast day"), is devoted to this dire situation, prescribing a series of public fasts, prayers, and other mourning practices to be observed in a communal effort to bring rain. Tractates Ta'anit of both the Bavli and Yerushalmi develop the Mishnah's rituals and also contain dozens of stories of rabbis, holy men, and sometimes entire villages praying for rain with varying degrees of success. Our story appears in this context, but begins immediately with a tension: the dream—a supernatural sign from above—directs R. Abbahu to ask a rogue to pray for rain, when we would expect that this weighty task be given to the most learned rabbi or most pious holy man. Only absolutely exemplary and righteous humans, the audience assumes, have the merit that their prayers for rain be answered by the Almighty. This tension immediately becomes apparent to the audience through the symbolic name Pantokaka, "Mr. Completely-Evil," as no further information is necessary to understand the disjunction between the character of the individual and the task for which he is selected. Thus with maximum economy—just seven words in the original Aramaic—the storyteller exploits the effectiveness of the symbolic name to prepare the audience for the story to come.

R. Abbahu summons Pantokaka, inquires after his occupation, and receives the details of his corrupt lifestyle [B]. Pantokaka seems to be portrayed as the owner of a high-class brothel, what we might call a pimp,

---

5 Lieberman, *Greek in Jewish Palestine*, 32 n. 22 proposes the emendation "drum and items belonging to my drum" for "bed and bedding," in which case the man sold his valuable professional tools to save the woman.

and he candidly discloses his daily routine of five sins. Some interpreters accordingly understand his name to derive from the Greek *pente* or *penta*, "five," and *kakos*, "evil" or "sin," hence "Mr. Five-Sins," which would be an equally symbolic name; the Aramaic consonantal text can also be read as Pentakaka. It is also possible that both meanings are intended—a doubly symbolic name. Apart from procuring and readying the prostitutes, Pantokaka provides musical and theatrical entertainment, a description that may suggest a mime or actor.[6] Because Greek courtesans were often trained in music and Roman actors had a low social status comparable to prostitutes, the combination of musical, theatrical, and sexual entertainment often went together.[7] One Roman author describes mimes, in particular, as little different from male prostitutes.[8] Though there was nothing illegal about these professions in antiquity, they certainly would have been judged immoral and decadent by the Jewish moral standards of the time. Indeed, the rabbis considered theaters and circuses as the cultural opposites of Judaism: a talmudic prayer thanks God "that You have given my portion among those who sit in the houses of study and houses of prayer, and You have not given my portion among the theaters and circuses. For I work and they work. I am diligent and they are diligent. I work to inherit the Garden of Eden, and they work [to inherit] a pit of darkness."[9] Why, the audience asks themselves, should the rabbi, who frequents both the house of study and synagogue, be directed to request a whoremonger and entertainer, a patron of theaters and circuses, to pray on behalf of the community?

The answer comes in the second half of the story, in Pantokaka's response to R. Abbahu's follow-up question [B']. The chronic sinner has a heart of gold. When a poor woman presented herself at his theater, apparently seeking work among his group of prostitutes, he noticed her tears and asked her what was wrong. Upon realizing that she was forced to sell her body in a desperate effort to raise money to free her husband,

---

6 See Martin Jacobs, "Theatres and Performances" and Zeev Weiss, "Theatres, Hippodromes, Amphitheatres, and Performances."

7 See Debra Hamel, *Trying Neaira*, 4–15.

8 T. D. Barnes writes: "Aristides depicted *pantomimi* as sexually promiscuous, no better than male prostitutes" ("Christians and the Theater," 175).

9 Yerushalmi Berakhot 4:1 (33a).

he does not allow such degradation, and instead himself provides her the needed funds. The sale of his bed and bedding (probably the bedding used by the prostitutes in their immoral sexual activity) for the funds necessary to preserve the woman's sexual purity creates a beautiful and ironic contrast: the instruments of decadence and corruption are transformed into the means of salvation. Instead of generating income for Pantokaka through depraved uses, their sale produces revenue for his most noble and generous deed on behalf of another.

The greatness of Pantokaka's deed is twofold. First, his deed is selfless and contrary to his personal interest. He could have earned money for himself by taking her into his brothel. Yet he not only forgoes that potential income but sells his own possessions in an extremely charitable act. Second, he reacts with empathy and immediacy in what seems to be a spontaneous response to the suffering of another human being. He is not acquainted with this woman or her difficulties. He could easily have said to himself: "How sad...but not my problem." Yet upon hearing her predicament he immediately responds.

Upon hearing this account, the rabbi immediately recognizes and acknowledges the virtue of Pantokaka, resolving the tension occasioned both by the symbolic name and the corrupt occupation. The compact chiastic structure contributes to this narrative dynamic. The reason the dream directs the rabbi to summon Pantokaka to pray [A] is spelled out at the end [A'], namely that he is "worthy." The rabbi asks Pantokaka two questions, about his profession [B] and about a good deed [B']. Pantokaka in turn recounts a depraved quotidian routine [B], which contrasts sharply with a singular act of extraordinary piety [B']. The first half of the story baffles the audience with what seems to be an incongruity between the individual and the crucial task for which he is called, while the second half illustrates that he is well suited for the mission. Surprisingly, Mr. Completely-Evil is not so completely evil after all: this is an ironically symbolic name, which points to the storyteller's message. Anyone and everyone, even those most dissolute and sinful, those who wear their wickedness like a banner, may have deeds of outstanding goodness to their credit that trump their misdeeds, such that they rank among the most "worthy." Who knows whether the scoundrel we behold is really a hidden *tzaddik* (righteous one)? Likewise, no matter how much individuals have sinned or failed to live up to their own moral standards, they can redeem themselves through one meritorious act.

## Symbolic Names and Narrative Themes

Let us look at another story featuring a hero whose symbolic name relates to the themes of his story. This story appears in Avodah Zarah, which deals in part with forbidden and permitted interactions between Jews and gentiles. The tractate contains various stories of evil and hostile gentiles, and others about virtuous and generous gentiles. This story features a protagonist with the unlikely and thoroughly symbolic name Ketiah bar (=son of) Shalom. His personal name comes from the root קטע/*k-t-a*, meaning "cut, bite, kill," and his patronymic שלום/*shalom* means "peace or wholeness," hence "Mr. Cut-One son of Peace":

**תלמוד בבלי, עבודה זרה י ע"ב**

קטיעה בר שלום מאי הוי?

[A1] דההוא קיסרא דהוה סני ליהודאי. אמר להו לחשיבי דמלכותא: מי שעלה לו נימא ברגלו יקטענה ויחיה או יניחנה ויצטער? אמרו לו: יקטענה ויחיה.

[A2] אמר להו קטיעה בר שלום: חדא דלא יכלת להו לכולהו, דכתיב, כי כארבע רוחות השמים פרשתי אתכם (זכריה ב:י). מאי קאמר? אלימא דבדרתהון בד' רוחות, האי כארבע רוחות, לארבע רוחות מבעי ליה. אלא כשם שאי אפשר לעולם בלא רוחות, כך אי אפשר לעולם בלא ישראל. ועוד קרו לך מלכותא קטיעה.

[A3] א"ל: מימר שפיר קאמרת. מיהו, כל דזכי מלכא, שדו ליה לקמוניא חלילא.

[B1] כד הוה נקטין ליה ואזלין, אמרה ליה ההיא מטרונית: ווי ליה לאילפא דאזלא בלא מכסא.

[B2] נפל על רישא דעורלתיה, קטעה. אמר: יהבית מכסי. חלפית ועברית.

[B3] כי קא שדו ליה אמר: כל נכסאי לר' עקיבא וחביריו.

[C1] יצא ר' עקיבא ודרש: והיה לאהרן ולבניו (שמות כט:כח). מחצה לאהרן ומחצה לבניו.

[C2] ויצתה בת קול ואמרה: קטיעה בר שלום מזומן לחיי העוה"ב.

[C3] בכה רבי ואמר: יש קונה עולמו בשעה אחת, ויש קונה עולמו בכמה שנים.

**Talmud Bavli, Avodah Zarah 10b**

What is [the story of] Ketiah bar Shalom?

[A1] There was a certain caesar who hated the Jews. He said to the notables of his empire: "One who has a growth on his leg—should he cut it off (*yakti'enah*) and live or leave it alone and suffer?" They said to him: "Let him cut it off (*yakti'enah*) and live."

[A2] Ketiah bar Shalom said to them: "First, you will be unable to [overcome] all of them (the Jews), as it is written, *For I have spread them out* ***like*** *the four winds of heaven (Zechariah 2:10)*. What [does the verse] mean? If it means, "He scattered them **to** the four winds of heaven," then this [phrase] "***like*** the four winds" needs to be "**to** the four winds"! Rather, [it means that] just as the world cannot exist without winds, so too the world cannot exist without Israel. Second, [if you kill all the Jews] they will call you 'a cut-off (*keti'ah*) empire.'"

[A3] He (the caesar) said to him (Ketiah): "You have spoken well. Nevertheless, whoever bests the emperor, they throw him into a furnace."[10]

[B1] When they were seizing him (Ketiah) and going out, a certain Roman lady said to him: "Woe to the ship that sails without [paying] the tax!"

[B2] He fell on the tip of his foreskin, and bit it (*keta'ah*) off. He said: "I have paid my tax. I will pass and proceed."

[B3] When they were throwing him [into the furnace], he said: "All my possessions [are bequeathed] to R. Akiva and his colleagues."

[C1] R. Akiva went out and expounded: "*And it shall be to Aaron and his sons (Exodus 29:28)*—half to Aaron and half to his sons."

[C2] A heavenly voice went out and said: "Ketiah bar Shalom is destined to the life of the world to come."

[C3] Rabbi [Yehudah HaNasi] wept and said: "There are those who acquire their [eternal] world in one instant, and there are those who acquire their [eternal] world over many years."

---

10 Literally a "hollow furnace," which was heated from below.

This is a strange story, and we must clarify its basic meaning before discussing the symbolic name.[11] The story can be divided into three parts: First, the discussion among the Roman emperor (caesar) and his notables [A], presumably his aristocratic supporters or his council of advisors, which includes Ketiah. Second, Ketiah's punishment and death [B]. Third, the reactions to his death [C]. Each part consists of three sections: the sections of the first and third parts are almost entirely dialogue, while the sections of the second part consist of three actions, each accompanied by a verbal utterance.

This emperor hates the Jews, analogizing them to a painful growth on one's leg. Just as one should excise the growth to end the pain it causes, prevent its spread, and restore the body to health, so the Jews, he suggests, should be excised from the body of the empire. The notion of the Jews as a disease or cancer is rare in ancient sources, though it would become more common in the Middle Ages; it would eventually come to feature prominently in Nazi propaganda.

As opposed to the rest of the nobles, who quickly affirm the emperor's suggestion to annihilate the Jewish people, responding like spineless yes-men, Ketiah counsels against the persecution [B2]. He offers two arguments, one based on a midrashic reading of a verse and the other focused on honor and reputation. The first derives from an awkward phrase in Zechariah 2:10, where God mentions having dispersed the Israelites "*like* the four winds," rather than "*to* the four winds" as we would expect with an image of scattering. Ketiah accordingly interprets this anomalous locution not in a geographic sense, but rather as a comparison indicating that the Jewish people are similar to the four winds: they both comprise a fundamental element of the world and hence cannot be destroyed completely. For this reason the emperor's efforts to expunge the Jews from his dominion are doomed to fail. Ketiah's second argument is that eliminating the Jews will be counterproductive, as it would render the empire incomplete such that it would be remembered in pejorative terms as a "cut-off empire." The meaning of this expression is not totally clear, but the sense is that the emperor will have destroyed a part of his own realm. As opposed to the great Roman emperors who conquered territory

---

11 On this story see Howard Jacobson, "Ketiah Bar Shalom"; Daniel Boyarin, "Homotopia"; Gray, "The Power Conferred"; Mira Beth Wasserman, *Jews, Gentiles, and Other Animals*, 57–60; and Shlomo Zuckier, "Cutting a Peace."

and subjugated other peoples, this emperor will have reduced the empire's population and strength, an undesirable legacy.

The emperor accepts these arguments and abandons his genocidal proposal [A3]. Unfortunately, Ketiah's efforts on behalf of the Jewish people boomerang such that in saving the Jews he dooms himself. He has dishonored the emperor by demonstrating publicly his superior wisdom and the weaknesses of the emperor's plan. The duty of the notables apparently is to approve whatever the emperor proposes, as Ketiah's associates do, rather than provide sage counsel. Although the story is set in Rome, this caricature of an emperor and his court probably derives more from the Bavli storytellers' familiarity with depictions of Persian and other Eastern emperors, who were considered divine, demanded absolute deference, and dispensed draconian and unpredictable punishments. The emperor sentences Ketiah to burn to death in a furnace, an image that may derive from Daniel 3, where King Nebuchadnezzar sentences three Jewish youths to be thrown into a fiery furnace.

The second section of the story recounts the death and final words of Ketiah [B]. This story, like the story of the arranged marriages discussed above, features the stock character of a Roman matron, an aristocratic woman. Here she makes a cryptic pronouncement as Ketiah is led forth to his death. In saying "woe," she seems to mean that because he is not Jewish, his noble deed and quasi-martyrdom will be unrewarded. A ship that sails without paying tax would not be allowed to dock in Roman ports and deliver its goods, and similarly Ketiah's soul will not be allowed to enter the world to come. The storyteller apparently believes either that only Jews are eligible for posthumous reward in the next world or that Ketiah's former wicked deeds (in collaboration with the evil emperor?) will not offset this one virtuous act: he has not paid the "tax" that other Jews (metaphorically) pay, namely a life dedicated to fulfilling the *mitzvot*. The fiery furnace is not only the means of his cruel, this-worldly death, but also portends his terrible posthumous punishment in the flames of hell.

Ketiah immediately takes this observation to heart. Having defended the Jewish people with his words, he now joins them by his deeds, performing an auto-circumcision in the nick of time [B2]. Some manuscripts of the Talmud make the image even more graphic by adding that he bit off his foreskin "with his teeth." In other words, Ketiah converts to Judaism by undergoing the essence of the conversion ritual, circumcision, thereby fulfilling one of the most important commandments. Ketiah's act does not fulfill the technical legal requirements for conversion, which would include instruction about the commandments and immersion in a *mikveh* (ritual bath), but the story here clearly considers it to be an "extra-legal" conversion; as we have noted, narratives tend to be somewhat flexible with legal details. This heroic deed relates to the symbolism of his name, "the cut one" who thereby brought himself "peace" in the next world. With his final words, Ketiah wills his property to R. Akiva and his students. In doing so, he performs another *mitzvah* by providing for the sages who study Torah, the greatest commandment of all. He will earn significant vicarious merit through their Torah study, and has also (concretely) paid the (metaphoric) tax, that is, the duty to support communal Torah study.[12] He therefore can state with confidence, "I will pass" into the world to come.

The final section concludes with three statements about Ketiah's death [c]. First, R. Akiva explains that Ketiah's deathbed bequest to "R. Akiva and his students" means that the property should be divided half to R. Akiva and half among the students, rather than, for example, the master and each student receiving equal shares. He bases this on Exodus 29:28, where the similar phrasing regarding the division of sacrifices "to Aaron and his sons" is also interpreted as a fifty-fifty division.[13] This clarification does not contribute much to the narrative and should be seen as a footnote of sorts. If the Talmud had been typeset in the style of modern books, this statement might have been placed in parentheses or at the bottom of the page.

However, the second statement, spoken by the heavenly voice, is absolutely crucial [c2]. Like the voice that made a similar pronouncement about the mother who committed suicide after watching her seven sons die, discussed in chapter 1 (p. 53), this supernatural sign informs the audience that Ketiah succeeded in his efforts and was duly rewarded with eternal life. Without this coda we might wonder whether his self-sacrificing intercession with the emperor and desperate conversion were in vain, whether God takes note of such heroism and responds. Ketiah thus becomes a "son of peace," בר שלום/*bar shalom*, enjoying the peace of

---

12 Perhaps this is also a gesture toward fulfilling the halakhic requirement that a convert study Torah, or at least receive instruction, before the conversion.

13 This midrash may have been adapted from a similar interpretation found in Yoma 17b and Sanhedrin 21a.

eternal life, which may also play on a second meaning of *bar* ("son of") as "worthy of": Ketiah is "worthy of" [the world of] peace.[14]

The story concludes, however, on a more ambivalent note. R. Yehudah HaNasi, who lived several generations after R. Akiva, reacts to Ketiah's story with tears and a bittersweet reflection. He contrasts the fate of Ketiah, who received eternal life due to this heroic but brief episode, with that of most Jews, including the rabbis, who each day dedicate themselves to the commandments, wrestle against temptation, struggle to resist sin, and sacrifice to live a holy life, in an extended process that lasts for years—and only then gain entrance to the next world. That Ketiah and the rabbis receive the same share in the world to come feels unfair, as if Ketiah took a shortcut (no pun intended) of sorts. R. Yehudah HaNasi does not protest the reward granted to Ketiah as much as lament the difficulty of leading a righteous Jewish life. "It's wonderful that Ketiah made it into heaven," he seems to say, "Would that the rest of us could find shortcuts too."

Though relatively compact, this story is complex and should not be reduced to a single message. It offers a portrait of the righteous gentile, a man who advocates on behalf of the Jewish people and prevents a threatened persecution, despite having everything to lose, which he in fact does—not only his aristocratic position but his life. Having constructed such a figure, the storyteller proceeds to grapple with the implications. Given the possibility for such righteousness and virtue among gentiles, do they deserve posthumous reward? Can they expect it? Perhaps only if they "go all the way" and convert to Judaism, joining the chosen people in body ("cut one") and not only in word and deed. While the divine voice grants a share in the next world to the righteous gentile or convert under these circumstances, R. Yehudah HaNasi seems conflicted about the fairness of this outcome.

The symbolism of both elements of the name "Ketiah bar Shalom" extends throughout the narrative, both explicitly and implicitly. In the first scene the emperor proposes "cutting off" the metaphoric growth, to which Ketiah retorts that he will be called a "cut-off" empire. This counterargument instructs the emperor to keep the empire "whole," שלם/*shalem*, a word closely related to Ketiah's patronym, Shalom (though the word "whole" does not appear explicitly in the story). Moreover,

14 "Bar" can also mean "resident of": Ketiah becomes a "resident of [the world of] peace."

Ketiah seeks to keep the Jews in peace/*shalom* and safety. In the second scene Ketiah "cuts off" his foreskin, the act that most clearly identifies him with this name. The final scene confirms that Ketiah reached the next world, the "world of peace," and was "worthy of peace," per his symbolic patronym. If the same story were told of a protagonist with an ordinary name, it would have been much less memorable and elegant. The connections between the symbolic name and the narrative themes render the story more cohesive and didactic: the audience associates the story's meaning with the name of the protagonist and not only with its plot and course of events.

## Symbolic Names as a Narrative Building Block

Let us conclude this section with a striking story that turns completely on the protagonist's name. Because of its richness and complexity, we will also consider the relationship between the story and its talmudic context, a crucial axis of interpretation, to be more fully explored in chapter 5.

This story appears in Nedarim ("Vows"), a tractate that deals with the laws of oaths and vows, related to the biblical injunction, "If a man makes a vow to YHVH or takes an oath imposing an obligation on himself, he shall not break his pledge; he must carry out all that has crossed his lips" (Numbers 30:3). So serious are oaths and vows that the third of the Ten Commandments instructs: "Do not swear falsely by the name of YHVH your God" (Exodus 20:7). In halakhic contexts the rabbis generally distinguish "oaths" from "vows" based on their linguistic formulation, but in other contexts, including narratives, this distinction is not important, and in the discussion below I use the terms interchangeably.[15]

These verbal expressions invoking the name of God served a variety of religious ends, among them motivation to acts of piety ("I swear to give one hundred coins to charity" or "I vow that this fine calf will be dedicated as a sacrifice to God") and guarantees of telling the truth ("I swear that I did

15 To simplify matters somewhat—as there are many different types of vows and oaths—a vow pertains to an object: one forbids oneself to benefit from an object that is normally permitted. An oath is based on the person: one swears to do or not to do something. Another type of vow is used to dedicate something, typically an animal, for a sacrifice, to God. Yet another type of oath is used to invoke punishment upon oneself if one is lying.

not take your axe"). However, oaths and vows can be formulated for just about any purpose, and those undertaken in anger or agitation could lead to very difficult and problematic situations. A man might become irate at his friend or uncle and state, "I swear that I will never speak to you again," or "I swear that you will never set foot in my house." Similarly, a husband incensed at his wife might swear, "I will never look at you again." Or a wife might react to her husband's negative comments about the dinner she prepared and vow never to cook him another meal. Later, the swearers might calm down, make up, and regret having made the oaths—but they were stuck, as the oaths were binding, and they had no choice but to fulfill them, for fear of divine punishment. Some vows might even require a husband and wife to divorce, as a couple could not remain married if one partner swore, for example, not to speak to, look at, or live in the same house as the other.

To cope with these situations, the rabbis ruled that a sage or a rabbinic court had the power to annul an oath or vow made in error or under mistaken assumptions, and they also adopted what we might call legal fictions to judge many oaths as errant. In this way they effectively "released" many swearers from vows they later regretted.

And now for the story:[16]

**תלמוד בבלי, נדרים סו ע"ב**

[A] ההוא דאמר לדביתהו: קונם שאי את נהנית לי עד שתראי מום יפה שבך לרבי ישמעאל ברבי יוסי.

[B] אמר להם:
שמא ראשה נאה? אמרו לו: סגלגל.
שמא שערה נאה? דומה לאניצי פשתן.
שמא עיניה נאות? טרוטות הן.
שמא אזניה נאות? כפולות הן.
שמא חוטמה נאה? בלום הוא.
שמא שפתותיה נאות? עבות הן.
שמא צוארה נאה? שקוט הוא.
שמא כריסה נאה? צבה הוא.
שמא רגליה נאות? רחבות כשל אווזא.
שמא שמה נאה? לכלוכית שמה.

[C] אמר להן: יפה קורין אותה לכלוכית, שהיא מלוכלכת במומין. ושרייה.

16 On this story, see Eli Yassif, *The Hebrew Folktale*, 172–73; Reuven Kiperwasser, "Wives of Commoners"; and Dina Stein, "The Untamable Shrew."

**Talmud Bavli, Nedarim 66b**

[A] A certain man said to his wife: I vow that you not benefit from me unless you can show a fair aspect (or: "fair blemish") that is in you to R. Yishmael b. R. Yose.

[B] He (R. Yishmael b. R. Yose) said to them:
"Perhaps her head is fair?" They said to him: It is round.
"Perhaps her hair is fair?"—It resembles stalks of flax.
"Perhaps her eyes are fair?"—They are blurred.
"Perhaps her ears are fair?"—They are doubled over.
"Perhaps her nose is fair?"—It is swollen.
"Perhaps her lips are fair?"—They are thick.
"Perhaps her neck is fair?"—It is stubby.
"Perhaps her abdomen is fair?"—It sags.
"Perhaps her legs are fair?"—They are as broad as a goose's.
"Perhaps her name is fair?"—Her name is Likhlukhit (=little soiled/ repulsive one.)

[C] He said to them: "It is fair (=fitting) that she is called Likhlukhit, since she is repulsive in [all of her] aspects (or: "blemishes"). And he permitted her (to her husband, i.e., released him of his vow.)

This husband has evidently become angry at his wife and makes a vow forbidding her any benefit from him unless she can show a certain well-known rabbi some attractive feature of her body. To forbid one's spouse all "benefit," a term that includes both use of his possessions and marital intimacy, would make married life impossible and necessitate a divorce if she fails to fulfill the vow's stipulation. The husband's purpose, however, is not to divorce but rather to humiliate and degrade his wife by forcing her to manifest her ugliness to the rabbi. We know this because, had he wanted out of his marriage, he could simply have issued her a divorce, as rabbinic law gives men great latitude to initiate divorce (even though the rabbis frowned on unilateral divorces and tried to discourage them). Or he could have made an unconditional vow forbidding his wife all benefit from him. In this case, however, he has made a stipulation, knowing that she must do everything in her power to fulfill it, as a divorced woman was not only stigmatized but also reduced to a precarious financial situation. Thus scholars have noted that vows could function as cutting instruments of social manipulation: "Such vows were probably intended to cause distress to the object of the vow...the vow is also employed as a method to gain coercive power, whether in domestic or wider social contexts, and to inflict harm."[17] This man's vow places his wife in a terrible quandary. To show herself to the rabbi would be demeaning and would make her ugliness into a public spectacle. To refuse would entail divorce.

The storyteller employs a strange but ingenious locution for the husband's stipulation: מום יפה/*mum yafeh*. The word *mum* means "blemish," but its close homonym מאום/*me'um*, spelled with the letter *alef* but probably pronounced identically or very similarly, means "something," or in this context, "aspect." The word יפה/*yafeh* means "fair" or "beautiful," but also "fitting" or "appropriate," a secondary meaning that becomes crucial later in the story. So the phrase can mean "fair aspect," though the audience would also apprehend it as the oxymoronic "fair blemish." Since no blemish can really be beautiful, the audience will imagine the woman as completely blemished such that the best she can hope for is that one of her blemishes has some attractive element. A pleasantly shaped mole on her cheek? A finely tinted growth on her neck? This is an extremely insulting, if also comical, image, though one borne out by the subsequent investigation.

The case comes before R. Yishmael b. R. Yose, who is asked to rule as to whether the vow is valid and the husband must issue a divorce. Does the woman have a single "fair aspect" that would void his vow, such that the marriage can continue? It is not clear who brought the case to the rabbi, as the rabbi responds to an unidentified "them." Perhaps it was the woman and her family, seeking to prevent the divorce, or the husband himself, now feeling remorse, together with those who heard the vow. Note that the storyteller spares the woman the extreme humiliation of presenting herself in person to the rabbi and subjecting her body to an examination, as was probably the husband's original intent. The verbal description of her body is still demeaning, though not to the same degree: this story could be rated PG rather than R.

R. Yishmael b. R. Yose inquires about her physical features, moving systematically from head to toe. Alas, each and every part of the woman is unattractive: head, hair, eyes, ears, nose, lips, neck, abdomen, and legs, an unrelenting series of homely features. These descriptions of parts of a woman's body were undoubtedly considered especially ugly in talmudic

---

17 Avigail Manekin-Bamberger, "The Vow-Curse in Ancient Jewish Texts," 346–49.

times, though the standards of beauty seem to be remarkably consistent with those of our day and age, such that no great exercise of imagination is necessary to appreciate the storyteller's point. The husband's vow, like other impetuous vows, seems to have backfired, as this wife is in fact so ugly that she cannot show the rabbi any attractive bodily feature. Having calmed down, the husband now finds himself in the predicament of having to divorce his wife, which he really does not want to do, and pay her the *ketubah*, the marriage payment, which may have been a considerable sum of money relative to his means.

Searching desperately for some way that the condition might be fulfilled and the divorce avoided, the rabbi shifts from physical and corporeal characteristics to the abstract and non-tangible. He asks about her name, hoping that it is *yafeh*, pretty. Alas, even her name, Likhlukhit—from the Hebrew לכלוך/*likhlukh*, meaning "soiled," "stained," "disgusting"—is decisively unappealing. In other sources this word is associated with the soiling/staining of wine dregs, semen, and feces. (The name is reminiscent of—though considerably worse than—"Cinderella," derived from "cinders," thus "Little Ash Girl," as the oppressed heroine of the fairy tale slept near the fireplace for warmth and awoke covered in ashes and dirt. In fact the original Hebrew translators of the Cinderella story rendered her name "Likhlukhit.")

Paradoxically, her unpleasant name provides the rabbi just the opening he seeks. Because the name "Little Soiled/Repulsive One" fits her physical appearance perfectly, the rabbi rules that she indeed possesses *mum yafeh*, a fitting aspect. Just as we might say that an artist has painted an ugly person "beautifully" by representing the ugliness in a fitting and perfect manner, so the rabbi asserts the woman's name beautifully matches her consummate repulsiveness: an ugly name for an ugly appearance. Ironically, because of this perfect correspondence, the vow is void and she is spared from divorce. Problem solved.

This story depends completely on the wife's symbolic name, as without the correspondence between name and physical appearance, the plot collapses. Indeed, the entire story is constructed so as to build up to the rabbi's question as to her name, which at first increases the tension by seeming to continue the litany of ugly aspects and the failure to find attractiveness, but then resolves the crisis with magnificent irony. Our storyteller could not agree with Shakespeare's Juliet: "What's in a name? That which we call a rose by any other name would smell as sweet." For him, everything depends on the name "Likhlukhit," and no other name could be as foul. Of course the name marks the story as fictional (like the story of Cinderella). It is a sign of the storyteller's genius and sophisticated narrative art.

Clearly the symbolic name is also meant to be humorous, though equally clearly this is a misogynistic type of humor.[18] The humor increases as each part of her body, from head to toe, is reported to be unattractive, and the imagery of "stalks of flax" and "wide as a goose's" contributes to the portrait of consummate ugliness. This type of misogynistic humor is found in many cultures, including "Yo Momma" jokes today, which have become a serious subject of academic study.[19] Greco-Roman and medieval literature also contain vignettes describing hideously ugly people, both men and women, including complete inventories of repulsive features.[20] Horace's *Epode* 8 (first century BCE) is a description of an old "crone," with such phrases as "flabby belly," "shriveled-up thighs," "swollen calves," "blackened teeth," "wrinkled forehead," and even more insulting terms for private parts that need not be detailed here.

Yet the husband can be considered a target of the humor, too. He presumably intends that the rabbi, and perhaps his students and assistants, acknowledge the ugliness of his wife, a kind of public affirmation of the private insults he hurls at her when angry. At first his judgment appears to be confirmed, as the investigation fails to discover a single attractive feature, and perhaps he takes some satisfaction at the start of the proceedings. But the rabbi turns the tables on the husband with an ingenious argument to identify a "fair aspect" that fulfills the stipulation. The husband may be consoled that this machination allows his marriage to continue, assuming again that he never intended to divorce her but only subject her to public humiliation. Still, he did not get the full recognition he sought. In addition, the husband may have intended to embarrass the rabbi by forcing him to examine his wife's body, placing the rabbi in an uncomfortable and awkward situation. Other rabbinic sources caution against looking at women's hair, much less entire bodies, as immodest and

---

**18** Eli Yassif, *The Hebrew Folktale*, 173.

**19** Steve Stanzak, "Manipulating Play Frames" and Mary Jane Kehily and Anoop Nayak, "'Lads and Laughter.'" For example, "Yo momma is so ugly, when she looks in the mirror, the reflection ducks….the psychiatrist makes her lie facedown….she made a blind kid cry."

**20** See Jan Ziolkowski, "Avatars of Ugliness in Medieval Literature."

potentially arousing behavior. Here the rabbi, if he is to save the woman, must search her body, part by part, until he finds the attractive feature, as if playing a lewd children's game of "doctor." However, by asking about the woman rather than examining her, and then undermining the husband's stipulation, the rabbi again gets the last laugh at the husband's expense.

Removed—or we might say "divorced"—from its literary context, the story can be read in several ways. Despite the humor, there are disturbing elements. We have an unhappy, mean-spirited husband and a woman so pathetically ugly she can only be an object of sympathy. The story subjects her to what feminist theory would describe as a type of "male gaze," the masculine, heterosexual perspective that objectifies female bodies. The storyteller attenuates the "gaze" somewhat by the rabbi's choice to ask about the parts of her body rather than having the wife actually stand before him. He also delicately skips over her breasts, moving from neck to abdomen to legs, unlike the description of the beautiful woman in the biblical Song of Songs: "Your breasts are like two fawns, twins of a gazelle" (7:4), a contrasting catalog of beautiful features that listeners to this story might well have had in mind. And of course the audience would have heard the tale, rather than seen any woman in flesh and blood. Yet the progressive interrogation about the details of a woman's appearance, even in this literary manner, also objectifies the female body and would seem to violate the rabbinic value of modesty. The attempt to humiliate a wife in public is also unsettling. While the rabbi ultimately saves the marriage and helps the woman, he accepts the responses that pronounce her ugly in every respect, participating in the husband's joke at her expense. Elsewhere the rabbis teach, "Do not look at the container but what is inside of it" (Mishnah Avot 4:20). We could have had a lesson here about true beauty lying within, or about not judging superficial appearances, or about the importance of virtue and character. The rabbi, in theory, could have said, "Her deeds are beautiful" or "Her concern for the poor is beautiful." But that was not the story that our storyteller chose to tell. Thus one way to interpret the story is as reflecting male misogyny and disrespect of women, as a type of locker-room humor.

This reading, however, is not fully convincing to me. The husband here is less a partner in the humor than the butt of it. Even if we consider the storyteller and audience as the in-group, the dynamic is not as much males versus females, as rabbis versus non-rabbis. We could therefore see the story as highbrow or elitist, celebrating the rabbis and their brilliance over against the petty squabbles, foolish vows, and repulsive physical appearance of the common folk, or against non-rabbinic males in particular. But this reading does not do full justice to the story, either. Nor were the rabbis ever an elite class like the Roman patricians or medieval nobility, for whom this reading might have been more apt.

Looking to the wider context of this story, in its setting within the Talmud, offers a different, and more layered, lens. The story appears in the Talmud's commentary to Mishnah Nedarim 9:10. This chapter of Mishnah deals with different ways that the rabbis released individuals from vows that had been made in error or were subsequently regretted. Mishnah 10 begins by ruling on the case of a man who vowed that he would not marry "so-and-so who is ugly, and it turns out she is beautiful." This vow is considered a "mistaken vow" and is not binding, as the man would not have vowed had he known the facts. The mishnah proceeds with other cases of mistaken vows, and then discusses a somewhat different scenario:

**משנה נדרים ט:י**

...ומעשה באחד שנדר מבת אחותו הניה. והכניסוה לבית רבי ישמעאל ויפוה. אמר לו רבי ישמעאל: בני, לזו נדרת? אמר לו: לאו. והתירו רבי ישמעאל.

באותה שעה בכה רבי ישמעאל ואמר: בנות ישראל נאות הן, אלא שהעניות מנולתן.

**Mishnah Nedarim 9:10**

...And once a man vowed he would derive no benefit from his sister's daughter [whom he was to marry]. They brought her into R. Yishmael's house and they beautified her. R. Yishmael said to him, "My son, did you vow to [not benefit from] this one?" He said to him, "No." And R. Yishmael released him [from the vow].

At that time R. Yishmael wept and said: "The daughters of Israel are beautiful, but poverty disfigures them."

This vow, too, is judged as mistaken, as the man acknowledges that he did not intend to avoid marrying his now-beautiful niece, but rather his formerly-ugly niece. However, we should immediately perceive how different this second case is, and how potentially radical the ruling, from the mishnah's previous example where he vowed not to marry "so-and-so who is ugly, and it turns out she is beautiful." In that scenario the man really was mistaken about the underlying facts, in that he vowed not to marry a certain woman whom he believed to be ugly, but who was actually beautiful. In the second case, however, he was not mistaken in the same way, as he was correct about the facts when he articulated his vow: the woman really was unappealing to him at the time he made the vow. Later, though, subsequent to the time of the vow, the woman's appearance improved such that the man regretted that he had made the vow. Had he known at the time of the vow (when the woman did not attract him) what he knew later (that the woman would soon become beautiful), he would not have vowed. In other words, this second vow is mistaken not due to an error as to the facts as they were known at the time, but due to the man's regret in light of subsequent developments. Moreover, in the first case the language of the man's vow explicitly includes the circumstances that motivate it: "So-and so who is ugly." In the second case, the man simply vows in an absolute manner that he will derive no benefit from that specific woman. He does not say that his vow is dependent on a particular condition such as "because she is ugly" or "because she can't cook" or provide any reason for it. Yet when the groom expresses regret, R. Yishmael is still willing to annul the vow. Finally, R. Yishmael proactively takes measures to undermine the vow and facilitate the marriage by becoming involved and beautifying the woman at his own expense.

The brevity of R. Yishmael's lament in the concluding lines of the mishnah accentuates its pathos, as does the image of the rabbi shedding tears as he utters it. We do not know the cause of the poverty, whether due to the general suffering of the Jewish people after the destruction of the Temple and Bar Kokhba revolts, the oppressive Roman taxes, or simply the perennial difficulties of earning a living in antiquity. Whatever the reason, his words set the mishnah in a tragic context. Poverty—with its inevitable suffering, hardship, hunger, and malnutrition—ruins bodies and physical appearances, resulting in this heartbreaking disruption in the relationships between brides and grooms. What should be happy and joyous occasions of newfound love and youthful marriage have been thrown into disarray due to the tragic material fortunes of the nation. The young men who vow not to marry women they consider ugly should not be seen as arrogant, picky, stuck-up, or misogynistic—as we may well consider them, especially from our contemporary perspective—but rather as caught up in the same distressing situation. Rabbinic intervention, however, can ameliorate the misery, at least to some degree, and foster happier relations.

In the context of the mishnah, the following talmudic story takes on more specific meanings. Clearly there are parallels between the mishnah's two cases and the husband's vow that Likhlukhit not benefit from him. True, the mishnaic cases involve designated grooms attempting to prevent their arranged marriages whereas the man in the talmudic story is already married, and the potential grooms in the mishnah issue unconditional vows whereas Likhlukhit's husband makes a conditional vow. However, all three cases deal with the issue of beauty and ugliness, and each culminates in the marriage going forward. In both the story of the mishnah and the talmudic story, the case comes before a rabbi named Yishmael: the R. Yishmael of the mishnah is R. Yishmael b. Elisha, who lived in the early second century CE, while R. Yishmael b. R. Yose of the Talmud lived several generations later. Most importantly, R. Yishmael in the mishnah exerts himself to bring together the groom and bride, both beautifying the woman and ruling that the vow was mistaken, despite the considerations mentioned above. R. Yishmael b. R. Yose in the talmudic story also finds a way to permit the husband and wife to stay together, devising an ingenious solution to deem the woman beautiful and rule that the stipulation of the vow has been fulfilled. The rabbi in the talmudic story follows in the path of the rabbi in the mishnaic story, continuing the work of reconciling men and women such that marriages can thrive. The meaning of the talmudic story thus becomes more focused on the rabbi's efforts to reunite the couple, and the imperative to find any way possible to release men from such vows.

In addition, R. Yishmael's lament at the end of the mishnah's story blames poverty for the woman's unattractiveness in her groom's eyes. Keeping this context in mind, too, shifts the message of the Likhlukhit story away from the nastiness of the husband and the ugliness of the wife to the tragic historical circumstances in which they both find themselves. Hardship and suffering can wreak havoc with marriages, but at least rabbis can play a small role in restoring marital harmony. And by extension, we might learn from the story that we should all emulate these rabbis and do whatever we can to bring couples together, whether by reconciling them when they have fallings out, or by providing funds for wedding garments so the couple will find each other desirable, or by beautifying the bride and groom in other ways. A delightful rabbinic tradition portrays God as the first matchmaker, who brought Adam and Eve together in the Garden of Eden.[21] To bring couples together and to help restore marital harmony

**21** See Bereishit Rabbah 18:1; Berakhot 61a.

is therefore part of the imperative of *imitatio dei,* the imitation of God, among the highest ethical and pious acts.

## Symbolic Names of Rabbis

The names of the rabbis themselves sometimes function symbolically within the story. That is, the storyteller chooses a particular rabbi as the protagonist of a given story because of the symbolism or meaning of his name. A fine example, found at Nedarim 66b, is another story of husbands and wives, in which a husband becomes angry at his wife and orders her to take two lamps and "break them on the head of the gate," intending to humiliate her by making her into a public spectacle. She will appear as a lunatic when she breaks the lamps on the top ("head") of the town gate in the public square. This story resembles that of Likhlukhit, although in this case the husband has stopped short of a vow. Still, there is the implied threat that if she refuses, he will vow that she not benefit from him unless she carries out his command. The word in Aramaic for "gate" is *bava,* and there just happens to be a sage by the name of Bava ben Buta who holds court in her town. The dimwitted wife, apparently misunderstanding her husband's intention, breaks the lamps on Bava ben Buta's head, understanding על רישא דבבא/*al reisha devava,* which the husband intends as "on the top (head) of the *bava* (gate)," as "on the head of Bava (ben Buta)."[22] This part of the story is entirely dependent on the name of the sage being Bava ben Buta, as otherwise the wife could not make such a mistake. The storyteller has constructed this story around the fact that the rabbi's personal name is a homonym for "gate."[23]

Another example of this phenomenon is the story of a rabbi who boasts of his ability to defeat Satan:

---

22 Unless she is not dimwitted at all, but rather incredibly crafty, capitalizing on the coincidence of the sage's name to deviate from her husband's order. For such a reading, see Jeffrey L. Rubenstein, *Land of Truth,* 59–65.

23 On this story, see Jeffrey L. Rubenstein, *Land of Truth,* 52–72; David Sperling, "Aramaic Spousal Misunderstanding"; Shmuel Faust, *Agadata,* 165–71; and Dina Stein, "Linguistic Liaisons."

**תלמוד בבלי, קידושין פא ע"א**

פלימו הוה רגיל למימר כל יומא: גירא בעיניה דשטן.

**Talmud Bavli, Kiddushin 81a**

Pelimo was in the habit of saying each day, "An arrow in Satan's eye."

In other words, Pelimo asserts that he can overcome Satan's attempts to cause him to sin, that his metaphoric weapons will injure Satan if the Evil One chooses to engage in this battle. "Pelimo" is an unusual name for a rabbi, though there was evidently a sage by this name, as several talmudic traditions are attributed to him. However, the storyteller probably chose Pelimo as the protagonist for this story because his name sounds like the Greek word *polemos*, meaning "war, battle," as in our English word "polemic." (It is possible that the sage's name was pronounced "Polemo" or something like that, as the pronunciation of the consonantal Aramaic text is uncertain.) In this way the name itself—(Rabbi) Battle—embodies the theme of the story, the wisdom of challenging Satan to a battle of wills.

## Flat and Round Characters

Another way of understanding characterization in talmudic stories derives from the distinction between what the novelist and literary critic E. M. Forster described as "flat" and "round" characters. "Round" characters, in his oft-quoted definition, are complex and multidimensional, whereas "flat" characters are "constructed around a single idea or quality" or are "stereotypical characters that exhibit/contain nothing surprising."[24] Round characters develop and change, and may surprise the reader, whereas a flat character can be summed up in a single phrase "which completely describes him; he has no existence outside of it."[25] Symbolic names generate flat characters, as the name provides all the information the talmudic storytellers need us to have about the characters. Even when

24 E. M. Forster, *Aspects of the Novel*, 67–68.

25 Ibid.

a symbolic name is not employed, most characters in talmudic stories are flat, so a brief description of one characteristic generally suffices.

We saw a good example of this in the story of Hillel in chapter 1, which opens: "One should always be a gentle man like Hillel and never be an impatient man like Shammai" (Shabbat 30b). The storyteller hits us over the head with the positive and negative qualities he wishes to model with the sages Hillel and Shammai, and the subsequent stories illustrate those traits.

Here are two other examples, in each of which the plot and didactic lesson derive from the single quality attributed to the character:

**תלמוד בבלי, תענית כ ע"ב**

נזדמן לו אדם אחד שהיה מכוער ביותר. אמר לו: שלום עליך רבי.

**Talmud Bavli, Ta'anit 20b**

He (R. Shimon) chanced upon a very ugly man, who said to him, "Peace be upon you, my master!"

This story will proceed with R. Shimon insulting the ugly man, realizing he has transgressed, and seeking forgiveness. The salient characteristic for the plot is the man's ugly physical appearance, nothing more. (See chapter 4, p. 140 for more on this story.)

**תלמוד בבלי, עבודה זרה יז ע"א**

אמרו עליו על אלעזר בן דורדיא שלא הניח זונה אחת בעולם שלא בא עליה.[26]

**Talmud Bavli, Avodah Zarah 17a**

It was said of Eleazar b. Dordia that there was not one prostitute in the world with whom he had not had sex.

In this example, Eleazar b. Dordia's carnal lust defines him for the purposes of the storyteller. This is all we know about him, and all we need to know. The story continues by telling us about a particular encounter with a prostitute, after which he felt remorse and tried to repent for this sin. But

26 The printed Talmud reads "Rabbi Eleazar b. Dordia." However, most manuscripts omit "Rabbi," which fits better with the story, discussed in detail in the following chapter.

we know nothing else concerning his character or history, nothing about his prior life, his place in society, family relations, and so forth.

Stories themselves may be complex; they may engage different issues or communicate several lessons. But with rare exceptions, the characters in talmudic stories are not complex, and for the purposes of the story, they embody one single characteristic.

An important step, therefore, in analyzing a talmudic story is to pay close attention to all names, both those of the non-rabbinic and the rabbinic characters. These names will often connect in a substantive way to the themes of the story. In some cases they will contribute to the narrative artistry and the aesthetics of the story, featuring as wordplays or allusions. Whether named or not, characters in talmudic stories are typically flat, identified with a single factor relevant for the story. But some of the more well-known rabbis appear in relatively highly developed stories and emerge as more rounded characters, almost to the point where we get glimmers of their personalities and proclivities, at least as they were remembered by their students. Later Jewish tradition would continue to "round out" characters, though in many cases interpreters read a great deal into subtle clues and turns of phrase.

because nothing else concerns his character or history, nothing about his private life, his place in society, his relations, and so forth.

[illegible] themselves into the complex. They are [illegible] adjusted to [illegible] mentioned above, [illegible] with the exception of the characters in [illegible] Talmudic stories are not complex, and for the purposes of the story they embody one single characteristic.

As opposed to this, therefore, in analyzing Talmudic stories we pay close attention to all details, both those of the [illegible] and the [illegible] details [illegible] way to the [illegible] of the [illegible] for the [illegible] of the story [illegible] as complete [illegible]

# CHAPTER 3
## Biblical Verses and the Quotation of Scripture

FOR THE RABBIS, the biblical texts, God's revealed words, were the key to understanding the cosmos: relevant to past, present, and future. Together with many ordinary Jews throughout antiquity, the rabbis knew the Bible by heart and constantly repeated chapters and even entire books to facilitate memorization. Every week they endeavored to study the portion of the Torah designated for reading during Shabbat services. Many psalms appear in the daily liturgy, and hundreds of biblical verses are integrated into rabbinic prayers. Like traditional Jews today, they also read entire biblical books in the course of the festival liturgy, such as the Book of Esther, chanted on Purim, and the prophet Jonah, recited during the afternoon service of Yom Kippur. Biblical passages, verses, and phrases were therefore always on the tips of the rabbis' tongues, and could be brought to bear on any situation or experience.

Through this deep familiarity, biblical verses essentially took on lives of their own, and were often known to the rabbis independently of their original contexts. Many verses appear in liturgical texts and folk proverbs, and therefore were encountered already apart from their biblical settings. Biblical verses were also integrated into still other literary texts and known from these secondary contexts. Verses rolled around in the rabbis' heads, so to speak, and would in turn call to mind related verses that shared common words or phrases. To some extent this is still true today for those familiar with the prayerbook (*siddur*) and the regular Torah, Haftarah, and other readings, as well as songs that quote verses. But this awareness was much more strongly the case in the rabbinic period when the stories were composed.

We can think of biblical verses among the rabbis analogously to famous quotations from Shakespeare in the general English language culture today. Many people recognize the quote "Neither a borrower nor a lender be." But only some of them also know that it quotes Polonius in *Hamlet*, Act 1, Scene 3. Likewise, many who quote the line "All the world's a stage" do not know that Jacques speaks this line in *As You Like It*. These quotations exist as independent sayings in many people's minds, perhaps associated with other famous quotations from Shakespeare and other authors. Rabbinic verses had a similar type of disembodied existence in the rabbinic culture, though the rabbis themselves also would have been able to identify, if they thought about it, the original biblical contexts.

Rabbinic storytellers often fashion their dialogue by placing biblical verses or parts of verses in the mouths of the characters. Again we can turn to Shakespearean quotations to understand this storytelling technique. A storyteller might integrate a biblical verse into the dialogue in similar fashion to how we might quote a phrase from Shakespeare in the middle of conversation. To say "the lady doth protest too much, methinks" suggests that someone who vociferously denies a charge is actually guilty or hiding the truth. (Gertrude, Hamlet's mother, speaks these words in Shakespeare's *Hamlet*, when watching a play in which the queen swears not to remarry if her husband dies.) The shared knowledge of the quotation's source and meaning unite the speaker and audience in a mutual experience, and invoking a familiar text also involves aesthetic and intellectual pleasure. Similarly, later storytellers and writers quote or allude to such famous quotations as a shorthand method of communicating with their audience. Thus, in a *New York Times* column entitled "These Artful Dodgers Doth Protest Too Much," criticizing citizens who refuse to pay taxes on the grounds that the government has no constitutional power to tax, the author uses the quotation in the heading to efficiently transmit his opinion of such protestors as shameless hypocrites who try to avoid paying taxes with spurious arguments that they themselves don't really believe.[1] The author could say this explicitly—and basically

1 Tom Zeller, "These Artful Dodgers Doth Protest Too Much."

does so in the rest of the column—but the quotation succinctly and effectively communicates the message—even without getting into an explicit discussion of *Hamlet.* One scholar describes the deployment of Shakespearean quotations in a culture where they were well known as follows: "In 19th-century America, where everyone from Tammany Hall politicians to Bowery Boys knew Shakespeare by heart...audiences had no problem sampling, burlesquing and generally messing around with his work. 'Get thee to a brewery' was a popular joke; 'To be or not to be' was frequently sung to the melody of 'Three Blind Mice.'"[2] Shakespearean quotations were adapted and used in new contexts and forms of cultural expression. Biblical quotations in rabbinic stories likewise reinforced the shared background, knowledge, and culture of the talmudic storyteller and the audience.

On another level, since the quotations in rabbinic stories come from the Bible, not from classical literary works or famous authors, they also exemplify the eternally relevant quality of scripture, God's revealed word. The rabbinic audience—including us, when we enter the rabbinic way of reading—understands that the verses operate in both their biblical contexts and their secondary contexts in the rabbinic stories, which confers authority upon the story while illustrating the enduring truth of the Bible.

Here is an elementary example of the use of biblical verses in a brief account of a conflict between rabbis:[3]

**ירושלמי פסחים ו:ב (לג ע"ב)**

שלש עשרה שנה עשה ר"ע נכנס אצל ר' ליעזר, ולא היה יודע בו.

וזו היא תחילת תשובתו הראשונה לפני ר' ליעזר.

אמר לו ר' יהושע: הלא זה העם אשר מאסת בו, צא נא עתה והלחם בו (שופטים ט:לח).

2 Tana Wojczuk, "How Shakespeare Paperbacks Made Me Want to Be a Writer."

3 This example is based on Moshe Halbertal, "Discipleship in Rabbinic Literature," 92–94.

**Yerushalmi Pesaḥim 6:2 (33b)**

For thirteen years R. Akiva would enter [the house of study] of R. Eliezer, but he (R. Eliezer) did not acknowledge him (R. Akiva).

This was his (R. Akiva's) first dispute with R. Eliezer.

R. Yehoshua said to him (R. Eliezer): *There is the army you sneered at; now go and fight it! (Judges 9:38)*

This account follows an extended legal debate between the senior sage R. Eliezer and his younger contemporary R. Akiva over a difficult halakhic question, in which R. Akiva has gotten the last word, implying that he has triumphed. The narrator informs us that, prior to this interchange, R. Akiva had studied for thirteen years in R. Eliezer's house of study without the two having exchanged so much as a word, and without R. Eliezer even acknowledging R. Akiva's presence. We should picture R. Akiva as among the most inferior students (at least in R. Eliezer's view), at the bottom of the academic hierarchy, and R. Eliezer the exalted head of the school. This debate was R. Akiva's "coming out," his explosion on the intellectual scene, when he suddenly displayed his full prowess by challenging the senior master in debate, demonstrating how much he had learned in those years. Here R. Yehoshua quotes part of a biblical verse to R. Eliezer, effectively saying that R. Eliezer has disdained R. Akiva by not giving him the proper respect, but now has to engage the young scholar. R. Yehoshua is telling his colleague that R. Akiva has come of age and proven his talents. The motifs of war and fighting are often used to describe academic debate, for arguments are "fighting words," so the verse fits the scholastic context nicely. But there is more to the use of the biblical verse; here it is in full, in its biblical context:

**שופטים ט:לח-מ**

[לח]ויאמר אליו זבל: איה אפוא פיך אשר תאמר מי אבימלך כי נעבדנו? הלא **זה העם אשר מאסתה בו צא נא עתה והלחם בו.**

[לט]ויצא געל לפני בעלי שכם וילחם באבימלך.

[מ]וירדפהו אבימלך וינס מפניו, ויפלו חללים רבים, עד פתח השער.

**Judges 9:38–40**

38"Well," replied Zebul, "where is your boast, 'Who is Abimelech that we should serve him?' **There is the army you sneered at; now go out and fight it.**"

39So Gaal went out at the head of the citizens of Shechem and gave battle to Abimelech.

40But he had to flee before him, and Abimelech pursued him, and many fell slain, all the way to the entrance of the gate.

The story in the Book of Judges from which this quotation is taken relates that the citizens of Shechem rebelled against Abimelech, whom they had previously accepted as their "judge" and protector. They turned to a man named Gaal son of Ebed to lead them, and Gaal boasted that he would rid them of Abimelech's tyranny. However, Abimelech mustered an army and took Gaal by surprise. Zebul, the governor of Shechem, had remained loyal to Abimelech, and when Abimelech arrived, he called Gaal to account for his boast, mockingly stating that Gaal must now actually confront Abimelech—and Gaal lost the battle. The rabbinic audience would be well aware of this larger context and understand R. Yehoshua's repartee with added depth: R. Eliezer has not given R. Akiva the honor he deserves, treating the young but intellectually powerful student with disdain. Like Gaal, who thought he could ignore Abimelech and rule Shechem, R. Eliezer thought he could ignore Akiva and dominate the house of study. The audience will understand from R. Yehoshua's quotation that R. Akiva has defeated R. Eliezer and will soon supplant him as the leading sage, the most powerful mind in the rabbinic house of study. Indeed, in the later rabbis' view of their own past, R. Akiva rose to greatness and attracted thousands of disciples, while R. Eliezer, previously one of the greatest of the sages, became marginalized and even ostracized. Quoting the verse clarifies that R. Akiva has won this argument and evokes the aftermath of this initial encounter between the two sages. The storyteller could have had R. Yehoshua say something like "You superciliously ignored this brilliant student, but now you have to face him in debate," which would communicate much the same message. But it would not be as effective as having the rabbi quote a verse that brings the broader biblical context to bear on the rabbinic story.

In many stories rabbinic characters argue with one another by exchanging biblical verses. A good example of this phenomenon appears in a story about an attempt by two rabbis, R. Meir and R. Natan, to depose Rabban Shimon ben Gamaliel from his position as head of the rabbinic academy.[4] Rabban Shimon ben Gamaliel manages, with some help, to foil their plot. He then decrees that traditions no longer be transmitted in these rabbis' names: henceforth subsequent generations of sages may not state "R. Meir said..." and "R. Natan said..." but rather must quote these sages as "Others say..." and "Some say..." This is an extremely harsh punishment in rabbinic culture; it denies all honor and status to these sages, as now their great contributions to rabbinic law and tradition can never be identified.

Many years later, Rabban Shimon ben Gamaliel's grandson, R. Shimon, protests to his father, R. Yehudah HaNasi (=Rabban Shimon ben Gamaliel's son), that it is time to terminate this penalty, though the latter demurs:

**תלמוד בבלי, הוריות יד ע"א**

אמר לו: מי הם הללו שמימיהם אנו שותים ושמותם אין אנו מזכירים? אמר ליה: בני אדם שבקשו לעקור כבודך וכבוד בית אביך.

אמר ליה: גם אהבתם גם שנאתם גם קנאתם כבר אבדה (קהלת ט:ו).

אמר ליה: האויב תמו חרבות לנצח (תהלים ט:ז).

**Talmud Bavli, Horayot 14a**

He (R. Shimon) said to him (R. Yehudah HaNasi), "Who are those [others] whose waters we drink and whose names we do not mention?" He said to him, "They are men who tried to uproot your honor and the honor of your father's house."

He (R. Shimon) said to him, *Their loves, their hates, their jealousies have long since perished (Kohelet 9:6).*

He (R. Yehudah HaNasi) said to him, *The enemy is no more; the ruins last forever (Psalm 9:7).*

R. Shimon's quotation from Kohelet 9:6 suggests that the acrimonious affair belongs to the distant past, whatever jealousy and hatred existed

4 On this story, see Jeffrey L. Rubenstein, *Talmudic Stories*, 176–211, and the literature cited there; Geoffrey Herman, *A Prince Without a Kingdom*, 67–71; and Shmuel Faust, *Agadata*, 230–38.

between these two rabbis and their father/grandfather is over and done, and consequently the names of R. Natan and R. Meir should be restored to their traditions. R. Yehudah HaNasi's reply, however, quoting Psalm 9:7, means that the damage done by the two rabbis endures, even if they themselves have passed away. Their challenge to the dynastic privilege of academic leadership set a dangerous precedent that others may imitate and repeat. Again, the storyteller could have expressed these sentiments straightforwardly without quoting the verses. However, the mobilization of biblical verses for narrative dialogue enhances the literary artistry of the storyteller. The audience, who recognized the original texts, undoubtedly enjoyed their application to this new context in a rabbinic story and found it meaningful that scripture continued to be relevant.

Yet there is more: as in the previous example, even though the verses appear in the story independently of their original contexts, the rabbinic audience would have known the entirety of the biblical passages from which they were excerpted:

**קהלת ט:ה-ו**

[ה]כי החיים יודעים שימתו והמתים אינם יודעים מאומה, **ואין עוד להם שכר כי נשכח זכרם**.

[וא]גם אהבתם, גם שנאתם, גם קנאתם כבר אבדה.

[וב]וחלק אין להם עוד לעולם בכל אשר נעשה תחת השמש.

**Kohelet 9:5–6**

[5]since the living know they will die. But the dead know nothing; **they have no more recompense, for even the memory of them has died.**

[6a]Their loves, their hates, their jealousies have long since perished;

[6b]and they have no more share till the end of time in all that goes on under the sun.

**תהלים ט:ו-ז**

[ו]גערת גוים, אבדת רשע, **שמם מחית לעולם ועד**.

[זא]האויב תמו, חרבות לנצח.

[זב]ועָרים נתשת, **אבד זכרם המה**.

**Psalm 9:6–7**

[6]You blast the nations; You destroy the wicked; **You blot out their name forever.**

[7a]The enemy is no more; ruins everlasting;

[7b]You have torn down their cities; **their very names are lost.**

The verse preceding R. Shimon's quotation, Kohelet 9:5, mentions "recompense," which suggests that R. Meir and R. Natan died without reward for their Torah, because the "memory of them has died" through the effacement of their names. The broader biblical context of Psalm 9:7 is also relevant to R. Yehudah HaNasi's quotation: the previous verse, 9:6, emphasizes that God destroys the wicked by "blotting out their names," while the continuation of 9:7 emphasizes that "their very names are lost," which was exactly the policy of his father. The effacement of the rabbis' names is therefore not unjust, but consistent with the divine policy. Again, the storyteller could have provided more typical dialogue for the characters without quoting the biblical verses. But by placing the verses in the mouths of the characters he accomplishes a great deal more, since the audience also picks up on the larger context of the verses, including the issues of deleting names, communal memory, and fairness of the punishment. In this way the storyteller rehearses and emphasizes the narrative themes and conveys a range of ideas beyond the words spoken by the characters.

The important point for us, as students of rabbinic stories, is that, to appreciate the layers of meaning contained within a rabbinic story, it is imperative to look up all biblical verses quoted within the story and study their wider contexts. We must always ask: Where do these verses come from? What is their original meaning? What are the proximate verses about? How are the verses applied in the rabbinic story? Contrasts between the original biblical contexts of the verses and their new use in stories create irony, pathos, humor, emphasis, and other effects. Understanding these contrasts provides a window into the narrative artistry of the storytellers and their ways of leveraging the meaning of the biblical corpus.

## Ironic Use of Biblical Verses

The story of the "Oven of Akhnai," probably the most frequently taught talmudic story in our times, employs biblical verses for a critical narrative purpose, which creates a powerful irony, though this dimension of the story often goes unnoticed. In this story, R. Eliezer has disagreed with "the sages," that is, all the other rabbis, over a detail of purity law pertaining to an oven constructed in an unusual way. After the sages have rejected both R. Eliezer's arguments and the miracles he performs as supernatural evidence for his ruling, R. Eliezer states, "If it [the law] is as I say, let it be proved from heaven," whereupon a heavenly voice answers, "What is it for you with R. Eliezer, since the law is like him in every place?" That is: why are you sages disputing with R. Eliezer and giving him a hard time, as the divine law accords with his ruling? There could hardly be stronger supernatural evidence in support of R. Eliezer. Yet the sages reject not only his position, but also God's intervention in the process of legal debate.[5]

Here is what happens next in the story:

**תלמוד בבלי, בבא מציעא נט ע"ב**

עמד רבי יהושע על רגליו ואמר: לא בשמים היא (דברים ל:יב).

מאי, לא בשמים היא?

אמר רבי ירמיה: אין אנו משגיחין בבת קול, שכבר כתבת בהר סיני בתורה, אחרי רבים להטות (שמות כג:ב).

**Talmud Bavli, Bava Metzia 59b**

R. Yehoshua stood on his feet and said, "*It is not in heaven (Deuteronomy 30:12).*"

What is, "*It is not in heaven*"?

R. Yirmiyah said, "We do not listen to a heavenly voice, since You already wrote in the Torah on Mount Sinai, *Incline after the majority (Exodus 23:2).*"

---

5 For literature on this story, see Jeffrey L. Rubenstein, *Talmudic Stories*, 34–63, and the references in n. 1 there; Charlotte Elisheva Fonrobert, "When Rabbis Weep"; and Moshe Simon-Shoshan, "A Doorway of Their Own."

R. Yehoshua asserts that the Torah is no longer with God in heaven, but has been transmitted to human beings to interpret and adjudicate. The revelation to Moses on Mount Sinai has essentially placed the Torah in the hands of rabbis and removed it from God's jurisdiction. God's affirmation of R. Eliezer's ruling is therefore irrelevant, as God no longer plays a role in the legal process. R. Yirmiyah fleshes out his colleague's words by quoting another verse that directs the court to follow the majority. If the majority of the sages rule one way, or interpret biblical law in a certain manner, then that becomes the law, irrespective of what God "intended." This, R. Yirmiyah claims, is how God charged the rabbis to act, hence following the majority of the sages is not rejecting God's rulings, but rather adhering exactly to God's directions.

This interchange raises fascinating questions concerning authorial intent, interpretive authority, and the adjudication of law, but here I would like to focus on the verses cited as the basis for the sages' position. In fact, the two verses mean something different in their original contexts.[6] Here is the full biblical context of the first verse, "It is not in heaven," cited by R. Yehoshua:

**דברים ל:יא–יד**

יא**כי המצוה הזאת** אשר אנכי מצוך היום לא נפלאת הוא ממך, ולא רחקה הוא.

יב**לא בשמים הוא**, לאמר: מי יעלה לנו השמימה ויקחה לנו וישמענו אתה ונעשנה?

יגולא מעבר לים הוא, לאמר: מי יעבר לנו אל עבר הים ויקחה לנו וישמענו אתה, ונעשנה?

ידכי קרוב אליך הדבר מאד, בפיך ובלבבך, לעשתו.

**Deuteronomy 30:11–14**

11Surely, **this Instruction** that I enjoin upon you this day is not too baffling for you, nor is it beyond reach.

12**It is not in heaven**, that you should say, "Who among us can go up to the heavens and get it for us and impart it to us, that we may observe it?"

6 This analysis is based on Daniel Boyarin, *Intertextuality and the Reading of Midrash*, 34–37.

[13]Neither is it beyond the sea, that you should say, "Who among us can cross to the other side of the sea and get it for us and impart it to us, that we may observe it?"

[14]No, the thing is very close to you, in your mouth and in your heart, to observe it.

The passage insists that "this Instruction," the Torah and its commandments, is accessible to all the people. It is neither too complicated to understand ("baffling") nor too hard to observe. There is nothing said about God giving human beings the authority to interpret the Torah and legislate on that basis. If anything, the passage implies the opposite: because the Torah is so close and so clear, we should be able to follow God's intentions and directions without difficulties. The words "It is not in heaven," in this original context, means that the Torah is neither remote nor difficult, but rather that it is easy to access and follow.

The larger context of the second verse, cited by R. Yirmiyah, is as follows:

**שמות כג:ב-ג**

[ב]לא תהיה אחרי רבים לרעת, **ולא** תענה על רב לנטת, **אחרי רבים להטת.**

[ג]ודל לא תהדר בריבו.

**Exodus 23:2–3**

[2]You shall neither side with the majority to do wrong—**you shall not** give perverse testimony in a dispute to pervert it so as to **incline after the majority.**

[3]You shall not show deference to a poor man in his dispute.

Here the Torah insists that one always act justly, and specifically that one *not* follow the majority if the majority perverts justice. R. Yirmiyah, however, adduces the verse to prove exactly the opposite position, that one *should always* follow the majority. It is much like quoting a statement without the negative, quoting "Do not do such-and-such" as "Do such-and-such," quoting the exact words uttered, but omitting the critical "do not." To be fair, the syntax of the verse is awkward. The literal translation is more like: "You shall not incline after the majority to do wrong. Do not give perverse testimony in a dispute. Incline after the majority." To make the best sense of the last two sentences we should connect them with an implicit "so as" or "such that you" or "with the result that you": "Do not give perverse testimony in a dispute *such that you* incline after the majority." According to rabbinic interpretive assumptions, however, R. Yirmiyah's understanding is not completely unfounded in seeing the last sentence as superfluous and therefore independent of the preceding sentences. He understands the words as a self-contained precept, and provides a different context, a judicial context, as if this clause relates to the court: "Incline after the majority" when voting over legal issues. Nevertheless, we can easily perceive that the way he uses this part of the verse is diametrically opposed to the biblical contextual meaning.

This use of the biblical verses adds an ironic dimension to the story and even renders the storyteller's message somewhat circular, as the rabbis in the story end up basing their claims to interpretive authority on the very authority that they claim. They interpret the verses in a manner that justifies their right to interpret the Torah...which is what justifies their interpreting the Torah in this way. In this maneuver they have little choice, as only God or God's revelation can provide them authority to reject God's explicit testimony. Yet by appreciating the original biblical context and the tension with the way the verse appears in the story, we understand the circular nature of this claim, and that a different perspective is both possible and reasonable. Ironically, the very same verses in theory could support R. Eliezer (and God!), by justifying the position that one *not* follow the majority if it perverts the interpretation of a statute (as the sages perhaps do here), and by underscoring that the Torah is not so distant, not so recondite (=not in heaven), that God's intended meaning cannot be understood. Awareness of the verses in the context of the story over against their biblical contexts points to many of the issues at the heart of the story: rabbinic interpretive authority as opposed to God's original intent, the integrity of the legal system, and the question of following the majority when that majority position is not objectively correct.

## Biblical Verses Undermine the Character's Words

Let us turn to another story that employs biblical verses within the dialogue to brilliant effect by undermining a character's duplicitous advice. The Talmud (Gittin 56b–57a) relates that a Roman named Onkelos son of Kalonikos, a nephew of the Emperor Titus, considered converting to Judaism. (In the previous chapter we discussed a different story about

Onkelos b. Kalonikos, the relationship of which to this story is unclear.) By means of necromancy, he raises the ghost of his uncle Titus from the dead and asks whether he should join the Jewish people. Titus tries to discourage Onkelos by warning that Onkelos will not be able to fulfill all the commandments, and advises him rather:

**תלמוד בבלי, גטין נו ע״ב**

> זיל איגרי בהו בההוא עלמא והוית רישא,
> דכתיב: היו צריה לראש (איכה א:ה).

**Talmud Bavli, Gittin 56b**

> "Go and attack them in that world and you will become a ruler,
> as it says, *Her enemies become rulers (Lamentations 1:5).*"

Although Titus is a gentile—and not even a philosopher or scholar, that is, not a particularly educated gentile—in the rabbinic imagination he apparently possesses comprehensive knowledge of scripture. He poignantly quotes from the Book of Lamentations, which mourns the destruction of the First Temple by the Babylonians in 586 BCE, but was understood by the rabbis to pertain equally to the destruction of the Second Temple in 70 CE—perpetrated by Titus himself. This book is recited on the Ninth of Av, the fast day commemorating that double disaster. The verse indeed mourns the bitter catastrophe and reversal of expectations, such that the wicked foes of the Jewish people triumphed and destroyed Jerusalem—the feminine "her" refers to the city, personified as a widow. Titus thus recommends that, if Onkelos wishes to succeed, he should not convert to Judaism, but should rather attack the Jewish people. As the story continues, however, Titus admits that he suffers horrendous punishment in the next world, which completely undermines his counsel. The audience understands that Titus is selling fools' gold, and that the wise choice is indeed to convert to Judaism, so as to avoid posthumous punishment and to enjoy the bounties of the world to come. At the same time, the story provides comfort by defusing the disturbing implications of a harsh biblical verse. Enemies of the Jews may "become rulers" in this world, but, like Titus, they will pay the price in the next.

Onkelos's discussion with his uncle's ghost does not resolve his doubts, so he proceeds to raise up the ghost of Bilaam, the gentile prophet who was hired by King Balak of Moab to curse the Israelites in the Book of Numbers, and asks him the same question about joining the Jewish people. Bilaam responds, "You shall never concern yourself with their welfare or benefit as long as you live." These words are a direct quotation from Deuteronomy 23:7. Note, however, that Bilaam does not first offer advice and then quote scripture to back it up (as Titus did): "You should do X, because it says Y." Rather the storyteller has placed the biblical verse in Bilaam's mouth directly as part of the dialogue, and the audience recognizes the words on the basis of their knowledge of scripture. The larger biblical passage that contains this verse reads as follows:

**דברים כג:ד–ז**

ד**לא יבא** עמוני ומואבי **בקהל ה׳**, גם דור עשירי לא יבא להם בקהל ה׳ עד עולם,

העל דבר אשר לא קדמו אתכם בלחם ובמים בדרך בצאתכם ממצרים, ואשר שכר עליך את־בלעם בן בעור מפתור ארם נהרים לקללך.

וולא אבה ה׳ א־להיך לשמע אל בלעם, ויהפך ה׳ א־להיך לך את הקללה לברכה כי אהבך ה׳ א־להיך.

ז**לא תדרש שלמם וטבתם כל ימיך לעולם.**

**Deuteronomy 23:4–7**

4No Ammonite or Moabite shall be **admitted into the congregation of YHVH**; none of their descendants, even in the tenth generation, shall ever be admitted into the congregation of YHVH,

5because they did not meet you with food and water on your journey after you left Egypt, and because they hired Bilaam son of Beor from Petor of Aram-Naharaim to curse you—

6But YHVH your God refused to heed Bilaam; instead, YHVH your God turned the curse into a blessing for you, for YHVH your God loves you—

7**You shall never concern yourself with their welfare or benefit as long as you live.**

In the original context God speaks the verse to Israel as part of a prohibition and its rationale, which are connected to the evil deeds of the Ammonites and Moabites. Because these nations hired Bilaam to curse the Israelites, the Israelites may not assist them in any way. Ironically, the misleading advice Bilaam gives Onkelos in this rabbinic story—to avoid, rather than join, the Jewish people—is essentially the penalty that the Bible prescribes for those who opposed Israel: the Israelites may not be concerned with "their welfare or benefit." In addition, these biblical nations can never "be admitted into the congregation of YHVH," understood by the rabbis to mean conversion and marriage, which perfectly suits the story's context, Onkelos's contemplation of conversion.[7]

Finally, just as Titus himself was (according to the rabbinic understanding) the enemy-become-ruler in the Lamentations verse that his ghost quoted, here the context mentions Bilaam himself as the cause of the punishment of the enemies of the Jews, completely undermining the credibility of his advice, too. In other words, the Bible prohibits the Ammonites and Moabites converting to Judaism (the rabbinic understanding of "admitted to the congregation of YHVH") because they hired Bilaam to curse the Israelites, and cautions the Israelites to "never concern yourself with their welfare…" In the rabbinic story, Balaam uses these very words to instruct a potential convert not to join the Jewish people. The storyteller could have had Bilaam say, "Don't join those people" or some similar expression. But this would lose the powerful irony created by putting God's words in Bilaam's mouth, and the deeper lesson that devolves from the biblical context: that those who oppose Israel are punished.

## Stories and Midrash

Midrash, the rabbinic interpretation of the Bible, anchors a large part of the rabbinic worldview, and features prominently in almost every rabbinic literary work. Many stories accordingly include midrash; that is, they quote not only the biblical verse but also the rabbinic interpretation of the verse, which may be quite different from its "simple" or "contextual" meaning, in Hebrew called *peshat*. In some cases the storytellers borrowed the midrashic interpretation from other midrashic compilations or

7 The rabbis limited this prohibition against conversion and marriage to Ammonite and Moabite men, as Ruth, who married Boaz, and from whom King David descended, was a Moabite.

from elsewhere in the Talmud; in others they seem to have created the midrashic interpretation for their own narrative purposes, although they may have drawn on sources available to them but unknown to us. A typical example of a story involving midrash is that of R. Yose and the Roman matron, discussed in chapter 1 (pp. 36–42). R. Yose advises the matron of the difficulty of arranging marriages by invoking a midrashic interpretation of a verse that analogizes marriage to the splitting of the Sea of Reeds. Another example is the midrash presented to the emperor by Ketiah bar Shalom in the story discussed in chapter 2 (pp. 76–82). Ketiah "proves" to the emperor that he cannot destroy the Jewish people through an interpretation of a biblical verse, and the emperor accepts this midrashic teaching. What is remarkable, even somewhat bizarre, about this scene is that both of these figures are gentiles who should know little, if anything, about the Bible, and care even less. Yet in these stories they behave in a quintessentially rabbinic manner, engaging in midrash like typical sages. (More on this below.)

A good example of the prominent role of the midrashic reading of biblical verses appears in a story that recounts a friendship between R. Yehudah HaNasi, the leading rabbi of the time, and a Roman emperor named Antoninos. The story portrays these two leaders engaging in mutually respectful dialogue, and even depicts the Roman emperor consulting the rabbi about his personal and political problems.[8] The emperor, in fact, thinks so highly of the rabbi that he sneaks away from Rome and travels through a secret subterranean tunnel every evening (!) to serve the rabbi food and drink, apparently returning to Rome in the morning. During one of those nocturnal visits the two engage in the following dialogue:

**תלמוד בבלי, עבודה זרה יא ע"א**

[A] א"ל: אתינא לעלמא דאתי? א"ל: אין.

[B] א"ל: והכתיב: ובית עשו לקש, ודלקו בהם ואכלום. ולא יהיה שריד לבית עשו (עובדיה א:יח).

[C] א"ל: בעושה מעשה עשו...

8 For literature on this story, see Jeffrey L. Rubenstein, "The Story-Cycles of the Bavli," 267–76; Gray, "The Power Conferred"; Shaye J. D. Cohen, "The Conversion of Antoninus"; Ofra Meir, "The Historical Contribution of the Aggadot of the Sages" and *Rabbi Judah the Patriarch*, 277–91; and Boyarin, "Homotopia," 41–71.

[D] א"ל: והכתיב: שמה אדום, מלכיה וכל נשיאיה, אשר נתנו בגבורתם את חללי חרב, המה את ערלים ישכבו ואת ירדי בור (יחזקאל לב:כט).

[E] א"ל: מלכיה – ולא כל מלכיה, כל נשיאיה – ולא כל שריה.

**Talmud Bavli, Avodah Zarah 11a**

[A] He (Antoninos) said to him (R. Yehudah HaNasi): "Will I enter the world to come?" He said to him: "Yes."

[B] He (Antoninos) said to him: "Is it not written, *The House of Esau shall be straw; they shall burn it and devour it. And no survivor shall be left of the House of Esau (Obadiah 1:18).*"

[C] He (R. Yehudah HaNasi) said: "The verse refers to those who do the deeds of Esau."....[9]

[D] He (Antoninos) said to him: "Is it not written, *Edom is there, her kings and all her chieftains, who, for all their might, are laid among those who are slain by the sword; they too lie with the uncircumcised and with those who have gone down to the Pit (Ezekiel 32:29).*"

[E] He (R. Yehudah HaNasi) said to him: "This applies to [some of] *her kings*, but not to all her kings, to *all her chieftains*, but not to all her ministers."

The emperor Antoninos first asks R. Yehudah HaNasi whether he will "enter the world to come" and receive eternal life together with the righteous [A]. When the rabbi answers yes, the emperor expresses doubt about that encouraging answer by quoting a biblical verse, Obadiah 1:18, which prophesies that the House of Esau will be destroyed [B]. The rabbis identified the Romans with the biblical people of Edom, whom Genesis 36:1 describes as having descended from Esau: "This is the line of Esau—that is, Edom." In the rabbinic understanding, therefore, this prophecy concerning the Edomites, and "the House of Esau," suggests that the Romans will be annihilated, hence no Roman will be admitted to the world to come. In this way the emperor asks the rabbi how he can enter the next world, considering that the Bible prophesies the total destruction of

9 The Talmud here interrupts the dialogue by quoting a source (a *baraita*) that supports this interpretation.

all Romans. To this the rabbi replies with a midrashic interpretation, "The verse refers to those who do the deeds of Esau" [C]. That is, the verse means that only those descendants of Esau who act like Esau will be obliterated, but not good and pious Romans like the emperor Antoninos! "Esau" in the verse should be understood as "Esau-types" or "followers in the ways of the wicked Esau," not merely genetic descendants of Esau/Edom.

Still not satisfied, the emperor responds by quoting Ezekiel 32:29, a prophecy that consigns Edom's "kings and all her chieftains," which the rabbis understood as the Roman emperors, to the "Pit," namely to hell, precluding heavenly reward [D]. Again, the rabbi answers midrashically, specifying that, since the word "all" is applied to chieftains but not to "kings," the verse only applies to *some of* the Roman kings. In other words, because the verse does not state explicitly "*all* her kings" but only "her kings," it implies that *some* Edomite/Roman kings must be exempt from this dire prophecy [E], and a good Roman emperor like Antoninos can still gain entry to the next world.

The storyteller portrays the Roman emperor as having an encyclopedic knowledge of the Bible, mobilizing verses at will from the prophets Obadiah and Ezekiel, and debating their meaning with the great rabbi. But though the emperor knows the Bible, he does not know the midrash. The emperor's doubts are based on his straightforward (and mistaken) understanding of the verses; they are resolved by the rabbi's midrashic interpretation of the same scriptures, which teach the emperor to understand their import properly. The story's point of the Jewish leader's superiority to the Roman emperor is thus in part a function of his knowledge of midrash, which gives him the ability to understand the true nature of things, including the emperor's future posthumous fate.

While the story and dialogue focus on the emperor Antoninos, they engage the broad theological question of the gentiles and the world to come. As with many aspects of rabbinic theology, rabbinic thinking on this issue was not uniform. Some rabbis had extremely negative views of gentiles and taught that they had no share in the next world: gentiles either would suffer in a type of hell or at death pass from existence into oblivion. Other views, however, were ambivalent or more nuanced, and held that righteous gentiles would share in heavenly rewards. Our storyteller appears to fall into this second trend, insisting that righteous emperors will enter the world to come, and presumably other righteous gentiles will, too.

## Biblical Verses, Authority, and (Quasi-) Prophecy

This ability to apply biblical verses to their present-day situations is crucial to the rabbis' claim to authority and to their self-understanding as the legitimate leaders of the Jewish people. Rabbinic knowledge of scripture and its correct interpretation provide the rabbis with a quasi-prophetic capacity to understand how the divine will applies to their present historical moment, and what the future has in store. The rabbis believed that the age of prophecy had concluded with Haggai, Zechariah, and Malachi, the last of the biblical prophets, who lived at the beginning of the Second Temple period (c. 530–500 BCE). God no longer disclosed the divine will through new prophecy, but rather through the existing biblical text, that is, through past revelations that were eternally relevant. But it required the right interpreter to understand how to make sense of the holy scriptures and to apply them to present circumstances. That interpretive ability, which the rabbis believed they alone possessed, gave them a key to understand reality and to negotiate its challenges. They stood in the place of the prophets as the only humans capable of understanding the divine will in their post-biblical age.

Rabbinic stories often feature a sage's mastery of scripture and interpretive ability as the key to his success and even survival. Let us take as an example three moments in the story of the destruction of the Temple and R. Yoḥanan b. Zakkai's escape from Jerusalem (Gittin 55b–56b). When the Romans besiege the city a stalemate develops between the rabbis, who counsel to sue for peace, and a war party of "thugs" (בריוני/*biryoni*) or zealots, who insist upon attacking the enemy. These thugs prevent any Jews from leaving the city, so as not to weaken the ranks of defenders. They even destroy the stocks of food and wine in order to force a confrontation, which quickly brings the Jerusalemites to the point of starvation. In the first of our three moments, the Talmud recounts that Martah, daughter of Baitos, "the richest woman in Jerusalem," tried in vain to purchase some bread to eat, first sending her servant to the market and then going herself to search, whereupon "a piece of dung stuck to her foot and she died." (Evidently she was disgusted to death, or perhaps an infection from the dung quickly caused her demise due to her weakened state.) Upon seeing her death, R. Yoḥanan b. Zakkai recalled an apposite biblical passage:

**תלמוד בבלי, גטין נו ע"א**

קרי עלה רבן יוחנן בן זכאי:

הרכה בך והענגה ,אשר לא נסתה כף רגלה הצג על הארץ מהתענג ומרך, תרע עינה באיש חיקה ובבנה ובבתה

ובשליתה היוצת מבין רגליה ובבניה אשר תלד, כי תאכלם בחסר כל בסתר במצור ובמצוק אשר יציק לך איבך בשעריך (דברים כח:נו-נז).

**Talmud Bavli, Gittin 56a**

R. Yoḥanan b. Zakkai applied to her the verse:

*And she who is most tender and dainty among you, so tender and dainty that she would never venture to set a foot on the ground, shall begrudge the husband of her bosom, and her son and daughter,*

*the afterbirth that issues from between her legs and the babies she bears; she shall eat them secretly, because of utter want in the desperate straits to which your enemy shall reduce you in your towns (Deuteronomy 28:56–57).*

These verses derive from a section of Deuteronomy known as the תוכחה/*tokheḥah* or "rebuke," a terrible prophetic warning of punishments and disasters that God will inflict upon the Israelites if they sin and abandon their religion.[10] The rabbi identifies Martah with the verses' reference to the "most tender and dainty among you," a woman so pampered that she would typically not leave her mansion "to set foot on the ground" but rather send her servants to do her errands, as she first attempted to do, and who experienced the terrible hunger so gruesomely depicted in the biblical passage. This means that the biblical prophecy has materialized, that God is punishing the Jewish people exactly as foreseen in the *tokheḥah.* Indeed, the same biblical passage warns in the preceding verses that "YHVH will bring a nation against you from afar, from the end of the earth, which will swoop down like the eagle, a nation whose language you do not understand" (28:49), which will besiege the people and reduce them to starvation. That nation, for R. Yoḥanan b. Zakkai, is clearly their present enemy, the Romans. That the eagle was the principal symbol of

---

10 This section is sometimes designated "The Greater Rebuke" to distinguish it from "The Lesser Rebuke" found in Leviticus 26.

the Roman army might strengthen his understanding, too. Now, the siege of Jerusalem and starvation are coming true before his eyes, precisely as foretold. Most importantly, the rabbi knows that the biblical passage predicts not only starvation but also other disasters, including defeat and massacre by enemies (28:25–26), enslavement to a foreign people (28:32–34), and servitude and exile (28:36–37, 41, 48). Now these, too, are guaranteed to transpire. R. Yoḥanan b. Zakkai thus perceives that the war against the Romans is futile, defeat inevitable, and that it can only be counterproductive to continue resisting. He therefore makes a secret deal with the leader of the thugs to escape from Jerusalem, and he slips out, hidden in a coffin.

At first glance this episode involving Martah appears to be a minor interlude within the larger story, serving primarily to illustrate the severity of the famine and the misery of the city's inhabitants. If this scene were removed, the plot would still flow smoothly and the story would be completely comprehensible. The audience would conclude that R. Yoḥanan b. Zakkai decided to escape from Jerusalem due to the acute famine and to his assessment that the Jews would lose the war. Yet to the storyteller and his message, this scene is absolutely crucial. Without it, the audience would wonder whether R. Yoḥanan b. Zakkai made the correct decision to abandon the city and his fellow Jews, and, as the story continues, to parley with the Roman general Vespasian. Perhaps he should have led the rabbis and their followers in a battle against the thugs who refused to sue for peace, and he could have then negotiated a settlement with the Romans. Perhaps he should have taken up arms against the Romans and led the people out to battle, or at least remained with them to provide moral and spiritual support. How could he be so sure that the Jews would lose the war, or that their prayers would not be heard, or that their God would not destroy their enemies? The audience might even think the rabbi had betrayed his people, consigning them to a miserable death while saving his own skin.

R. Yoḥanan b. Zakkai, however, could be sure of all this because he knew that God was now on the side of the Romans and that resistance was useless. He knew that the city was doomed because he witnessed the *tokheḥah* prophecy coming true in Martah's death, and therefore he knew that the other curses would soon follow, including defeat and exile. His understanding of scripture and his ability to apply it to his present circumstances provided the key to recognizing the historical moment. By means of this scene—and especially its use of biblical citation—

the storyteller communicates to his audience that the rabbi made the absolutely correct decision and embarked on a phenomenally courageous course of action, to escape the doomed city and salvage what he could.

Having escaped from Jerusalem, R. Yoḥanan b. Zakkai approaches Vespasian, in the second of our three moments, and salutes him, "Peace to you O king, peace to you O king."[11] Vespasian replies that R. Yoḥanan deserves death for this greeting. For a general to accept such a salutation entails treason against the reigning emperor, so Vespasian must make it crystal clear that he rejects the title of king. Unfazed, the rabbi replies with a midrashic proof that Vespasian is, or is destined to be, the king:

**תלמוד בבלי, גטין נו ע"א–ב**

[A] אמר ליה: דקאמרת לאו מלכא אנא, איברא מלכא את. דאי לאו מלכא את, לא מימסרא ירושלים בידך, דכתיב: והלבנון באדיר יפול (ישעיהו י:לד).

[B] ואין אדיר אלא מלך, דכתיב: והיה אדירו ומשלו מקרבו יצא ממנו (ירמיהו ל:כא).

[C] ואין לבנון אלא בית המקדש, שנאמר: ההר הטוב הזה והלבנון (דברים ג:כה).

[D] ...אדהכי, אתא פריסתקא עליה מרומי. אמר ליה: קום, דמית ליה קיסר, ואמרי הנהו חשיבי דרומי לאותיבך ברישא.

**Talmud Bavli, Gittin 56a–b**

[A] He (R. Yoḥanan b. Zakkai) said to him (Vespasian): As for what you said, "I am not a king"—in truth you are a king. For if you were not a king, Jerusalem would not be delivered into your hands, as it says, *Lebanon shall fall to the mighty one (Isaiah 10:34).*

[B] And "mighty one" refers to a king, as it says, *His mighty one shall be of themselves, His ruler shall come from his midst (Jeremiah 30:21).*

---

11 This and the following example were brilliantly analyzed by Yonah Frankel, "Bible Verses Quoted," and I borrow here a great deal from Frankel's discussion. Frankel, however, does not discuss the episode with Martah b. Baitos, which I believe is crucial to understanding why the rabbi resolved to escape the city. See Jeffrey L. Rubenstein, *Talmudic Stories*, 153–55. The Martah episode also helps explain why R. Yoḥanan b. Zakkai did not ask that Vespasian give the Jews another chance or spare Jerusalem and the Temple—he knew that the destruction was inevitable.

[C] And "Lebanon" refers to the Temple, as it says, *That good hill country and the Lebanon (Deuteronomy 3:25).*

[D] ...Just then a messenger came from Rome. He said to him: "Rise, for the emperor has died, and the nobles of Rome voted to make you (=Vespasian) the leader."

His proof quotes three different verses. The logic is as follows: R. Yoḥanan b. Zakkai knows that Vespasian will win the war and conquer Jerusalem because he realizes from Martah's demise that the *tokheḥah* is materializing. He understands Isaiah 10:34 to describe precisely this event, as he interprets "Lebanon" to refer to the Temple. This interpretation, in turn, derives from his reading of Deuteronomy 3:25, where Moses petitions God to allow him to enter the Land of Israel, to "cross over and see the good land on the other side of the Jordan, that good hill country and the Lebanon" [C]. In the rabbi's understanding, Moses is not referring to Mount Lebanon in the north (probably the contextual or *peshat* meaning), but rather the "good hill country" of the Land of Israel and the Temple, or future site of the Temple, namely Jerusalem. That the place name "Lebanon" refers to the Temple was a widespread ancient tradition, in part predicated on the fact that Solomon had imported cedars from Mount Lebanon to construct the Temple (1 Kings 5:19–24). Moreover, why would going to Mount Lebanon be so important to Moses? He must rather mean Jerusalem, the most important part of the Land of Israel.

Isaiah calls the conqueror a "mighty one," and the rabbi understands from the mention of the same word in Jeremiah 30:21 that it is a synonym for "king." That verse states, "His **mighty one** shall be of themselves; His **ruler** shall come from his midst" [B]. In this verse's parallel structure, a "mighty one" is equivalent to a "ruler," that is, a king. Isaiah's prophecy therefore reveals, when read with R. Yoḥanan b. Zakkai's midrashic insight, that the "fall of Lebanon," that is, the destruction of the Temple and the Temple-city of Jerusalem, will come at the hands of a "mighty one," a king. So Vespasian, who is about to conquer the city (as evidenced by the Martah episode), must be a king.

Almost immediately after this exchange, the story continues with the arrival of news that Vespasian had been chosen as the new emperor [D]. Exactly as R. Yoḥanan ben Zakkai asserted, Vespasian has in fact already become king, even though he did not yet know it. The ability to interpret scripture, that is, to engage in midrash, gives the rabbi a quasi-prophetic ability to understand the true state of things and course of history. The writing was on the wall, so to speak, for those who know how to read; our only surprise is that the announcement came so soon after the rabbi mentioned it to Vespasian.

R. Yoḥanan b. Zakkai continues to prove his worth to Vespasian in the next scene:

**תלמוד בבלי, גטין נו ע״ב**

הוה סיים חד מסאניה. בעא למסיימה לאחרינא. לא עייל. בעא למישלפיה לאידך. לא נפק. אמר: מאי האי?

אמר ליה: לא תצטער. שמועה טובה אתיא לך, דכתיב: שמועה טובה תדשן עצם (משלי טו:ל).

אמר ליה: מאי תקנתיה? (אמר ליה:) ליתי איניש דלא מיתבא דעתך מיניה ולחליף קמך דכתיב: ורוח נכאה תיבש גרם (משלי יז:כב).

עבד הכי. עייל.

**Talmud Bavli, Gittin 56b**

He (Vespasian) had put on one shoe. He tried to put on the other. It would not go on. He tried to take off the first. It would not come off. He said, "What is this?"

He (R. Yoḥanan b. Zakkai) said to him, "Don't worry. You received good news, as it says, *Good news puts fat on bones (Proverbs 15:30)*."

He (Vespasian) said to him, "What is the remedy?" (R. Yoḥanan b. Zakkai said to him,) "Bring someone who annoys you and have him pass before you, as it says, *Despondency dries up the bones (Proverbs 17:22)*."

He (Vespasian) did this. It (the shoe) went on (his foot).

There is something comical about the newly-elected Roman emperor unable to put on his combat boots, stuck like a small child with one shoe on and one shoe off. The rabbinic storyteller is likely making a little joke at the villain's expense. More significantly, R. Yoḥanan b. Zakkai solves these podiatric difficulties through his knowledge of scripture. Proverbs 15:30 advises that "good news," namely the message that Vespasian was elected emperor, "puts fat on the bones," which caused his foot to swell such that his boot would no longer fit. Impressed by the rabbi's explanation,

Vespasian turns to him for a solution, readily supplied from another biblical verse. "Despondency," literally a "downcast spirit" or "dejected mind" (רוח נכאה), the rabbi knows, will "dry up the flesh" and cause the foot to contract, so he proposes a simple way for the emperor to experience a depressed mood—and simultaneously to test his wisdom. Voilà! Problem solved. R. Yoḥanan b. Zakkai can approach the emperor not as a supplicant or subordinate, but as an equal, because of his mastery of the Bible. On the surface, the Roman general-emperor is arguably the most powerful man on earth, certainly far more powerful than a defenseless Jewish sage, but at a deeper level he is inferior and less potent. For the storyteller, indeed, the rabbi's abilities render him superior to the Roman, much as we saw above in the case of R. Yehudah HaNasi and Antoninos.

Vespasian proceeds to grant R. Yoḥanan b. Zakkai a request, "Ask something of me and I will give it to you," and the rabbi replies, "Give me Yavneh, and its sages, and the line of Rabban Gamaliel, and doctors to heal R. Tzadok." The rabbi ensures that despite the destruction of Jerusalem, rabbinic Judaism will endure, securing the safety of the leading rabbis and a haven for them to continue their studies. Knowledge of scripture, and the ability to understand reality through that prism, saves rabbinic Judaism. The rabbis' ability to read the verses and apply them to the historical moment justifies their claim to authority and position as the heirs of biblical prophets. This ability to interpret Torah thus serves both as the key to the survival of rabbinic Judaism and as the end, the purpose of the rabbinic project of understanding God's will and observing it in practice. And this project, the audience should understand, will outlast the Roman Empire and army, despite the destruction of the Temple and the Romans' seeming triumph in battle.

In these ways the biblical verses mobilized within a rabbinic story sometimes operate on another level to transmit larger messages to the audience. Those messages can support the surface message of the story, as they do in these passages about R. Yoḥanan b. Zakkai, or they can nuance or even undermine it, as we might consider them to have done in the "Oven of Akhnai" story. One way or another, far from being mere decorative flourishes with a loose connection to the story, verses will almost always be important for understanding both the dynamics of the plot and the storyteller's larger message.

## The World Speaks the Language of Torah

In rabbinic stories, not only do all human beings quote the Bible, but even inanimate objects do so. In the previous chapter (p. 94) we briefly mentioned the characterization of Eleazar b. Dordia who, in contemporary terms, might be called a sex addict: "There was not one prostitute in the world with whom he had not had sex." As the story continues, he eventually feels remorse for his actions but thinks himself too much a sinner, such that his "repentance will never be accepted."[12]

**תלמוד בבלי, עבודה זרה יז ע"א**

[A] הלך וישב בין שני הרים וגבעות.

[B1] אמר: הרים וגבעות, בקשו עלי רחמים. אמרו לו: עד שאנו מבקשים עליך נבקש על עצמנו, שנאמר: כי ההרים ימושו והגבעות תמוטינה (ישעיהו נד:י).

[B2] אמר: שמים וארץ, בקשו עלי רחמים. אמרו לו: עד שאנו מבקשים עליך נבקש על עצמנו, שנאמר: כי שמים כעשן נמלחו והארץ כבגד תבלה (ישעיהו נא:ו).

[B3] אמר: חמה ולבנה, בקשו עלי רחמים. אמרו לו: עד שאנו מבקשים עליך נבקש על עצמנו, שנאמר: וחפרה הלבנה ובושה החמה (ישעיהו כד:כג).

[B4] אמר: כוכבים ומזלות, בקשו עלי רחמים. אמרו לו: עד שאנו מבקשים עליך, נבקש על עצמנו, שנאמר: ונמקו כל צבא השמים (ישעיהו לד:ד).

[C] אמר: אין הדבר תלוי אלא בי. הניח ראשו בין ברכיו וגעה בבכיה עד שיצתה נשמתו. יצתה בת קול ואמרה: ר"א בן דורדיא מזומן לחיי העולם הבא.

**Talmud Bavli, Avodah Zarah 17a**

[A] He went and sat between two mountains and hills.

[B1] He said, "Mountains and hills! Pray for me." They said to him, "Before we pray for you, we should pray for ourselves, since it says, *For the mountains may move and the hills be shaken (Isaiah 54:10).*"

[B2] He said, "Heaven and earth! Pray for me." They said to him, "Before we pray for you, we should pray for ourselves, since it says, *Though*

---

12 For analysis of this story, see Mira Balberg, "Between Heterotopia and Utopia," 206–14.

*the heavens should melt away like smoke, and the earth wear out like a garment (Isaiah 51:6).*"

[B3] He said, "Sun and moon! Pray for me." They said to him, "Before we pray for you, we should pray for ourselves, since it says, *Then the moon shall be ashamed, and the sun shall be abashed (Isaiah 24:23).*"

[B4] He said, "Stars and constellations! Pray for me." They said to him, "Before we pray for you, we should pray for ourselves, since it says, *All the hosts of heaven shall wither (Isaiah 34:4).*"

[C] He said, "Then the matter depends exclusively on me." He put his head between his knees and broke out in sobs until his soul departed. A heavenly voice went forth and said, "R. Eleazar b. Dordia is destined for life in the world to come."

As we saw in chapter 1, repetition is characteristic of rabbinic stories. Here Eleazar solicits four different components of the natural world to pray for him [B1–B4]. Alas, these natural phenomena each respond that they must pray for themselves, and each quotes a biblical verse in explanation. The four verses suggest that terrestrial and celestial objects themselves are vulnerable to dissolution and extinction. Thus heaven and earth quote a verse from Isaiah's prophetic vision that describes the heavens "melting away like smoke" and the earth "wearing away like a garment," that is, passing away into nothingness. Heaven and earth must pray for their own existence, must beseech God not to bring about this apocalyptic destruction, and therefore cannot take the time to pray for poor Eleazar. Similarly, the other biblical verses, in this context, mean that the hills and mountains may be uprooted, the stars and constellations "wither" away and decay into nonexistence, and the sun and moon go dark—being ashamed is associated with blushing, which in rabbinic Hebrew is described as darkening of the face—and die out. Failing to receive help from any of these sources, Eleazar realizes that he must take matters into his own hands [C]. He assumes a contrite posture, weeps to express his anguish, and presumably pours his heart out in prayer, too. And although he dies in this abject state, we learn from the heavenly voice that his penitential prayers and remorseful tears succeeded in atoning for his sins and he has gained entry into the world to come. Even the most chronic and inveterate sinners, the storyteller instructs us, have the potential to repent for their sins and receive divine forgiveness.

As we would expect, the original contexts of several of these verses also have some bearing on the themes of the story. For example, the verse quoted by the mountains and hills in its broader context reads as follows:

**ישעיהו נד:ח-י**

ח בשצף קצף, הסתרתי פני רגע ממך, ובחסד עולם רחמתיך, אמר גאלך ה'.

ט כי מי נח זאת לי, אשר נשבעתי מעבר מי נח עוד על הארץ, כן נשבעתי מקצף עליך ומגער בך.

י **כי ההרים ימושו והגבעות תמוטינה** וחסדי מאתך לא ימוש, וברית שלומי לא תמוט, אמר מרחמך ה'.

**Isaiah 54:8–10**

8 In slight anger, for a moment, I hid My face from you; but with kindness everlasting I will take you back in love—said YHVH your redeemer.

9 For this to Me is like the waters of Noah; as I swore that the waters of Noah nevermore would flood the earth, so I swear that I will not be angry or rebuke you.

10 **For the mountains may move and the hills be shaken** but My loyalty shall never move from you, nor My covenant of friendship be shaken, said YHVH who takes you back in love.

Here God promises to always accept those who wish to return to God's favor, and will always be ready with "kindness," "friendship," and "love" to restore the covenantal relationship when it has been disrupted by sin. Verses 8–9, immediately preceding the verse quoted in the story (which the audience, knowing the larger context, would have had in mind, too) emphasize that God will always "take you back," no matter how severe the sin. Eleazar b. Dordia need not have worried that his repentance "would never be accepted" without outside intervention; on the contrary, God was waiting for him all along! Ironically, the evidence of God's perpetual openness to repentance is another natural phenomenon—the waters—as God promised after the flood that he would never destroy the world again (Genesis 9:12–16). Within the story, these verses are quoted as evidence that great works of nature signify the inherent instability of the cosmos, but in their original, biblical context they suggest almost the opposite: the endurance of both the natural order and of God's covenant with the Jewish people. Even the reference to the mountains and hills in the biblical context essentially means the opposite of what the verse seems to mean in the story. The verse suggests that *even if* the mountains were to move and hills to be shaken—an extremely unlikely if not impossible occurrence—still God's loyalty and covenant would remain in force. In contrast to the story, for the prophetic speaker the mountains and hills, like the waters, symbolize the permanence of God's covenant and the possibility of repentance.

This is a beautiful example of the verses quoted in the story conveying a meaning that supports and communicates the overall message of the storyteller, in contrast to their function within the characters' dialogue. It is almost a secret message shared by storyteller and audience, beyond the purview of the characters. Both the biblical passage and the storyteller therefore teach a fundamental principle of Jewish theology, that repentance is always possible as God, the Merciful One, always welcomes those who return.

For traditional readers who treated talmudic stories as historical or biographical, as factually true, stories like this one present a problem. How can these natural phenomena speak? How are they able to quote biblical verses? Some medieval commentators claim that the mountains, sun, and stars did not really speak, but that Eleazar b. Dordia imagined them speaking, or that he himself articulated what they would have said had they been sentient beings.[13] Their speech was just his vision, or hallucination, or a type of concretization of his thought processes. Understanding the speech of objects in this way allowed them to hold on to a view of talmudic stories in general as realistic.

I am not fully satisfied with this explanation. Rabbinic storytellers knew how to distinguish imagination from "reality" in their stories: we have some stories that portray characters experiencing visions or dreams, and in other cases the storytellers tell us what the characters mistakenly thought. True, as we have seen, it is not always clear whether speech is articulated aloud or only in the character's head. Thoughts are often represented as speech, as interior monologues: "R. So-and so said…" sometimes means

---

**13** See the commentaries in Ein Ya'akov, ad loc.

"R. So-and-so said to himself"—which is close to "R. So-and-so thought" in contemporary terms. But our story's case seems very different to me. Here the storytellers are attributing speech and the quotation of scripture directly to natural phenomena, and the same question applies whether the speech is voiced or internal (whatever that would mean for these objects).[14]

Moreover, attributing the speech of natural phenomena to a projection of the characters in those stories still doesn't resolve the question of whether it is realistic for Romans and other gentiles to quote biblical verses and produce midrashic interpretations. Some intellectually inclined gentiles in antiquity took an interest in the Jewish scriptures and may have had a general sense of their contents. That they had encyclopedic knowledge and the ability to mobilize relevant verses at will, however, that some of them would interpret those verses with midrashic techniques like a rabbi, and that even Roman emperors (and Persian emperors in other stories) would know details of what is written in Jewish scriptures—this is all far beyond the realm of possibility.

The most plausible way to understand the pervasive deployment of biblical verses by all characters in rabbinic stories—rabbis and non-rabbis, Jews and gentiles, humans and natural phenomena—is that rabbis understood the Bible as the framework that underlies the past, present, and future. Rabbinic traditions consider the Torah to have antedated the world and to have served as the blueprint for creation, asserting that "God looked into the Torah and created the world."[15] Placing biblical verses in the mouths of gentiles or natural phenomena reflects this worldview. Gentiles may not have studied the scriptures, and the sun and stars cannot speak, but this quasi-mystical rabbinic understanding of the cosmos entails that they can quote Torah when apposite. In slightly different terms, the prevalence of biblical verses in rabbinic stories points to a deep religious sensibility that characterizes the rabbinic worldview and that continued throughout the Middle Ages, and that for many of us continues to be relevant today. The rabbis understood the world through the prism of

---

14 See too Avot D'Rabbi Natan, Version A, chapter 3, which tells of a pious man whose boat sank. He tells how he was saved: "I heard the sound of a great noise of the waves of the sea, one wave saying to the other and the other to another, 'Hurry! And let us raise the man out of the sea, for he practiced charity all his days.'"

15 Bereishit Rabbah 1:1.

the scriptures, and it was that connection of biblical text to contemporary times that gave their lives meaning.

At the same time, I believe that this use of biblical verses and midrash reflects a cultural convention shared between storytellers and their audience. Both parties understood that mountains do not really speak and gentiles do not really know midrash, much as we understand today that stories about speaking animals, superheroes, and magic are not real in any literal or factual way. This literary technique functions as a type of learned and sophisticated cultural "play" that articulates values, norms, ideas, and other sociocultural elements shared by the storytellers and their audience. It is an act of religious imagination on their part, that is available to us all as well: a way of engaging readers religiously in an imaginative world where all humans, animals, and natural phenomena speak the language of Torah.

## Verses as Narrative Frames

Apart from serving as components of the characters' dialogue, biblical verses sometimes provide a framing device for the plot or offer a general perspective on the story. We encountered a good example of this phenomenon in the story of the mother and her seven sons in chapter 1 (pp. 46–53). That story opened with the verse *It is for Your sake that we are slain all day long, that we are regarded as sheep to be slaughtered (Psalm 44:23)* and a comment by Rav Yehudah that the verse refers to the martyrdom of the mother and her sons. Here the biblical verse functions as a framework for the entire story: the death of the sons and the mother exemplify those who are "slain all day long" and went like "sheep to be slaughtered." As the storyteller proceeds to narrate their deaths one by one, the audience understands them under this conceptual rubric.

Another example is found in a story of a struggle between rabbis in Babylonia and in the Land of Israel for authority over the calendar. In rabbinic times, the Jewish calendar was not fixed, as it is now, but depended on observations of the moon and other criteria to determine the beginning of the new month and the addition of the leap month of Second Adar. The rabbis in the Land of Israel traditionally held this authority, but at one point faced a challenge from Babylonian rabbis who sought to wrest it away. The story recounts that the rabbis of the Land of Israel sent emissaries to the Babylonians to reassert their authority and convince their rivals to abandon this challenge. This mission succeeded, and the story concludes:

**תלמוד בבלי, ברכות סג ע"ב**

וכל כך למה?

משום שנאמר: כי מציון תצא תורה, ודבר ה' מירושלים (ישעיהו ב:ג).

**Talmud Bavli, Berakhot 63b**

Why all this?

Because it says, *For Torah shall come forth from Zion, and the word of YHVH from Jerusalem (Isaiah 2:3).*

Here the narrator offers a general perspective to understand the events of the story.[16] The Bible designates Jerusalem as the center of Torah, the source from which "the word of YHVH" radiates outward to the diaspora. Hence it is fitting that the rabbis of the Land of Israel make the legal determinations over calendrical matters, and send forth their decisions to far-flung Jewish communities. Moreover, the beginning of the verse reads: "Come, let us go up to the Mount of YHVH , to the house of the God of Jacob; *that He may instruct us in His ways*, and that we may walk in His paths." The Land of Israel, home to the "Mount of YHVH," and not cities in Babylonia, should be the source of instruction in "His ways," including the correct workings of the calendar. Without this coda the audience might have been more sympathetic to the possibility that calendrical authority be vested in the most learned rabbis, or the most brilliant rabbis, or the rabbis most knowledgeable in astronomical "science," wherever they reside.

## Rabbinic Stories as Narrative Exegesis

Rabbinic stories generated from the interpretation of biblical verses, that is, through a midrashic process, are most commonly rabbinic retellings of stories of the biblical characters, filling in gaps in the biblical text, resolving difficulties, and providing additional color. Narratives produced

16 On this story see Isaiah Gafni, *Center and Diaspora*, 108–11; Aharon Oppenheimer, "The Attempt of Hananiah,"; Jeffrey L. Rubenstein, *Culture of the Babylonian Talmud*, 23–26.

through midrash in this way are sometimes called "exegetical narratives." Found throughout the collections of midrash as well as in the Talmuds, exegetical narratives remain within the biblical world. Many of these stories achieved legendary status, such as the disputes between Cain and Abel that led to the fratricide (Midrash Bereishit Rabbah 22:7), Satan's attempts to prevent Abraham from carrying out God's commandment of the binding of Isaac (Sanhedrin 89b), and Leah and Rachel conspiring to deceive Jacob into marrying the wrong sister (Bava Batra 123a, Bereishit Rabbah 70:19).

Occasionally, however, stories about the sages or post-biblical characters develop in part from biblical interpretation or from a process of interpretation of early rabbinic sources. This method produced several stories of Elisha b. Abuya or Aḥer, "the Other," the arch-heretic and Roman collaborator.[17] Rabbinic texts preserve disparate and conflicting traditions about Elisha b. Abuya such that the historical or "biographical" kernel (if one exists) is impossible to discern. The earliest tradition lists Elisha among four rabbis who "entered the orchard" (פרדס/*pardes*), which scholars understand as a type of esoteric study or a form of mystical experience. This type of mysticism, known as מעשה מרכבה/*maaesh merkavah*, "chariot mysticism" or "throne mysticism," preceded Kabbalah as the main form of Jewish mysticism. Its goal, based on the prophet Ezekiel's vision (chapter 1–3), was to visualize, and perhaps even ascend to, God's celestial chariot-throne in the heavenly Temple.

An extremely cryptic source in the Tosefta mentions that Elisha b. Abuya was among four rabbis who attempted to "enter the orchard" and describes the results of their esoteric-mystical activity. It then associates each of the rabbis with a biblical verse:

**תוספתא חגיגה ב:ג–ד**

[A] ארבעה נכנסו לפרדס: בן עזאי, ובן זומא, אחר, ורבי עקיבה.

[B] אחד הציץ ומת. אחד הציץ ונפגע. אחד הציץ וקיצץ בנטיעות. ואחד עלה בשלום וירד בשלום...

[C] אלישע הציץ וקיצץ בנטיעות.

[D] עליו הכתוב אומר: אל תתן את פיך לחטיא את בשרך, ואל תאמר לפני המלאך כי שגגה היא, למה יקצף הא־להים על קולך וחבל את מעשה ידיך (קהלת ה:ה).

17 Elisha b. Abuya's story was fictionalized and popularized through Milton Steinberg's novel *As a Driven Leaf*.

**Tosefta Ḥagigah 2:3–4**

[A] Four entered the orchard: Ben Azzai, Ben Zoma, Aḥer ("Other"), and R. Akiva.

[B] One gazed and died. One gazed and was harmed. One gazed and cut the shoots. And one went up in peace and went down in peace….

[C] Elisha gazed and cut the shoots.

[D] Scripture says about him, *Let not your mouth lead your flesh to sin, and do not say before the messenger that it was an error, else God may be angered by your talk and destroy the work of your hands (Kohelet 5:5).*

Exactly what happened to Elisha/Aḥer is by no means clear, as both the phrase "cut the shoots" and the meaning of the biblical verse in relation to him are opaque. (In fact, the meaning of Kohelet 5:5 itself is unclear even in its biblical context.) Esoteric and mystical sources often obscure their meaning, as the sensitive nature of the subject requires secrecy and concealment from the unworthy. It appears that even the sages of the talmudic era no longer understood the original meaning of this earlier tradition of the Mishnah-Tosefta, and did their best to puzzle out the enigmatic references. The Talmud Yerushalmi provides three explanations to the Tosefta passage (which appears below in boldface):[18]

**תלמוד ירושלמי, חגיגה ב:א (עז ע״ב)**

**אחר הציץ וקיצץ בנטיעות.**

[A1] מני אחר? אלישע בן אבויה, שהיה הורג רבי תורה.

[A2] אמרין: כל תלמיד דהוה **חמי** ליה משבח באוריתא הוה קטיל ליה.

[B1] ולא עוד, אלא דהוה עליל לבית ווערא והוה **חמי** טלייא קומי ספרא. והוה אמר: מה אילין יתבין עבדין הכא? אומנתיה דהן בנאי. אומנתיה דהן נגר. אומנתיה דהן צייד. אומנתיה דהן חייט.

[B2] וכיון דהוון שמעין כן הוון שבקין ליה ואזלין לון. **עליו הכתוב אומר: אל תתן את־פיך לחטיא את בשרך, ואל תאמר לפני המלאך כי שגגה היא, למה יקצף הא־להים על קולך וחבל את־מעשה ידיך (קהלת ה:ה).**

---

18 On this text, see Jeffrey L. Rubenstein, *Talmudic Stories,* 82–89 and "Elisha ben Abuya"; Alon Goshen-Gottstein, *The Sinner and the Amnesiac*; Jay Rovner, "Structure and Ideology in the Aher Narrative."

[B3] שחיבל מעשה ידיו שלאותו האיש.

[C1] אוף בשעת שומדא, הוון מטענין לון מטולין, והוון מתכוונין מיטעון תרי חד מטול, משם שנים שעשו מלאכה אחת.

[C2] אמר: אטעוננון יחידאין. אזלון ואטעונינון יחידיין.

[C3] והוון מתכוונין מפרוק בכרמלית.

[C4] אמר: אטעונינון צלוחיין. אזלון ואטעונינון צלוחיין.

**Talmud Yerushalmi, Ḥagigah 2:1 (77b)**

**Aḥer gazed and cut the shoots.**

[A1] Who is Aḥer? Elisha ben Abuya, who would kill the young students of Torah.

[A2] They said: He would kill every student whom he **saw** distinguish himself in Torah.

[B1] Not only that, but he would go to the meeting-place and **see** children in front of their teacher, and he would say, "What are these sitting and doing here? This one's profession is a builder. That one's profession is a carpenter. This one's profession is a hunter. That one's profession is a tailor."

[B2] When they heard this they would leave him and go away. **Scripture says about him, *"Let not your mouth lead your flesh to sin, and do not say before the messenger that it was an error, else God may be angered by your talk and destroy the work of your hands (ma'aseh yadekha, Kohelet 5:5)."***

[B3] For he destroyed the works (*ma'aseh yadav*) of that man (i.e., himself).

[C1] Also, when there was a persecution, they made them (Jews) carry burdens, but they (Jews) arranged to have two [people] carry one burden, on account of [the rule that] two who perform one labor [on Shabbat are not culpable].

[C2] He (Elisha) said, "Make them carry individually." They went and made them carry individually,

[C3] but they arranged to set [the burdens] down in a *karmelit* [in order that they not carry out from a private domain to a public domain].

[C4] He said, "Make them carry flasks." They went and carried flasks.

The first account [A] derives from the Tosefta's phrase, "Aḥer gazed and cut the shoots," quoted at the outset of the passage (in bold). This reading understands "cut" to mean "cut down" or "kill" and takes "shoots" or "new growths" (נטיעות/*netiot*) to refer to young students [A1]. The seeming redundant restatement in the next line adds that he would kill the students he **saw** excel in Torah, in order to account for the Tosefta's word "gaze" [A2]. Thus this first explanation provides a narrative exegesis of the first part of the toseftan tradition: What does the cryptic phrase "gazed and cut the shoots" mean? That Elisha saw and killed youths studying Torah.

The second account [B] starts with another variation of the first explanation that again interprets the Tosefta's "gaze" as seeing and "shoots" as youngsters (here "children" rather than "young students"), but interprets "cut" metaphorically to mean "cut off" from their studies [B2]. Elisha cut off the children from their studies by speaking, by convincing them to abandon their study of Torah in favor of a profession. This scenario begins to incorporate interpretations of Kohelet 5:5, which states that the "mouth lead…to sin" (in bold): Elisha's mouth led to the sin of persuading the children to desist from Torah [B2]. The last phrase of the verse, "work of your hands" (מעשה ידיך/*ma'aseh yadekha*), which appears frequently in the Bible, is understood here as merit and good deeds, in line with a widespread rabbinic tradition.[19] Elisha destroyed the "work of his hands," his own merits, by this sinful act, as stated explicitly in [B3]. In other rabbinic traditions, however, "work of your hands" also refers to one's children, the "work" or "products, fruit" of one's metaphoric hands. So we should probably see a double entendre: Elisha destroys children (=the work of one's hands) in causing them to lose the merit (=work of one's hands) of Torah study.

19 For biblical usage, see for example Deuteronomy 14:29, 16:15, 24:19, and Jeremiah 32:30. For the rabbinic understanding, see Vayikra Rabbah 16:5, ed. M. Margulies, 398; Kohelet Rabbah 5:2; Bavli Ketubot 5a and Ta'anit 5b.

The third account of Elisha's sin has him collaborate with persecutors to force the Jews to desecrate Shabbat, despite the victims' efforts to avoid the most serious types of violations [c]. According to *halakhah*, if two people together perform a forbidden labor on Shabbat, neither one is guilty of violating biblical (דאורייתא/*de'oraita*) Shabbat law, which, as understood by the rabbis, only applies to individuals—and so the Jews attempted to avoid this culpability by carrying in pairs [c1]. Seeing this, Elisha then instructed that they be compelled to carry individually, not in pairs [c2]. Similarly, biblical law (as understood by the rabbis) prohibits carrying from a private domain to a public domain or the reverse, and from carrying four cubits in a public domain, but not carrying from one of these domains to a כרמלית/*karmelit*, an intermediate domain that is considered neither public nor private. Again, the people tried to avoid the most serious violations by setting the objects down momentarily in a *karmelit* and then picking them up again, as in this way they avoided carrying from a private to a public domain or four cubits in a public domain in one and the same act [c3]. Elisha then instructed that the people be forced to carry fragile flasks that could not be set down lest they break [c4]. This scenario also fulfills the first part of the verse, "mouth lead your flesh to sin" (in bold), since Elisha twice told the persecutors how to force the Jews to sin by violating biblical Shabbat law. Elisha thus destroyed the "work of [his own] hands," namely the merits he had earned through former acts of piety, by collaborating in this heinous manner. There is again a double or triple meaning, as the phrase can also be understood to refer to commandments: Elisha "destroys the work of one's hands," that is, the commandments that the Jews attempt to observe. Furthermore, the Jews are being forced to work with their hands by carrying things, and the flasks will break (be destroyed) if they are set down. The "work of your hands" thus refers to Elisha's merits, to the commandments, and also to the carrying. The "destruction" is the loss of Elisha's merits, the violation of the commandments, and the potential breaking of the flasks. The story is thus a product of the narrative exegesis of the verse, in which every detail of the strange scenario derives from an intricately crafted interpretation.

Note too that the first explanation is based exclusively on the Tosefta's enigmatic description ("gazed and cut shoots"), the second explanation is based on both the Tosefta's description and the verse, and the third is based exclusively on the verse. The storytellers had little, if any, idea as to the meaning of the Toseftan tradition, and generated multiple narrative scenarios based on interpretations of different proportions of the two clues.

~

Biblical verses are a critical dimension of the narrative art of talmudic stories. Only occasionally do verses appear that simply embellish the action or dialogue and that could be omitted without detracting from the story. But even in these cases the verses serve an aesthetic function by mobilizing texts familiar to the audience. In most cases the verses contribute to the meaning in substantive ways by alluding to relevant texts and drawing on the broader biblical context to transmit other messages. Often the storytellers incorporate formal rabbinic midrash, either drawing on pre-existent midrashic compilations or innovating new interpretations. In rare cases much of the story is generated through a process of narrativization of a biblical passage. Finally, all of these ways of quoting biblical texts also serve a religious function, in that they link the story to scripture, the ultimate source of connection to the Divine—for the storyteller and their contemporary audience, and also potentially for religious readers today. Understanding a rabbinic story thus requires thorough study of the verses quoted and their contexts.

# CHAPTER 4
## Wordplay

THE SOPHISTICATED NARRATIVE art of talmudic stories involves a great deal of wordplay (paronomasia) and punning. These rhetorical devices are found in literature throughout the world, and especially in oral literature, where the audience is attuned to the sounds of every utterance. Wordplays are often used to create meaning by fashioning connections among words in the story so as to point to a deeper significance beyond the surface meaning. In this respect wordplay can serve a mnemonic function, too. But puns and wordplay can also be employed purely for aesthetic pleasure and entertainment—jokes and humor often involve punning—and even for stimulating intellectual excitement. Working primarily in Aramaic, with copious use of the Hebrew of the Bible and Mishnah and sprinklings of words in other languages, the rabbis had access to a wide linguistic and auditory palette with which to enliven their texts with wordplay of this kind; as we will see below, some wordplays even include more than one language. For contemporary readers, this, like the repetition of words and phrases we saw in chapter 1, is an especially valuable element of analysis to focus on—with attention to the original language of the text whenever possible.

To fully appreciate a translated talmudic story in all its richness requires a translation that is sensitive to this issue. Unfortunately, many translators do not bother to identify wordplay for the reader working with this literature in translation, either because of the difficulty of capturing it in a different language, or because they do not consider it important but a "mere" rhetorical flourish, or because they do not even notice it. This is one area where knowledge of Hebrew and Aramaic provides a great advantage in understanding the narrative art, and in some cases the meaning too, of talmudic stories. Translators should always endeavor to signal wordplay to their readers, if only by adding transliteration of the key words.

The connections established through wordplay generally disclose, clarify, or emphasize relationships among narrative elements. Here is a wordplay that helps us understand the punishment of Rav Reḥumei, who failed to return home to his wife and family for Yom Kippur after spending close to a year away studying at the academy. (We will discuss the story at greater length, in connection with its context, in chapter 5, pp. 171–77).[1] When his wife, who had been waiting and hoping for his return, realizes that he will not arrive before the holiday, the narrator relates:

**תלמוד בבלי, כתובות סב ע״ב**

חלש דעתה. **אחית** דמעתא מעינה.
הוה יתיב באיגרא. **אפחית** איגרא מתותיה ונח נפשיה.

**Talmud Bavli, Ketubot 62b**

She became distressed. A tear **fell** (*aḥit*) from her eye.

He (Rav Reḥumei) was sitting on a roof. The roof **fell in** (*ifḥit*) under him and he died.

The verbs in these two lines are not actually etymologically related, but their sounds are very similar. The wordplay between אחית/*aḥit* in the first line, here meaning "fell" (from the Aramaic root נ-ח-ת/*n-ḥ-t*, "to descend, to go down, to lower") and אפחית/*ifḥit* in the second line, meaning "fell in" (from the Aramaic root פ-ח-ת/*p-ḥ-t*, "to diminish, cave in, collapse") connects the two events and indicates a causal relationship. The reason the roof collapsed under Rav Reḥumei is because he caused his wife to shed tears. His death, the audience should understand, was divine punishment for the insensitive treatment of his wife. If this were a biblical story the narrator might explicitly have God strike Rav Reḥumei down. In rabbinic stories, however, God is rarely an acting character, and largely works behind the scenes. Without the wordplay the audience probably

---

1 See Frankel, *Aspects of the Spritual World*, 99–103.

would have come to the same conclusion about divine consequences, since the events follow each other in the plot. Nevertheless, the wordplay renders this interpretation more certain, even linking the two events in a measure-for-measure manner: the roof "falling in" constitutes measure-for-measure punishment for the rabbi causing the tear to "fall."

Another good example of a wordplay that emphasizes a cause-and-effect relationship between events appears in the story of the attempt by R. Meir and R. Natan to depose Rabban Shimon b. Gamaliel from his position as *nasi*, Head of the Academy. (In chapter 3, pp. 102–4 we analyzed the dialogue in a scene that takes place years later in the next generation, long after the failed coup.) R. Meir's and R. Natan's disaffection with Rabban Shimon b. Gamaliel stemmed from a change in protocol he instituted to promote his own honor at their expense. Formerly, whenever any one of these three sages entered, all had received the same honor of having the other members of the academy rise before them. Now, however, Rabban Shimon b. Gamaliel has decreed a distinction: henceforth, whenever he enters the academy, all the other rabbis must rise and not sit back down until he instructs them to do so, but whenever R. Meir or R. Natan, who also occupied positions in the academic hierarchy, enter, they will be shown a lesser degree of honor.

When R. Meir and R. Natan arrive at the academy one day, they are surprised and insulted at the change of protocol:

**תלמוד בבלי, הוריות יג ע״ב**

[A] חזו דלא קמו מקמייהו כדרגילא מילתא. אמרי: מאי האי?

[B] אמרו להו: הכי **תקין** רשב״ג.

[C] אמר ליה ר״מ לרבי נתן: אנא חכם ואת אב״ד. **נתקין** מילתא כי לדידן.

[D] מאי **נעביד** ליה? נימא ליה: גלי עוקצים דלית ליה. וכיון דלא גמר, נימא ליה: מי ימלל גבורות ה׳ ישמיע כל תהלתו (תהלים קו:ב)? למי נאה למלל גבורות ה׳? מי שיכול להשמיע כל תהלתו.

[E] **נעבריה** והוי אנא אב״ד ואת נשיא.

**Talmud Bavli, Horayot 13b**

[A] They (R. Meir and R. Natan) saw that they (the rabbis of the academy) did not stand before them as usual. They said, "What is this?"

[B] They (the rabbis in the academy) said to them, "Thus Rabban Shimon b. Gamaliel **enacted** (*takken*)."

[C] R. Meir said to R. Natan, "I am Sage and you are Head of the Court. Let us **fix** (*netakken*) something for ourselves.

[D] What will we **do** (*na'aveid*) to him? We will say to him, 'Teach Uktzin,' [a tractate] that he does not know. And because he has not learned it, we will say to him: *Who can tell the mighty acts of YHVH, make all His praise heard (Psalm 106:2)?* For whom is it pleasing to *tell the mighty acts of YHVH?* For him who is able to *make all His praise heard.*

[E] We will **depose** him (*ne'abreih*) and then I will be Head of the Court and you will be Head of the Academy."

When apprised by the rabbis of the academy that Rabban Shimon b. Gamaliel has changed the honorific protocol [A–B], R. Meir plots revenge, to "fix" or devise a way to unseat their rival [C]. He suggests that during the day's academic session they call on Rabban Shimon b. Gamaliel to teach Uktzin, the last tractate in the Mishnah, which deals with the laws of impurity of stalks of vegetables, a particularly obscure and recondite topic [D]. They know that Rabban Shimon b. Gamaliel has not mastered this tractate and will be unable to teach the material. This is a type of academic ambush—unexpectedly summoning a colleague to demonstrate expertise in a very difficult subject that he has not prepared. They anticipate that Rabban Shimon b. Gamaliel will be publicly humiliated, his lack of knowledge apparent to all members of the academy.

To argue that he cannot legitimately continue as the Head of the Academy, they will then cite a biblical verse and apply it to the current situation—similar to the way R. Shimon and his father R. Yehudah HaNasi debated academic policy by quoting biblical verses, as we saw in chapter 3. Here R. Meir explicates the first half of Psalm 106:2, *Who can tell the mighty acts of YHVH,* in terms of teaching (telling) God's Torah (mighty acts). He understands the clause to mean: "Who is entitled to teach the Torah of God?" In its biblical original context the second half of the verse simply expresses a parallel idea, presenting the same thought in different words, as is typical of biblical poetry: *Who can tell the mighty acts of God? = [Who can] make all His praise heard?* However, R. Meir interprets the second half as the response to the first half's question—and he puts the emphasis on "all": the one who can teach Torah is the one who can make **all** God's praise [=Torah] heard [=heard by others, taught]. R. Meir thus interprets the entire verse as: Who is the legitimate teacher of Torah, the legitimate leader of the academy? He who can teach **all** of God's Torah. This, it turns out, excludes Rabban Shimon b. Gamaliel, who is unable to teach Uktzin, and thus unable to teach **all** topics of Torah.

R. Meir and R. Natan anticipate that the rabbis of the academy, having witnessed Rabban Shimon b. Gamaliel's failure and humiliation, will depose him from his position of *nasi*, literally "prince/leader" but here referring to his position as Head of the Academy. In the background lurks a tension, found in many sources, among merit, lineage, and other considerations (including wealth) as the most important qualification for the position of Head of the Academy and other positions of leadership in rabbinic society.

In the continuation of the story, another rabbi overhears the plot and, appalled at the prospect of Rabban Shimon b. Gamaliel's public humiliation, intimates to him that he should review Uktzin. When R. Meir and R. Natan issue their challenge, Rabban Shimon b. Gamaliel is therefore prepared to teach the tractate; he then turns the table on his antagonists by exiling them from the academy. After some additional drama the story shifts to the next generation, with the dialogue analyzed in chapter 3 (pp. 102–3).

This compact scene contains two wordplays. First, when R. Meir and R. Natan are told that Rabban Shimon b. Gamaliel תקין/*takken* ("enacted" or "instituted") the change in protocol [B], they resolve that they will נתקין/*netakken* ("fix" or "devise") a plot to further their own interests [C]. The wordplay involves two grammatical forms of the same verb with different meanings. It connects the two actions and, as in Rav Reḥumei's case, emphasizes a causal relationship between them: one is a reaction to the other. Second, R. Meir asks rhetorically, "What will we נעביד/*na'aveid* (do)?" [D], and, after detailing the mechanism of the plot, states the ultimate goal: "we will נעבריה/*ne'abreih* (depose him)" [E]. Here, as in the story above, the wordplay is between two unrelated verbal roots, ע-ב-ר/*a-b-r* and ע-ב-ד/*a-b-d* that have similar sounds and, in this case, written appearances. The *b* and *v* in the English transliteration here represent the same Aramaic letter and the *r* and the *d* are nearly identical orthographically. Here too the wordplay connects the two actions: the purpose of R. Meir and R. Natan's machinations is to depose their rival. The two wordplays make the scene more cohesive and enhance the narrative artistry.

A fine wordplay in the opening of the story about R. Shimon b. Eleazar and the ugly man that we discussed in chapter 2 (p. 94) helps us understand the rabbi's mistaken reasoning in drawing connections between appearance and underlying reality:[2]

**תלמוד בבלי, תענית כ ע"ב**

נזדמן לו אדם אחד שהיה **מכוער** ביותר. אמר לו: שלום עליך, רבי!

ולא החזיר לו. אמר לו: **ריקה**! כמה **מכוער** אותו האיש! שמא כל בני **עירך** **מכוערין** כמותך?

**Talmud Bavli, Ta'anit 20b**

He (R. Shimon b. Eleazar) chanced upon a very **ugly** (*mekho'ar*) man, who said to him, "Peace be upon you, Rabbi!"

But he (R. Shimon b. Eleazar) did not answer. He said to him, "**Scoundrel** (*reikah*)! How **ugly** (*mekho'ar*) is that man (=you)! Perhaps all the people in your **village** (*irekha*) are as **ugly** as you are?"

The rabbi here encounters an ugly man and disparages him with a gratuitous and nasty insult; the rest of the story will go on to recount the rabbi's efforts to apologize and repent. The storyteller chooses a word for "scoundrel," ריקה/*reikah*, because of its similar sound to the words for "ugly," מכוער/*mekho'ar*, and "your village," עירך/*irekha*. This wordplay underscores the erroneous logic behind the rabbi's comment: he mistakenly infers that an ugly man must be a scoundrel, that the unpleasant outward appearance indicates a morally deficient inner character. Moreover, the rabbi wrongly concludes that the man lives in a place where everyone is ugly. To call a man "ugly" is bad enough, to then impute ugly character on the basis of the physical appearance is even worse, and to insult the whole village is a still greater transgression. The wordplay helps the audience appreciate the triple offense and the faulty reasoning that provoked it.

---

2 This discussion is based on Yonah Frankel, "Paronomasia in Aggadic Narratives." See too Admiel Kosman, "R. Simeon ben Eleazar and the Offended Man" and Jeffrey L. Rubenstein, *Land of Truth*, 95–115.

## Wordplay and Plot

Wordplays are often connected to issues central to the plot and help focus the audience on the issues at the heart of the story. Here is an example of such a wordplay from the Bavli's story of the sin, death, and legacy of Elisha b. Abuyah, also known as Aḥer, the "Other" (we looked briefly at part of the Yerushalmi's version of this story in chapter 3, pp. 129–34).[3] Elisha's mystical endeavors lead to his being punished by losing his merits and denied the opportunity to repent. Having lost any possibility of heavenly reward, Elisha understandably leads a sinful life. However, his disciple, R. Meir, refuses to give up on his teacher, and endeavors to persuade Elisha to repent:

**תלמוד בבלי, חגיגה טו ע״א**

[A] תנו רבנן: מעשה באחר שהיה רוכב על הסוס בשבת והיה רבי מאיר מהלך אחריו ללמוד תורה מפיו.

[B] אמר לו: מאיר, **חזור** לאחריך, שכבר שיערתי בעקבי סוסי עד כאן תחום שבת.

[C] אמר לו: אף אתה **חזור** בך.

[D] אמר לו: לאו כבר שמעתי מאחורי הפרגוד, שובו בנים שובבים (ירמיה ג:כב) – חוץ מאחר.

**Talmud Bavli, Ḥagigah 15a**

[A] Our sages taught: It once happened that Aḥer was riding his horse on Shabbat and R. Meir was walking after him to learn Torah from his mouth.

[B] He said to him, "Meir, **return** (*ḥazor*) back, since I have already measured by the footsteps of my horse that the Shabbat boundary is here."

[C] He said to him, "Then you too should **repent** (*ḥazor*)."

[D] He said to him, "No, I have already heard from behind the curtain, *Return, rebellious children (Jeremiah 3:22)*—except Aḥer.'"

---

3 On this scene, see Yonah Frankel, *Methods of Aggadah and Midrash*, 263–66. And see the studies of the entire story listed on p. 130 note 18 above.

This scene begins with Elisha/Aḥer riding his horse on Shabbat, a violation of rabbinic law [A]. Because he has been denied a share in the world to come, he has nothing more to lose, and riding is less tiring than walking. That R. Meir was "walking after him" seems incongruous; we might assume that a pious sage would distance himself from such a sinner, especially one engaged in the very act of sinning. The final clause explains the baffling scenario: although Aḥer has lost his merits and piety, he has retained his Torah, and R. Meir still desires to "learn Torah from his mouth" [A]. The conundrum of a sinning sage and the propriety of learning from such a figure are two of the main questions that the larger story addresses.

Presumably the two engage in discussions of Torah for a period of time as they proceed—the previous scenes of the story provide some examples of their deliberations. At a certain point, however, Aḥer warns R. Meir to "turn back" (חזור/*ḥazor*) because they are approaching *teḥum Shabbat,* the Shabbat limit. According to rabbinic law, one may not travel more than 2000 cubits from the boundaries of the city or area where one is located when Shabbat begins. Aḥer, despite his sinful way of life, remains conscious of this law, brilliantly keeping track of the distance they travel by monitoring the paces of his horse while simultaneously discussing Torah with R. Meir [B]. This scenario creates an interesting irony, in that the paces of the horse simultaneously cause Aḥer to sin while providing the means to preserve R. Meir's virtue. Seeing that Aḥer continues to be aware of the law and concerned that his student not violate it, R. Meir responds that Aḥer himself should חזור/*ḥazor.* This word also means "return" in the specific sense of "repent," which creates a beautiful wordplay: R. Meir means both that Aḥer should *ḥazor* (=repent) and *ḥazor* (=turn back) from the Shabbat limit, just as Aḥer had warned R. Meir to *ḥazor* (=turn back). The wordplay poignantly points to their continuing, if tragic, relationship: Aḥer tries to safeguard his student from sin, while R. Meir likewise tries to rescue his teacher from apostasy. Alas, as Aḥer explains, he cannot *ḥazor*/repent, as he had earlier heard a heavenly voice denying him this possibility. This renders irrelevant the decision whether to *ḥazor*/turn back or to sin by continuing onward. Crossing the "Shabbat limit," the boundary between inside and outside, between Shabbat observers and violators, symbolizes Aḥer's departure from the Jewish community. In this way the plot and the wordplay converge to convey the storyteller's message: Aḥer cannot turn back, cannot repent, and cannot remain within the fold.

In theory the storyteller could have communicated the message without the wordplay by having R. Meir say something like: "You know so much Torah?! You should repent," followed by Aḥer's response about the voice from behind the curtain. But it would have been a much inferior story. The wordplay points to questions central to the plot: Is repentance always possible? If a sage refuses to repent, should his students continue to learn from him and try to save him from the consequences of his sins?

Some wordplays, however, do not contribute substantively to the content of the story. The following scene is from one of the stories told of Ḥoni the Circle-Drawer (whose symbolic name is discussed in chapter 2), who slept for seventy years in Rip Van Winkle fashion:[4]

**תלמוד בבלי, תענית כג ע"א**

יתיב כריך ריפתא. אתא ליה **שינתא**. נים אהדרא ליה **משוניתא**
איכסי מעינא. ונים שבעין **שנין**.

**Talmud Bavli, Ta'anit 23a**

He sat down to eat his meal. **Sleep** (*shinta*) came upon him. While he slept a mound of **earth** (*meshunita*) encircled him and he was concealed from sight. He slept for seventy **years** (*shnin*).

This wordplay between "sleep," שינתא/*shinta*, "years," שנין/*shnin* and "mound," משוניתא/*meshunita*, is entertaining and connects the three: Ḥoni slept for years within a mound of earth. But otherwise the wordplay does not add much to the content, which would work equally well if Ḥoni slept in a cave or mountain crag. Indeed, a different version of this story, found in the Yerushalmi, relates that Ḥoni entered a cave and slept there for seventy years.[5] The Bavli storyteller seems to have changed the cave to the rare word *meshunita* to create the wordplay, even at some expense of coherence: it is strange to think of someone covered with earth and not discovered for seventy years (how did he breathe?), but more straightforward to picture someone tucked away in a cave. Some scholars have conjectured that caves are common in the Land of Israel but rarely

4 On this story, see Jeffrey L. Rubenstein, *Stories of the Babylonian Talmud*, 62–76, and the scholarly studies cited in n. 1 there; and Jeffrey L. Rubenstein, *Land of Truth*, 3–20.

5 Yerushalmi Ta'anit 3:10 (66d).

found in the topography of Mesopotamia, so the Babylonian storyteller changed the cave to a more familiar geological feature. But regardless of the geography, this suggestion doesn't really make sense as an explanation for our story. Many stories in the Bavli mention caves, and some tell of sages hiding in caves. Rather, the Bavli storytellers wished to create a wordplay simply to make the story more entertaining and easier to remember.

## Bilingual Wordplays

There are even a few wordplays in the Talmud that involve two languages. A rare example of a bilingual wordplay appears in a story of the sages Hillel and Shammai when they are confronted by a prospective convert:[6]

**תלמוד בבלי, שבת לא ע״א**

שוב מעשה בנכרי אחד שבא לפני שמאי. אמר לו: גיירני על מנת שתלמדני כל התורה כולה כשאני עומד על **רגל** אחת.

דחפו באמת הבנין שבידו.

בא לפני הלל. גייריה.

אמר לו: דעלך סני לחברך לא תעביד. זו היא כל התורה כולה. ואידך פירושה הוא. זיל גמור.

**Talmud Bavli, Shabbat 31a**

Another time a gentile came before Shammai. He said to him, "I will convert to Judaism on the condition that you teach me the entire Torah while I stand on one **leg** (*regel*)."

He (Shammai) drove him away with the builder's measuring stick that was in his hand.

He came before Hillel [with the same condition]. Hillel converted him.

He (Hillel) said to him, "That which is hateful to you, do not do to your fellow. That is the entire Torah. The rest is commentary. Go and learn it."

---

6 For studies of this story, see Amram Tropper, "On Condition That," 267–86; Jeffrey L. Rubenstein, *Land of Truth*, 254–64.

Shammai does not believe that the gentile is serious about conversion. This man wants a shortcut, an abbreviated version of Judaism, and sets a ridiculous and frivolous stipulation: to learn all of Torah in an extremely brief amount of time. Shammai accordingly rebuffs him with the stick "that was in his hand." The nice touch of characterization suggests Shammai is impatient and irascible; he regularly equips himself with a measuring stick to be ready to lash out at annoying questioners or at misbehaving students. When the gentile comes before Hillel with the same terms, however, Hillel surprisingly converts him and teaches him a core tenet of Judaism. This is hardly "the entire Torah," so Hillel adds a stipulation of his own: "The rest is commentary. Go and learn it." For the gentile to learn the content of Judaism, he has to master all the other parts of the Torah too. Hillel meets the gentile on his own terms, treats him with dignity and respect, and tries to move him to a deeper understanding and more serious commitment.

Why does the gentile make the condition "while I stand on one leg" as opposed to another indication of a brief span of time: "while I hold my breath," or "while I count to two hundred" or suchlike? Some scholars have suggested that a Latin-Hebrew pun underlies this anecdote. The Latin word *regula,* meaning "principle" or "general rule" (related to our English words "regular" and "regulation"), sounds like the Hebrew word for leg, *regel.* The gentile's question can be understood as "teach me the entire Torah in one basic principle." He may be asking Shammai and Hillel about the essence of Judaism, for an overriding belief behind the myriad of laws, observances, and practices. Moreover, *regula* can also mean a ruler or straightedge, namely a measuring stick. While Shammai rejects the gentile's request to distill the Torah down to one *regula* (rule, principle) that can be communicated while standing on one leg (*regel*) by brandishing his own *regula* (measuring stick), Hillel provides the desired *regula* (principle).[7]

We cannot be sure that the audience would appreciate the wordplay, though it seems likely to me that the original storyteller constructed the story on that basis. The main message of the story can be appreciated even without the wordplay: the impatient Shammai portrayed as a negative role model contrasted with the gentle and understanding Hillel. The story grapples with the question of whether there is an essence to Judaism, an overriding general principle, and offers a paradoxical answer. The

---

7 See Raphael Jospe, "Hillel's Rule"; Jeffrey L. Rubenstein, *Land of Truth,* 256–57; and Naphtali S. Meshel, "Measure for Measure." See too Galit Hasan-Rokem, "An Almost Invisible Presence."

wordplay enhances these didactic points and contributes to the narrative art of the story.

Hillel's instruction to the gentile, "What is hateful to you, do not do to your fellow," has often been compared with Jesus's saying, "In everything, then, do to others as you would have them do to you. For this is the essence of the Law and the Prophets" (Matthew 7:12). In that passage Jesus explicitly states that this precept is the core teaching of the Torah (=Law) and Bible, i.e., of Judaism. Much ink has been spilled on contrasting Hillel's negative formulation ("do not do") to the positive formulation of Jesus ("do to others"), often by those trying to prove Christianity is a superior religion to Judaism. But this is a silly debate: this idea, sometimes known as the "golden rule," is found in many other religions and cultures, in both positive and negative forms.[8] In any case, the heart of Hillel's teaching is in his concluding exhortation or challenge, זיל גמור/*zil gemor*, "go and learn it," at the end of his instruction, though this part of his saying is sometimes omitted from quotations of his words. The storyteller teaches that one should not be satisfied with any one general principle of Judaism, no matter how foundational, but must "go and learn" the rest, its "commentary." In rabbinic Judaism, commentary is as important as the main text. The Talmud is a commentary to the Mishnah, and midrash a commentary on the Torah, yet the rabbis would consider Talmud and midrash every bit as important as their underlying text, if not more so, as the Talmud is the key to understanding the Mishnah, and midrash is necessary to interpreting the Bible correctly. The storyteller probably meant to direct the saying he placed in Hillel's mouth more to his rabbinic audience than to problematic converts. He was challenging his audience, and audiences throughout the generations including us today, never to be satisfied with their knowledge of Torah but always to pursue more.

---

8 W. A. Spooner, "The Golden Rule"; Simon Blackburn, *Ethics: A Very Short Introduction*, 51: "a rule sometimes claimed by Christianity as its own, but found in some form in almost every ethical tradition, including that of Confucius."

# PART 2
# Stories and Contexts

# CHAPTER 5
## Context

WHY DO THE stories appear in rabbinic texts where they do? How do these textual contexts impact their meaning? And how do the stories, in turn, shed light on our readings of the rabbinic discussions in which they are embedded?

The Talmud's structure and organization follow that of the Mishnah. The primary reference point, then, for every talmudic *sugya* (passage, or literary unit) is the proximate mishnah—the unit of Mishnah that the talmudic passage follows and comments upon, which we might call its "mishnaic context."[1] This holds true whether the talmudic passage is comprised of legal commentary, biblical exegesis, stories, or any other genre of material. After the first printings of the Talmud in the late fifteenth and early sixteenth centuries, it became conventional to refer to passages in the Babylonian Talmud by the page and side of those printings, and this pagination has been replicated by almost all subsequent printings and re-printings of the Talmud down to the present day. "Shabbat 54a" thus refers to the talmudic text found in the tractate called Shabbat, on page

1 Books of midrash have a different textual context: they are structured and organized according to biblical verses, as midrash is above all biblical interpretation. The primary context of a midrashic story is therefore the biblical verse commented upon by that unit of midrash. The standard printed editions of midrash are typically divided into chapters and paragraphs, but these are divisions of convenience, used to locate and reference a passage, rather than drivers of meaning.

54, side a, of the standard printed edition; "Yoma 18b" indicates page 18, side b of the tractate called Yoma. This system, however, is an accident of the decisions of the printers and of the dimensions and limitations of the printed page, and means very little in terms of the actual organization of the Talmud. More important for meaning and understanding is that the talmudic editors placed the former talmudic passage in conjunction with Mishnah Shabbat 5:3 and the latter with Mishnah Yoma 1:3. Indeed, references to passages in the Talmud Yerushalmi, study of which was very much neglected in traditional Jewish culture until modern times, retained their connection to the Mishnah. "Yerushalmi Shabbat 12:7 (13d)" refers to the talmudic text juxtaposed with Mishnah Shabbat 12:7 and found on page 13, column d in the first printing of 1523, and also replicated in subsequent printings.[2] (For a more detailed description, see the Appendix, "Guide to the Main Works of Rabbinic Literature.")

Many stories of both Talmuds connect directly to their mishnaic contexts, though the nature of these connections varies a great deal. Most common are stories that illustrate and exemplify the topic of the mishnah that they follow. For example, the mishnaic tractate Ta'anit sets forth a series of fasts that the community undertakes if rain fails to fall at the proper time in autumn, and, as we saw in chapter 2 (pp. 72–75), the talmudic commentary includes stories of rabbis who decreed fasts when faced with such droughts. Some stories complement or supplement the Mishnah. Mishnah Ketubot 6:5 rules that the community must spend fifty *zuz* for the wedding of an orphan girl, and, if more charity funds are available, must "provide her according to her honor." The talmudic commentary on that mishnah includes stories of rabbis who distributed charity funds to the poor, sometimes providing formerly wealthy indigents with very fine and expensive food, thus also supporting them "according to their honor" (see chapter 6, pp. 192–97, for analysis of some of these stories). Still other stories challenge or subvert the mishnah they follow. In most of these cases, the law of the mishnah and content of the talmudic story—the halakhic and aggadic material—shed light on each

---

2 "Column d" refers to the second column on the back of page 13, as the printers set the Yerushalmi with two columns on each side of each page. There are thus four columns per page: a and b on the front; c and d on the back. In 1860–67, the Yerushalmi was reprinted in a new format, similar to the Bavli, with commentaries around the text, and with new pagination. However, this new pagination is not the standard reference system of scholars.

other in both directions, so that in learning settings where the entire *sugya* rather than the story itself is the unit under discussion, we may read the relationship between the two in complex and layered ways. The primary point of departure when trying to understand the context of a talmudic story is therefore the proximate mishnah with which the talmudic *sugya* containing the story is juxtaposed.

Yet talmudic discussions are renowned for their meandering, associative, and almost stream-of-consciousness style that typically takes them far afield from the initial commentary on the proximate mishnah. The Talmud may move from an issue directly related to the mishnah to discussion of a secondary legal issue, not related to the mishnah but raised in the initial analysis of that mishnah, and then proceed to an unrelated tradition quoted in the name of the same rabbi who commented on that secondary legal issue, and then digress to yet a different topic that happens to quote the same biblical verse that appeared in the discussion of that unrelated tradition, and on and on. This chain of associated units eventually ends, sometimes sooner and sometimes later, and the Talmud then returns to the next mishnah (or to the next clause of the same mishnah) and begins again. Talmudic discussion does not proceed in a random, haphazard, or arbitrary manner: one can almost always understand the links that connect one part of the discussion to the next. The Talmud is just not arranged in the manner that we typically think complex texts should be organized, namely according to content, with major topics divided into subtopics that proceed and unfold in a logical way. The Talmud, rather, proceeds *associatively*: each subsequent unit is associated with the previous one, though the association may be based on content, form, a rabbi's name, an unusual word, a biblical verse, or other connections. Again, this manner of organization reflects the Talmud's oral provenance, as these associations create mnemonic links that are conducive to memorization.

A talmudic story, therefore, may not connect substantively to the proximate mishnah but rather may be related to the talmudic *sugya* with which it is integrated, especially when, following the initial exposition of the mishnah, a protracted and complex discussion wanders to other topics. In these cases the local context of the preceding *sugya* will be more straightforward, and any relationship to the mishnah more distant. In this respect, analysis of the literary context of a talmudic story is similar to analysis of the literary context of stories in literature in general, as one should always pay attention to the larger swath of text in which a story appears when seeking to understand its meaning and function. It is important to ask: How has the author introduced the story? What leads up to the presentation of the story and why?

Accordingly, some talmudic stories have a very thin relationship both to the proximate mishnah and to the preceding talmudic discussion. For example, a story about a certain rabbi that is relevant to the talmudic discussion may be followed by another story about that same rabbi that has no connection to that discussion. The reason the second story appears is that it features the same rabbinic protagonist, which provides a convenient mnemonic link to the story, though not a substantive connection to the legal, theological, or ethical issues of the talmudic *sugya*. In such cases the story must be analyzed primarily on its own terms, as an almost independent textual unit. I say "almost" because even the associative link provides some minimal amount of context: in our example of a second story about the same rabbi, the first story may provide some information about the rabbi that contributes to our understanding of the second story.

There is nothing fundamentally wrong with interpreting a story purely on its own terms, with no consideration whatsoever of its mishnaic or literary contexts. Indeed, most of the stories in the previous chapters were analyzed in precisely this way. The context, however, typically provides more insight into the meaning of the story. It may confirm the internal analysis by featuring the same themes, thus making the interpretation more secure, as if the editors were informing the audience: while we are dealing with such-and-such a topic, here is a relevant story. In other cases it may add a layer of complexity or tension, providing a different and opposing perspective to what we have just read (or heard). In some cases the context focuses attention on a particular dimension of the story, or directs the audience to interpret aspects of the story in a specific way. In general, a decontextualized reading of a story will be less rich and less certain, while taking the contexts into account can make the reading more persuasive and add levels of complexity. More importantly, reading the story in its talmudic context can help us gain perspective on the larger issues, conflicts, and tensions that surface in the proximate passages.

## Mishnah as Context

A story in Berakhot 32b–33a offers a good example of how the internal reading may be strengthened and also nuanced by engaging the story's larger context. Mishnah Berakhot 5:1 deals with the proper demeanor for praying, here referring specifically to the recitation of the Amidah or "Silent Devotion," the centerpiece of each of the three daily services:[3]

**משנה ברכות ה:א**

[A] אין עומדין להתפלל אלא מתוך כובד ראש.

[B] חסידים הראשונים היו שוהין שעה אחת ומתפללים, כדי שיכוונו את ליבם למקום.

[C] אפילו המלך שואל בשלומו, לא ישיבנו. ואפילו נחש כרוך על עקבו, לא יפסיק.

**Mishnah Berakhot 5:1**

[A] One does not stand up to pray except in a serious frame of mind.

[B] The *ḥasidim* (pious man) of olden times would wait an hour before praying, in order that they might direct their hearts to the Omnipresent.

[C] Even if a king greets him [while praying], he should not answer. And even if a snake winds itself around his heel, he should not stop.

The first section of this mishnah mentions the seriousness required for the prayer [A], and the second provides an illustration: the *ḥasidim*, extremely pious "holy men" of yore, would prepare themselves for a full hour beforehand to ensure that they approached God with awe and reverence [B]. The third section then illustrates the high value and importance placed on the act of addressing God directly in prayer [C]: it prohibits interrupting one's prayer even when failing to do so puts the worshipper at risk, such as to respond respectfully to the most powerful human beings, or when a menacing animal threatens the worshipper's life.

The Talmud's discussion of this mishnah limits the scope of these final prohibitions by ruling that the "king" referred to is a "king of Israel," that is, a Jewish king. However, if "a king of the nations of the world," that is, a gentile king, addressed the worshipper, one may, in fact, desist from prayer to reply (Berakhot 32b). This ruling, on the one hand, makes some sense, as a Jewish king can be expected to understand the nature of prayer, and perhaps should not even have interrupted the worshipper in the first place.

---

3 This example is based on Yonatan Feintuch, "Anonymous *Hasid.*"

A gentile king, by contrast, probably does not understand the importance of prayer to the Jew, and likely does not care. To ignore the king would be rude at best and, at worst, might provoke a violent response or even death. On the other hand, the mishnah itself does not specify explicitly that this ruling relates to a Jewish king and not a gentile king. And the principle underpinning the precept would seem to apply equally to all human kings, namely that it is disrespectful to God to break off one's prayer in order to show honor to a mortal.

After a few lines of discussion the following story appears:

**תלמוד בבלי, ברכות לב ע"ב-לג ע"א**

[A] מעשה בחסיד אחד שהיה מתפלל בדרך, בא שר אחד ונתן לו **שלום**, ולא החזיר לו **שלום**. **המתין** לו עד שסיים תפלתו.

[B1] לאחר שסיים תפלתו, א"ל: ריקא! והלא כתוב בתורתכם: רק השמר לך ושמור נפשך (דברים ד:ט). וכתיב, ונשמרתם מאד לנפשותיכם (דברים ד:טו). כשנתתי לך **שלום** למה לא החזרת לי **שלום**? אם הייתי **חותך ראשך בסייף** מי היה תובע את דמך מידי?

[B2] א"ל: **המתן** לי עד **שאפייסך** בדברים.

[B1'] א"ל: אילו היית עומד לפני מלך בשר ודם ובא חברך ונתן לך **שלום**, היית מחזיר לו?
א"ל: לאו.
ואם היית מחזיר לו מה היו עושים לך?
א"ל: היו **חותכים את ראשי בסייף**.

[B2'] א"ל: והלא דברים ק"ו. ומה אתה שהיית עומד לפני מלך בשר ודם שהיום כאן ומחר בקבר כך, אני, שהייתי עומד לפני מלך מלכי המלכים הקב"ה, שהוא חי וקיים לעד ולעולמי עולמים, על אחת כמה וכמה?

[A'] מיד **נתפייס** אותו השר, ונפטר אותו חסיד לביתו **לשלום**.

**Talmud Bavli, Berakhot 32b–33a**

[A] It once happened that a certain *ḥasid* (pious man) was praying on his way, and a certain [Roman] governor came and greeted him with **peace**, and he did not greet him back with **peace**. He (the governor) **waited** until he finished his prayer.

[B1] After he finished his prayer, he (the governor) said to him, "Scoundrel! Does it not say in your Torah, *Take utmost care and guard yourselves scrupulously (Deuteronomy 4:9)*. And it is also written, *Be most careful for yourselves (Deuteronomy 4:15)*. When I greeted you with **peace**, why did you not greet me back with **peace**? If I had **cut off your head with a sword**, who would hold me accountable for your blood?"

[B2] He (the *ḥasid*) said to him: "**Wait** for me and I will **appease** you with words [of explanation]."

[B1'] He (the *ḥasid*) [then] said to him: "If you were standing before a mortal king and your friend had come and greeted you with **peace**, would you have answered him?"
He (the governor) said to him, "No."
"And if you had answered him, what would they have done to you?"
He said to him, "They would have **cut off my head with a sword.**"

[B2'] He (the *ḥasid*) said to him, "Is there not a logical inference here: If in your case, when you stand before a king of flesh and blood, who is here today and in his grave tomorrow—[you would have acted] thus, then in my case, standing before the King, the King of kings, the Holy One blessed be He, who lives eternally and for all time—how much the more so?

[A'] Immediately that governor was **appeased**, and the *ḥasid* departed for his house in **peace**.

Starting with an internal analysis of the story itself before we turn back to its context, we see that, structurally, this story divides into two parts: the governor's approach and criticism of the *ḥasid* [A–B], followed by the *ḥasid*'s convincing response and safe departure [B'–A']. The two parts are in a chiastic relationship: in the middle, the governor's accusation corresponds to the *ḥasid's* response [B versus B'], while the opening, with the *ḥasid* praying "on his way," apparently his journey home, is complemented by the ending, his return to his house. The chiastic two-part structure suits the narrative dynamic: the transition from danger to deliverance, from vulnerability to safety, from a precarious situation to its resolution.

As we have seen in other cases, this story consists almost exclusively of dialogue. The main conflict consists of the Roman governor's speech and the *ḥasid*'s answer. Their interchange is contentious, heated, even violent in its imagery: the governor essentially threatens to murder the *ḥasid*, while the *ḥasid*'s hypothetical scenario envisions the governor's death. Yet this violence is purely verbal, an attack parried by a well-articulated defense. The two characters' narrated actions, in contrast, are thoroughly mundane—the governor coming upon the *ḥasid* praying and the *ḥasid* departing to his house—and merely set the stage for and follow this verbal drama.

The primary conflict in the story is between two values, which the governor and the *ḥasid* respectively articulate. Interestingly, the Roman admonishes the *ḥasid* not as much for failure to return the greeting as for violating his own religious principle of the obligation to preserve one's life. Though this idea is not stated explicitly in the Bible, the rabbis anchored it in a midrashic reading of various biblical verses, including the two the governor adduces here. Though in their original biblical contexts the commands to "guard yourselves" and to "be most careful about yourselves" warn against forgetting the Torah and sinning, the rabbis interpreted them as mandating self-preservation: since the soul is a gift from God, one must do everything possible to preserve and safeguard it. This same principle generally requires a Jew to violate almost any commandment in order to remain alive, for example by eating forbidden foods if starving, and also prohibits suicide. The conditions that call for martyrdom are exceptions to this principle, and are few and far between, despite some famous examples. The story's scenario, at all events, involves no persecution or oppressor's command to violate any law. All the *ḥasid* needed to do to "guard his life" was to avoid ignoring the governor's greeting, and no rabbinic source would consider him innocent if he lost his life in this way. (Incidentally, we should not be surprised by the Roman's facility with the biblical text: as we have seen in the previous chapter, in the world of the rabbinic story, just about all characters quote biblical verses.)

The key didactic point emerges from the *ḥasid*'s parable and logical inference, which counters the governor's argument by invoking a different theological consideration. Like many rabbinic teachings, the parable points to the difference between the immortal King of kings, the God of the Universe, and a mortal king of flesh and blood, in particular the Roman emperor. The story of Onkelos the Convert, which we discussed in chapter 3 (pp. 108–11), appealed to this same contrast between God and the Roman emperor to illustrate God's care for the Jewish people and God's ability to protect them, as opposed to the human king's need for an army to protect him. Here, too, the contrast focuses on the human king's limitedness and powerlessness when compared to God's eternal and consummate power, though to the opposite effect, the potential for retribution. If the Roman governor himself would not risk offending his mortal king, who, though ephemeral, could nevertheless kill him with impunity, how much more should a human being not risk offending the immortal God. Thus the *ḥasid* does not dispute the governor's theological principle; rather, he trumps it with a higher one. The story essentially delineates a conflict in rabbinic values between the duty to preserve one's life and the obligation to honor God, and it argues for the latter, at least in this situation.

Four verbal repetitions contribute to the storyteller's message. First, the governor intimidates the *ḥasid* with the claim that he could have "cut off your head with a sword" and then answers the *ḥasid* that the king would have "cut off my head with a sword," using much the same language, adding a nice literary touch [B1, B1']. Applying to himself the same words with which he castigated the *ḥasid*, the Roman realizes that all humans are fundamentally vulnerable to a more powerful human authority, but that all of these authorities pale in comparison to the Divine. Second, the *ḥasid*'s initial response to the governor is curious: "Wait for me and I will appease you" [B2]. The governor has already waited for him to finish the prayer [A], so this additional imposition, phrased in the imperative voice, seems to border on insubordination, adding insult to insult. Even if he means "just give me a chance to explain" before you kill me, the *ḥasid*'s choice of expression is odd. By repeating the governor's need to wait, the storyteller emphasizes the true hierarchical relationship, that all humans are inferior to the eternal God. The repetition also contributes clarity to the structure, in that the two sections of the first half contain references to waiting [A, B2]. Third, the storyteller repeatedly stresses the word "peace," שלום/*shalom*, which appears in the many mentions of the expression "greet/greeted him with peace" (ונתן לו שלום), and then at the end when the *ḥasid* departs in peace: it is literally the last word of the story and the storyteller's "last word" [A, A′]. The *ḥasid*'s calculus proved correct, and he emerged from the predicament having honored God appropriately while securing peace from the threatening official.

Finally and most important, the protagonist states that he will "appease" the governor "with words," אפייסך בדברים [B2], and the storyteller notes his success, concluding with the governor's immediate appeasement [A′]. The word "appease" is certainly appropriate, though other locutions were equally possible, such as "satisfy you with a reason" or even "persuade you I acted appropriately." The verb "appease," לפיים, sometimes refers to prayer, to propitiate or appease God, and the full expression "to appease with words [of prayer]" can refer to a prayer for divine mercy. To the astute audience, the contrast between the prayer to God mentioned at the outset and appeasing/propitiating the governor—expressed with a term that could be used for prayer but here means something less—evokes their shared authority, while simultaneously underscoring the difference between them. In addition, the governor's mention of the *ḥasid*'s "blood," דם/*dam*, in his rebuke that he had license to kill him is matched by the *ḥasid*'s reference to a king of "flesh and blood," בשר ודם/*basar vadam*, in his didactic parable [B1, B2′]. Connoting mortality and vulnerability, the two mentions of blood also point to the common humanity shared by all people, even the greatest human king, in contrast to the eternal King of kings.

The storyteller's concluding phrase that the *ḥasid* "departed" (נפטר/*niftar*) for his home [A′], where he could have used any number of alternatives—returned home, went home, traveled home, and so forth—is another fine touch. The word "depart" is frequently used for someone found innocent in a legal trial and "dismissed" or "freed" from punishment. The *ḥasid*'s departure thus also indicates his vindication in the governor's eyes, the charges against him dismissed. Furthermore, the same word can be used to mean "die," to depart this world. Upon hearing "that *ḥasid* departed," ונפטר אותו חסיד, the audience initially decodes the phrase as "the *ḥasid* died," the very possible outcome explicitly threatened by the governor, which makes palpable the peril he experienced until the last word in the sentence, "to his home," לביתו, resolves the tension. The triple entendre—departed/dismissed/died—provides a virtuoso conclusion to the narrative.

Taken in and of itself, the story's message emerges from the exemplary conduct of the *ḥasid*. He displays courage in the face of danger, risking his life out of devotion to God, and not desisting even when faced with potential death from a gentile authority. Minimally the audience learns a lesson about never interrupting one's prayer, and maximally a message about all commandments: all sacred rituals should be fulfilled even in similar perilous situations.

With this complex internal analysis of the story in hand, let us now consider the story in its context. First of all, there is tension between the story and the talmudic limitation of the mishnah's rule to a Jewish king, which entails a dispensation to interrupt prayer when addressed by a gentile king. While the story concerns a governor rather than a king, the same principle is at issue: does one cease praying when approached by a gentile authority who may be incensed and retaliate if ignored? The Talmud's legal commentary to the mishnah says yes, while the story seems to say no. This discrepancy opens several interpretive possibilities. We might claim that ordinary people should follow the talmudic ruling, whereas those at a higher spiritual level, extremely pious *ḥasidim* or holy rabbis, should act in accordance with the story—perhaps they can count on extra divine protection due to their holiness. We might suggest that one is permitted to reduce one's risk in accordance with the Talmud's limitation of the mishnah, but if someone wishes to aspire to a higher spiritual standard, to go beyond the letter of the law, they may ignore the talmudic ruling and emulate the *ḥasid*. Note that the earlier part of the talmudic passage speaks in a legal-normative manner, in the language of *halakhah*, while the story is part of the *aggadah*, a non-legal mode of discourse. We might say that the legal discussion represents reality, while the story presents a hypothetical ideal that we can imagine but need not risk attempting ourselves. Presumably the talmudic editors could have rejected the ruling that one may interrupt one's prayer if addressed by a gentile king had they so wished, or not quoted that ruling at all and left the mishnah without any nuancing. Instead, they left the legal ruling in place but juxtaposed it with a story that pushes in the opposite direction. This juxtaposition moves the audience to a more complex perspective on the issue—but does not fundamentally reject the legal commentary.

The interpretive possibilities become more complex if we take the mishnah into account, too. Now we might see the story as returning to the policy of the mishnah, which does not distinguish between Jewish and gentile kings [c], over against the talmudic tradition, which limits the mishnah's ruling to the latter. Whoever added the story—later talmudic sages or the talmudic editors—may have felt uneasy with the limitation of the mishnah's explicit and absolute reference to a king, implying any and all kings, and sought to balance this unwarranted restriction by adding the story. Or the talmudic editors may have wished to provide more concrete expression of the theology underlying the mishnah's ruling, so they included the story with the *ḥasid*'s explanation. In this case they did not necessarily side either with the mishnah or with the Talmud's commentary, as they would have if they had instead offered an alternative halakhic claim, but sought to augment both with an illustrative narrative. Or again, they might have incorporated the story to suggest that the mishnah's ruling applied in a time when gentile authorities could be expected to respond like this Roman governor, with patience and a willingness to discuss the matter, but that such gentile authorities no longer exist, and therefore we must act in accord with the Talmud's limitation. It is also possible, though less likely in my opinion, to take the story as supporting the Talmud's limitation of the mishnah, in that it manifests the danger quite concretely. Here we have a story of someone foolish enough to have risked the wrath of a non-Jewish governor—not even a king, who would be even less forbearing—and almost got himself killed. He was lucky enough to survive—but do we want to risk our lives in this manner? (I say this reading is less likely because a hypothetical, alternative story that would have ended with the gentile official cutting off the worshipper's head would have made this point far more effectively.) At all events, if we wish to try to understand the story's meanings for the talmudic audience, we should read it in this wider context and take the proximate mishnah and the Talmud's legal commentary into account too.

There is no absolutely right or wrong answer to these interpretive questions, and several possibilities seem equally plausible. At this point it becomes the responsibility of attentive readers or audiences to play a larger role in the interpretive process. We should ask: Which of these readings makes the most sense to me? Why? Which values and ideas deserve emphasis, and which should be considered secondary? The answers to these questions will probably have to do with the audience's cultural and historical conditions. Some readings will resonate more powerfully, for example, for those living under authoritarian or totalitarian governments, and other readings for those in democratic and liberal societies. One's attitude toward prayer—its function, efficacy, and meaning—will likely make some readings more attractive than others. The audience always plays a role in interpretation, as no text speaks for itself. But a *sugya* that, like this one, offers multiple layers and perspectives without clearly resolving the relationships among them involves the audience to an even greater degree than usual, making us partners in the unfolding and creation of rabbinic tradition.

## Story as Historical Context

In some cases, a story uses the same legal language and concerns the same legal issue as its proximate mishnah, and in these cases the relationship between the two is particularly strong. Here is an example where the story provides a narrative of historical background, at least as imagined by the storytellers, for the promulgation of the law transmitted in the mishnah, and seeks to justify that law. Recall that, as discussed in the Introduction (pp. 9–10), rabbinic stories are not historical or biographical in our contemporary understandings of these genres; they are not intended to be accurate reconstructions of events as they actually happened. The rabbis, like almost all traditional societies, transformed, constructed, and refashioned memories from the past for a variety of purposes, including self-definition and shaping their collective identity. In this case the storyteller mobilizes a historical memory to justify a legal development.

The first three chapters of Mishnah Sanhedrin deal with laws of witnesses, trials, and judges, including the disqualification of certain individuals from these functions. Mishnah Sanhedrin 2:2 begins as follows:

**משנה סנהדרין ב:ב**

המלך - לא דן ולא דנין אותו.
לא מעיד ולא מעידין אותו.

**Mishnah Sanhedrin 2:2**

A king—he does not judge [others] and is not judged [in court].
He does not testify and is not testified against.

The king thus stands outside of the authority and purview of the judicial system. Why is this the case? Why should the courts be unable to put a king on trial or summon him as a witness?[4] To explain the reason for this

4 The Talmud restricts the mishnah's ruling to "kings of Israel" as opposed to "kings of the house of David," that is, the kings of the Davidic dynasty, who are permitted to serve as judges and judge others.

ruling, the Talmud tells a story of an event that happened hundreds of years earlier in the time of King Yannai (103–76 BCE), called Alexander or Jannaeus in Josephus and other Greek sources, a scion of the Hasmonean dynasty, great-nephew of Judah Maccabee. The rabbis remembered the Hasmoneans with great ambivalence. While Judah and his brethren were undoubtedly the heroes of Hanukkah, fighting for independence and purifying the Temple, some of their descendants became kings and tyrants, usurped the high priesthood, and, according to Josephus, even ordered massacres of their own people. Here is the talmudic story, with its quotations of the mishnah presented in bold:[5]

**תלמוד בבלי, סנהדרין יט ע״א–ב**

[A] מלכי ישראל מ״ט **לא [דנין אותו]**? משום מעשה שהיה. ד –

[B] עבדיה דינאי מלכא קטל נפשא. אמר להו שמעון בן שטח לחכמים: תנו עיניכם בו ונדוננו.

[C1] שלחו ליה: עבדך קטל נפשא. שדריה להו.

[C2] שלחו ליה: תא אנת נמי להכא. [ואם שור נגח הוא מתמול שלשם] והועד בבעליו [ולא ישמרנו והמית איש או אשה השור יסקל וגם בעליו יומת] (שמות כא:כט).
אמרה תורה: יבא בעל השור ויעמוד על שורו. אתא ויתיב.

[C3] א״ל שמעון בן שטח: ינאי המלך! עמוד על רגליך ויעידו בך. ולא לפנינו אתה עומד אלא לפני מי שאמר והיה העולם אתה עומד, שנאמר: **ועמדו** שני האנשים אשר להם הריב לפני ה׳ לפני הכהנים והשפטים אשר יהיו בימים ההם (דברים יט:יז).
אמר לו: לא כשתאמר אתה אלא כמה שיאמרו חבריך.

[D1] נפנה לימינו, כבשו פניהם בקרקע. נפנה לשמאלו, וכבשו פניהם בקרקע.

[D2] אמר להן שמעון בן שטח: בעלי מחשבות אתם? יבא בעל מחשבות ויפרע מכם. מיד בא גבריאל וחבטן בקרקע ומתו.

[A′] באותה שעה אמרו: **מלך לא דן ולא דנין אותו. לא מעיד ולא מעידין אותו.**

---

5 For further analysis of this story, see Jeffrey L. Rubenstein, *Land of Truth*, 205–21, and the references there.

**Talmud Bavli, Sanhedrin 19a–b**

[A] Why are kings of Israel "**not [judged]**"? Because of what once happened. For it was that–

[B] The slave of King Yannai killed someone. Shimon b. Shetaḥ said to the sages, "Set your eyes upon him (Yannai) and let us judge him."

[C1] They sent [a message] to him (Yannai), "Your slave killed someone." He (Yannai) sent him (the slave) to them.

[C2] They sent to him (Yannai), "You also come here. *[But if the ox were in the habit of goring] and it has been testified to its owner, [and he has not kept him in, and it kills a man or a woman; the ox shall be stoned, and its owner too shall be put to death] (Exodus 21:29)*. The Torah stated, 'Let the master of the ox come and stand by his ox.'" He (Yannai) came and sat down.

[C3] Shimon b. Shetaḥ said to him, "King Yannai! Stand on your feet and let them give testimony regarding you. You do not stand before us but before He-Who-Spoke-and-the-World-Came-into-Being, as it says, *The two parties to the dispute shall* ***stand*** *before YHVH, before the priests or magistrates in authority at the time (Deuteronomy 19:17)*." He (Yannai) said to him, "[I will] not [act] as you say but as your colleagues say."

[D1] He turned to his right, but they looked down to the ground. He turned to his left, but they looked down to the ground.

[D2] Shimon b. Shetaḥ said, "Are you preoccupied with your thoughts? Let the Master of Thoughts come and punish you." [The angel] Gabriel came and struck them [the sages] to the ground and they died.

[A'] At that time they said, **A king—he does not judge [others] and is not judged [in court]. He does not testify and is not testified against.**

At the heart of the story are the three demands made of King Yannai by the court [C1–C3]. He complies with the first two but resists the third, which leads to tragedy. These interchanges are preceded by the exposition recounting the crime [B] and followed by the tragic consequences that ensue [D1–D2].

The core conflict is between Shimon b. Shetaḥ, the head of the rabbinic court, and Yannai, the king. As is typical of rabbinic stories, political, national, and military conflicts are conceptualized as a conflict between two leading characters. It therefore would be only slightly anachronistic to consider this a conflict between the chief justice and the sovereign, or between the judicial and executive branches of government. One way to get a handle on the story's message is to ask: Who bears the blame for the disastrous ending? King Yannai? Shimon b. Shetaḥ? If they share the responsibility, do they share equally or is one party more at fault? Typically we would assume the rabbinic figure is the hero and his opponent the villain. But this case may be more complicated: does the storyteller portray Yannai negatively?

When the rabbinic court, prompted by Shimon b. Shetaḥ, informs Yannai of the crime perpetrated by his slave (or "servant," as the Aramaic word עבדא/*avda* can refer to either), the king dutifully sends the slave to trial [C1]. Yet the rabbis are not satisfied. They submit a midrashic teaching, an interpretation of Exodus 21:29, "proving" that Yannai himself must appear as well. This verse deems the owner of a violent ox guilty of negligence if he fails to prevent the animal from causing harm [C2]. The verse states *it has been testified to its owner,* suggesting that there had been a court "hearing" in the presence of the owner with the presentation of evidence that the ox is dangerous. If the ox subsequently causes a death, then *the ox shall be stoned, and its owner too shall be put to death.*[6] In the rabbis' understanding, the owner and the ox must appear together in court for the hearing, and the owner too is liable for the damage caused by the ox. The sages in the story draw an analogy between the owner of the ox in the biblical law and the owner of a slave, and insist that King Yannai appear in court together with his accused slave. Presumably, he too will be held responsible if the slave is judged to be culpable, just as the owner of the ox would be.

---

6 This is the King James Version translation, which is closer to the rabbinic understanding. The NJPS translation reads: "If, however, that ox has been in the habit of goring, and its owner, though warned, has failed to guard it, and it kills a man or a woman—the ox shall be stoned and its owner, too, shall be put to death."

Whatever the merits of this analogy between ox and slave according to rabbinic legal thinking or our own sensibilities (including ethical objections of analogizing human slaves/servants to domestic animals), one can imagine an ancient king respectfully insisting on his own grounds that an ox is an ox, while a slave is a slave. The former acts according to animal instinct alone, while the latter has free will to perform evil or to resist their impulses. Rabbinic law generally holds the slave, not the master, responsible for the damage he causes, though the storyteller may not be concerned with these sources, or may be portraying Shimon b. Shetaḥ as judging this case an exception, since the slaves/servants of kings typically carry out their masters' bidding.[7] The slave may have done the deed—but are we seriously to believe that Yannai had nothing to do with it? Would a king's servant have the audacity and autonomy to commit murder without the king's tacit—or explicit—instruction? The Bible verse about the ox deals with a case of negligence, and yet requires the owner to stand trial along with his animal. How much more so should a murderous slave's owner, who may have been complicit or directly responsible, and not merely negligent, stand trial for the crime!

In any event, Yannai acquiesces a second time: he comes to the rabbinic court and sits down quietly. What more could be asked of a king? Many rulers, ancient and modern alike, would not think twice about refusing to appear, perhaps even sending in some soldiers to deliver the message with a little calculated violence. To show up in and of itself can be perceived as a humiliating submission to the authority of others.

King Yannai's presence, however, still does not satisfy Shimon ben Shetaḥ. Quoting another biblical verse, he commands the king to stand up—to honor the rabbis not only by his appearance but by his posture [C3]. How are we to read Shimon ben Shetaḥ's motives: Does he feel that Yannai has insulted the court by refusing to abide by the standard protocol—standing—demanded of all other litigants? Or is this a power struggle, an effort to demonstrate to everyone that he possesses the higher authority and status? Shimon ben Shetaḥ seems to disavow a personal stake in the conflict by declaring: "It is not before us that you stand, but before He-Who-Spoke-and-the-World-Came-into-Being." He insists on

7 See Mishnah Yadayim 4:7, which attributes to the Pharisees the position that a master is not liable for the damages caused by his slave, while the Sadducees hold the opposite. The rabbis generally sided with the Pharisees, or inherited the legal tradition of the Pharisees.

God's honor, not his own. Should we take this rhetoric seriously? Does the shift from *the court* addressing Yannai, "*They* sent to him" in [C1–C2], to "*Shimon ben Shetaḥ* said to him" in [C3], imply that Shimon b. Shetaḥ now acts alone and that his colleagues believe he has gone too far?

At this point King Yannai balks. Yet he neither refuses Shimon ben Shetaḥ outright nor issues a warning or a threat. He resists the rabbi's individual authority, but he acknowledges, at least on the surface, the collective authority of the sages, of Shimon ben Shetaḥ's colleagues, the judges of the court. He will defer to the institution but not to Shimon ben Shetaḥ, whom Yannai seems to think is on a power trip. This court case has become too personal. It has turned into a test of wills, a power play. Yannai appeals to a more neutral judiciary.

"He turned to the right..." [D1]: who turned, Yannai or Shimon ben Shetaḥ? The ambiguity here is masterful. Does the pronoun refer to Shimon ben Shetaḥ, who looks to his colleagues for support, but they turn away and let him down? Or does the pronoun refer to Yannai, who stares at the rabbis seated at Shimon ben Shetaḥ's flanks, but they cannot bring themselves to meet his imperious glance? In either case, how do we assess the sages' averted eyes? Is this abject cowardice, a failure of nerve when confronted by a powerful king? Or, do they believe that Shimon ben Shetaḥ has exceeded his rightful authority? Initially they "set their eyes" on the king, summoning him to judgment, but now they avert their eyes, unable to meet the eyes turned toward them, either for support (if by Shimon) or intimidation (if by Yannai).

The divine intervention supports Shimon ben Shetaḥ's strong stance [D2]. He invokes the measure-for-measure principle: are you "preoccupied with your thoughts"? (literally, "Are you **masters of thoughts**"?). Then "let the [true] **Master of Thoughts** come and punish you." The sages turn their eyes to the ground in fear of the king, and are then struck down from their judicial positions to that very ground. They fail to "stand up" to Yannai, whom Shimon had commanded to stand, and are struck down prostrate, their reduced posture indicating the loss of honor. By declining to support Shimon in his confrontation with Yannai, they have failed in their capacity as leaders and judges.

Nevertheless, we should take the story neither as a total endorsement of Shimon ben Shetaḥ's actions nor as a consummate indictment of King Yannai. First, the narrator hints with the formulation of his call to his colleagues, "Set your eyes upon him (Yannai) and let us judge him" [A], that Shimon ben Shetaḥ's motives were not pure. The expression "set eyes upon" generally has negative connotations, and is frequently used for a man who "sets his eyes upon" a woman for illicit sex.[8] Second, however we view Shimon ben Shetaḥ's motives—pure or impure, self-interested or selfless—many sages die as a result of his actions.

The disastrous ending, rather than pinning the blame on one side or the other, teaches a tragic lesson of the incompatibility of power and justice. It is extremely difficult, if not impossible, to bring the sovereign to justice, because the presence of power disrupts the functioning of the judicial system. In many societies kings were considered the source of the law, and hence above the law: "The king is the law." In the Bible and in Judaism, by contrast, the king is human and, like all others, subject to God's law. Yet our story complicates this normative view. While the subordination of the king to the law may be true in theory, our story suggests that it does not work in practice, at least not in a human court. The difficulty, we are to understand, is not due solely to a sovereign's ability to use violence and to human weakness (the judges' failure of nerve), but also to the escalation and personality conflicts that can develop when judges attempt to exert their own authority.[9]

Let us now turn to the Talmud's contextualization of the story, the bracketing provided by sections [A] and [A'], which link the story directly to the mishnah. "At that time"—meaning, as a result of this incident—"they said, *A king—he does not judge [others] and is not judged in court. He does not testify and is not testified against*" [A']. The Talmud claims that the earlier law was changed so that kings would never again be tried or participate in the judicial system. Originally the law had held that a king was permitted to serve as a judge, offer testimony as a witness, and appear as a litigant. As a result of this disastrous event, however, the sages promulgated the ruling in our mishnah that disqualifies a king from functioning as a judge ("a king does not judge"), witness ("he does not testify"), or litigant ("is not judged in court...is not testified against").

This bracketing, on one level, supports an understanding of the story that attributes responsibility for the disaster both to Shimon b. Shetaḥ and to Yannai, for the Talmud does not conclude that those particular sages

---

**8** See, for example, Bava Batra 3b–4a and Ta'anit 22a.

**9** For connections between the story and the doctrine of "judicial review" and some aspects of political theory, see Jeffrey L. Rubenstein, *Land of Truth,* 214–21, and Yair Lorberbaum, *Disempowered King,* 100–7.

were unworthy and that, in order to bring kings to justice, better qualified judges should be appointed to the judiciary. In theory, the Talmud could have followed the story with the coda, "At that time they said, 'Let only the most courageous judges be appointed to the high court,'" or "At that time, they said, 'Let only judges who support one another completely serve on the court together.'" Instead, the Talmud asserts that the law was changed to avoid such conflicts in the future, because the situation of judging a king is itself untenable.

More importantly, the story functions as a narrative justification for Mishnah Sanhedrin 2:2. Typically the talmudic commentary points to scripture as the source of the Mishnah, offering a midrashic exegesis of a biblical law. In some cases the Talmud provides a logical basis for the Mishnah's rulings grounded in common-sense reasoning, fleshing out the conceptual basis of the statute. In still other cases the Talmud extrapolates one mishnaic ruling from another or from a more general legal principle. Here, by contrast, the Talmud provides a story to explain the origin of the ruling.

This explanation makes an enormous difference to how we understand both the mishnah and the story. Were it not for the story, we would have had no reason to consider Mishnah Sanhedrin 2:2 as a reformulation, a less-than-ideal revision of the way things were meant to be, a compromise with the messiness of reality. On the contrary, we would think that this ruling, as formulated in the mishnah, reflects the ideal law and embodies God's will (to the extent that the Mishnah and the rabbinic Oral Law embody God's revelation). We would probably interpret the disqualification of the king from the judiciary as a healthy policy of (what we would call) the "separation of powers," and understand the ruling that a king cannot serve as witness because he would be too influential and nobody would dare testify for the other party. Similarly, we would perceive the provision that a king cannot be a litigant as a kind of "executive immunity," much as some government officials enjoy today. Indeed, the Talmud Yerushalmi does not quote this story in its commentary to the mishnah, and offers no evidence that it considered Mishnah Sanhedrin 2:2 as anything but the original and ideal law. The Yerushalmi's commentary here is very rudimentary, quoting only a few biblical verses to explicate the mishnah's rulings in standard talmudic fashion. There is no awareness of any larger drama precipitating a reformulation of a putative original law.

We would also read the story itself differently without this framing that presents it as a narrative justification of a change in mishnaic law. Note that this contextualization appears in the bracketing of the story, in the introduction and concluding lines [A, A'], both of which can be omitted easily, and were probably added by the talmudic editors when they mobilized the story for this purpose. That is, it is likely that the story had circulated independently or in another context that has been lost, and the bracketing was added to connect the story to this legal context. Without the bracketing, the story could be interpreted in any number of ways. One could understand the message as delineating the type of judges required for effective justice—those willing to look a king in the eye and insist that justice be done despite the danger. Or one could take the story as an attack against the very institution of the monarchy, as arguing that kings disrupt the justice system to the point of sometimes bearing responsibility for a tragic loss of life. Or the story could be a polemic against Hasmonean kings specifically, those wicked kings who committed a litany of abuses, as we know from other sources, and who here threatened the court rather than submit to its authority, as pious kings ought to do. (Here I have sneakily re-contextualized the story among other anti-Hasmonean sources—which shows that some context is generally needed for interpretation.) Or again, the story could be arguing for judicial and rabbinic restraint, counseling rabbis not to confront sovereigns lest disaster result, but not forbidding such measures outright or in exceptional circumstances. But in its present context, a cogent interpretation of the story should construe the narrated events as so momentous as to have precipitated a change in rabbinic law for ever more.

## Stories Undermine the Law of the Mishnah

While many stories, like the one above, support or justify the laws with which they are juxtaposed, other stories may have the completely opposite relationship to the proximate law. Some stories contest a talmudic or mishnaic law, or provide warning that following the law is problematic. Placed in these contexts, the stories work to subvert the law and caution against putting it into practice. One powerful example of this phenomenon is a story whose wordplay we looked at briefly in chapter 4, about a rabbi and his wife, which appears in Ketubot 62b in the context of a discussion about the relationship between spousal obligations and the value of Torah study.

The Bible rules that a husband is obligated to provide his wife food, clothing, and sex:

**שמות כא:י**

אם אחרת יקח לו, שארה, כסותה, וענתה לא יגרע.

**Exodus 21:10**

If he marries another [wife], he must not withhold from this one her food, her clothing, or her conjugal rights (*onah*).

While the biblical law actually relates to a husband marrying a second wife, it references and presupposes those three "rights" of the first wife. The Mishnah, as is typical, provides many more details related to the biblical commandment, including the amount of food, value of clothing, and frequency of sex to which the wife is entitled. (Biblical scholars debate the exact meaning of the third term, *onah*, but the rabbis understood it to mean marital sex.) Rulings about the obligation and frequency of marital sex may strike us moderns as odd. However, the entitlement of a wife to conjugal sex makes sense in polygamous societies, as there is always a danger of a man marrying one wife for her wealth or lineage and completely neglecting her, then marrying a second wife for her attractiveness. Even in American law, both partners in a marriage have a right to sex, and in some states may be able to sue for divorce if their spouse consistently refuses on legal grounds known as "constructive abandonment."[10]

This biblical ruling supplies the background for Mishnah Ketubot 5:6:

**משנה כתובות ה:ו**

[A] התלמידים יוצאין לתלמוד תורה שלא ברשות שלשים יום.

[B] הפועלים, שבת אחת....

[C] דברי רבי אליעזר.

10 Although most states have "no fault" divorce, the charge of "constructive abandonment" may influence the settlement.

**Mishnah Ketubot 5:6**

[A] Students [of Torah] may depart for Torah study without permission [from their wives] for thirty days.

[B] Laborers—for one week.....

[C] These are the words of R. Eliezer.

The mishnah attempts to compromise between two rabbinic values, that of Torah study on the one hand, which the rabbis considered the greatest *mitzvah*, and that of marital obligations and domestic responsibilities more broadly on the other. The compromise permits rabbis and their students to leave home for up to one month in order to travel to a center of Torah study, thus temporarily denying the wives their rights to companionship and conjugal sex. Laborers receive a briefer exemption of up to one week, as they are not "professional" or full-time Torah students, and presumably engage in less frequent and shorter study. Longer periods of absence from the wife and home, even for this noble purpose, are prohibited, as they infringe on her rights.

The Talmud's commentary, however, skews this delicate balance in favor of Torah study. A tradition attributed to Rav Adda bar Ahava in the name of Rav states:

**תלמוד בבלי, כתובות סב ע״ב**

[D] אמר רב אדא בר אהבה אמר רב: זו דברי ר׳ אליעזר.

[E] אבל חכמים אומרים: התלמידים יוצאין לתלמוד תורה ב׳ וג׳ שנים שלא ברשות.

**Talmud Bavli, Ketubot 62b**

[D] Rav Adda bar Ahava said that Rav said: This (=the mishnah above, [A–C]) is the view of R. Eliezer [alone].

[E] But the sages say: Students may leave for Torah study for two or three years without permission [from their wives].

Now it is true that the mishnah attributes the ruling to R. Eliezer [C]. But the mishnah provides no other opinion, no sage who disagrees with R. Eliezer, which would typically indicate that his is the majority or consensus opinion. We might suspect that Rav Adda bar Ahava has invented a dissenting opinion that allows for much greater absences from home and attributed it to "the sages," the majority, in order to marginalize R. Eliezer's view and allow contemporary rabbis lengthier periods of study.

In any case, the Talmud follows this surprising move with an even more surprising tradition:

[F] אמר רבא: סמכו רבנן אדרב אדא בר אהבה ועבדי עובדא בנפשייהו.

[F] Rava stated: The rabbis relied on the words of Rav Adda bar Ahava and acted accordingly at the cost of their lives.

The Talmud then provides the following story (which we briefly examined in chapter 4 (pp. 136–37) for its wordplay):

[A] רב רחומי הוה שכיח קמיה דרבא במחוזא. הוה רגיל דהוה אתי לביתיה כל מעלי יומא דכיפורי.

[B] יומא חד משכתיה שמעתא.

[C] הוה מסכיא דביתהו, השתא אתי השתא אתי.

[D] לא אתא.

[E] חלש דעתה. אחית דמעתא מעינה.

[F] הוה יתיב באיגרא אפחית איגרא מתותיה ונח נפשיה.

[A] Rav Reḥumei would study with Rava in Maḥoza. He would regularly come home every Yom Kippur eve.

[B] One day his studies captivated him.

[C] His wife was looking out [for him, thinking], "He is coming now. He is coming now."

[D] He did not come.

[E] She became distressed. A tear fell (*aḥit*) from her eye.

[F] He (Rav Reḥumei) was sitting on a roof. The roof fell in (*ifḥit*) under him and he died.[11]

---

11 On this story see Yonah Frankel, *Aspects of the Spiritual World*, 99–115; Shulamith Valler, *Woman and Womanhood*, 51–72; Daniel Boyarin, *Carnal Israel*, 142–56; Jeffrey

It is a brief story, though dense with pathos and emotion. Rav Reḥumei studied with Rava, among the greatest talmudic masters, whose school was located in Maḥoza, a town on the Euphrates River near Be-Ardashir, one of the two capital cities of the Persian Empire. We don't know exactly where Rav Reḥumei lived, though it was evidently far from Maḥoza, such that the great distance and the difficulty of travel in antiquity prevented him from returning home frequently. He managed to return home once each year to see his wife (and perhaps other family members), on the eve of Yom Kippur. This does not necessarily imply that he remained home for only one day, though we probably should not rule out this possibility entirely. Rather, the sense is that he traveled home only at that time each year. Even if he may have remained a while before returning to his studies, the rabbinic audience would certainly be struck, as we are, by the lack of balance between the time invested in learning Torah and that devoted to his wife and family. The storyteller makes this negative assessment of Rav Reḥumei's priorities absolutely clear with a masterful use of irony: Rav Reḥumei "regularly" came home…once per year! The audience understands that the opposite is the case: Rav Reḥumei "regularly" can be found pursuing his studies with his fellow rabbis and disciples in the study house, and is very irregularly at home.

This tenable, if suboptimal, situation set forth in the exposition [A] is ruptured "one day" when Rav Reḥumei could not tear himself away from his study of Torah to depart even for that annual visit home [B]. More "captivated" by his studies than by his wife, Rav Reḥumei treated the Torah as his true love, his real passion, and his wife a distant second. The word "captivated him" (משכתיה, literally "drew him in") may even have some erotic overtones; apparently whatever erotic or romantic life the rabbi shared with his wife paled in comparison to his attraction and passion for Torah study. The story poignantly makes the wife's point of view the focus of the scene, as we picture her watching eagerly for her husband to return, excitedly thinking that he will arrive at any moment for their annual reunion, perhaps sitting on her stoop and peering down the road toward the horizon in the hope of discerning a traveler approaching the town [C]. And then, as the day passes and twilight descends, as she slowly realizes "he did not come" (לא אתא), we too feel her crushing

---

L. Rubenstein, *Culture of the Babylonian Talmud*, 103-7; Ruth Calderon, *A Bride for One Night*, 31–38; Haim Weiss and Shira Stav, *The Return of the Missing Father*, 11–20.

disappointment and despair. This brief sentence, right in the middle of the story, consisting of but two staccato words in the original Aramaic, *la ata*, expresses with absolute finality the devastated hopes of an entire year of waiting. For her, there is nothing more. *La ata.*

That his annual return takes place on the eve of Yom Kippur is significant in this respect. Theoretically the story would work equally well if he returned at any other time of year, say for Purim or for the first day of summer. But the symbolism of Yom Kippur is particularly apposite when pondering Rav Reḥumei's conduct. This is the day set aside for atonement, repentance, and forgiveness, for reconciliation not only between God and human beings but also between humans who have offended one other. On the days leading up to Yom Kippur, the rabbis call upon all Jews to increase charity, deeds of lovingkindness, and acts of piety as signs of sincere repentance. Yet Rav Reḥumei seems oblivious to the meaning of the holy day, oblivious to the pain he causes his wife by his failure to return.[12]

When the wife expresses her inner suffering through a tear, her pain ripples forth and—so the audience is to understand—brings about her husband's punishment. He was sitting on the roof of a house or of the school to enjoy some solitude or to rest at leisure, perhaps even to review his Torah studies. As we noted in chapter 4 (pp. 136–37), a wordplay connects the words "fall," אחית/*aḥit,* and "fell in," אפחית/*ifḥit,* suggesting that the one caused the other. The tear that fell from her eye *caused* the roof to collapse. *Because* Rav Reḥumei caused that tear to fall, he was punished, measure for measure, with the falling in of the roof.

Rav Reḥumei is a sage whose traditions appear elsewhere in the Talmud, albeit infrequently. The storyteller selected him as the protagonist of this story, however, because the verbal root ר-ח-מ/*r-ḥ-m* in Aramaic means "love." His name essentially corresponds to "Rabbi Lover." Yet it is clear that Rav Reḥumei loves not his wife but rather...his Torah. We have seen the function of symbolic names in rabbinic stories in chapter 2, and here the symbolic name points to the key theme and tension of the story: what should be the proper object of a rabbi's love? For the storyteller, Rabbi Lover loved the Torah inappropriately at the expense of the love for his wife, and paid for it with his life.

---

12 Some argue that Rav Reḥumei's offense is particularly outrageous because Yom Kippur is a day when marital relations are forbidden. However, as noted above, the simple meaning is not necessarily that he stays for just one day.

We now turn to the story's contextualization. The juxtaposition of the story with Rav Adda bar Ahava's permissive legal ruling that rabbis may absent themselves for "two or three years without permission" warns rabbis against following this view in practice. The story does not reject the ruling as the accepted law, and a rabbi who chooses to remain away for this period of time cannot be accused of a transgression. Yet the story undermines this ruling by presenting the dire fate of Rav Reḥumei. A rabbi studying this portion of Talmud would think twice about remaining away from home for a lengthy period, lest he suffer a similar consequence. Ideally he would also be sensitized to think more of his own wife's feelings as he considers the scene of Rav Reḥumei's wife waiting forlornly and weeping for her absent husband.

To see the power of this juxtaposition, imagine an alternative contextualization of the story in some other *sugya* of Talmud, in a different tractate far removed from this legal discussion. In this case Rav Adda bar Ahava's ruling following this mishnah here in Ketubot would have stood without challenge, and the talmudic audience would have had no reason to question its force, no reason not to act accordingly. When coming upon the story of Rav Reḥumei in that other (hypothetical) tractate, the audience would not necessarily have connected it with Mishnah Ketubot 5:6 at all. Taken in and of itself, the story of Rav Reḥumei is clearly a cautionary tale, but its target could be interpreted variously. The audience might have understood the offense as related to Yom Kippur, that Rav Reḥumei violated the spirit of the day by failing to spend the holy time with his wife and family. In this case the didactic point would have centered on observance of Yom Kippur and the importance of the interpersonal aspects of the day, namely the urgency of reconciling with one's loved ones, and not only atoning for sins against God. This understanding would have been particularly attractive if the story were contextualized with other traditions about observance of Yom Kippur, for example in Yoma, the tractate devoted to the laws and traditions of that day. Alternatively, the audience might have understood that Rav Reḥumei's failing was having appointed a specific time to return home, creating expectations that he cruelly dashed. The audience might then have concluded that it is better to be vague and unpredictable about visits home so as to avoid this eventuality, rather than understanding that long absences per se are the problem.

Any of these interpretations also apply, at least in part, to the story in its current context in Ketubot. Likewise, those other talmudic passages exist and would be known to the learned talmudic audience, who might choose, when studying them, to consider this story too, distant as it is. Indeed, some rabbinic stories appear in several locations, sometimes in different versions. In those cases, just as we interpret variations in the story itself to illuminate structure and language, we can hold multiple contexts in mind to layer different kinds of meaning onto the story. (Chapter 6 explores this phenomenon.)

But in this case, interpretations flowing from those other more distant talmudic passages are necessarily less prominent in our interpretation of the story of Rav Reḥumei. Juxtaposed as it is here with a talmudic ruling that permits long absences, which in turn follows a mishnaic tradition limiting those absences (albeit identified as the minority position), the story prompts its audience to interpret the thrust of the story as centered on Rav Reḥumei's protracted absence itself. Despite the technical permissibility of such behavior, the story's contextualization provides a powerful disincentive against this practice.

This story, for the rabbis, was about the tension between their vocation, Torah study, and domestic obligations—between two virtues but also between two sets of obligations. The story invites us to think about the balance between our vocations, such as demanding careers in medicine, law, or business, and our obligations to spouses and children. Because a career involves the earnings that support a family, the conflict is particularly acute and complex. It can be difficult to judge when devotion to work, despite the financial benefit to one's spouse and children, nevertheless has other costs due to long hours in the office or extensive travel. Likewise, it is hard to know when pursuing a promotion or greater status at work, which confers some material benefits, nevertheless takes too high a toll on the family, as it entails additional time with clients and longer absences.

By extension, the story alerts us to the danger that an individual's commitments to an important value or virtuous cause can be taken too far, and ultimately become more about self-gratification, leading to a blindness to the needs of others. Many elected officials throughout history have faced marital challenges, as they become so consumed by their public duties and the quest to serve their constituents that they neglect the emotional and familial needs of their own spouses and children. Even those working for charities, nonprofit and non-governmental organizations, and advocacy groups can become so devoted to the needs of these enterprises—typically understaffed and underfunded—that they lose sight of what is going on in their own homes. The story serves as a reminder that virtuous behavior should never come at the expense of empathy, compassion, and attentiveness toward those closest to us. Striking a balance between service to the greater good and personal relationships is vital to maintaining a harmonious and fulfilling life.

At a still more general level, the story can be seen as addressing conflicts between the two main classes of *mitzvot,* between human and human, בין אדם לחבירו/*bein adam la-ḥaveiro,* and between a human and God, בין אדם למקום/*bein adam la-Makom.* Rav Reḥumei devotes himself to Torah study, to the ultimate *mitzvah* between a human and God (בין אדם למקום), and arguably the highest *mitzvah* in the rabbinic worldview. His devotion to this laudable goal, however, has caused him to neglect his responsibilities to other human beings (בין אדם לחבירו), namely his wife and family. Tensions such as these between *mitzvot* of these two classes can often arise, as a focus on the Divine through study, prayer, meditation, mysticism, and other such spiritual practices can take time and focus away from the needs of other people. The storyteller warns that however important these Godly pursuits, they should not negatively impact real human beings and their needs. Holiness and piety, in other words, are as much—or even more—expressed in our conduct toward other people as they are in our relationship with God.

~

All rabbinic compilations are carefully edited works, and the Babylonian Talmud, in particular, went through a long and protracted editing process over the course of centuries. While in some cases stories and other sources were integrated purely on an associative basis, in most cases the editors juxtaposed sources for substantive reasons. To analyze a talmudic story comprehensively therefore requires the reader to assess its literary context or contexts. I say "contexts" because the immediate literary context, the broader context or literary unit (*sugya*), the proximate mishnah, and even the entire chapter of Talmud are all potentially relevant contexts in which to consider a story.

After analyzing the story itself as an independent text, the reader should therefore proceed to examining its contexts and pondering the relationship among them. In some cases the story will nuance or complicate the mishnah or the Talmud's interpretation of the mishnah, as we saw with the story of the praying *ḥasid* and Roman governor. The Talmud had narrowed the scope of the mishnah's ruling to permit, or perhaps require, interrupting prayer when in the presence of a gentile king—the opposite of the *ḥasid*'s behavior in the story. In other cases the story will justify the mishnah, as in the case of the story of King Yannai and Shimon ben Shetaḥ. The story explains why the mishnah rules that a king stands outside the judicial system, claiming that this law was promulgated following the disaster that followed the efforts of the sages to summon a king for judgment. In still other cases the story undermines the mishnah or the preceding talmudic legislation, as in the case of Rav Reḥumei. His untimely death, despite his having acted in conformity with the Talmud's ruling, warns the audience against following the ruling in practice, due to the pain it would cause one's spouse. And there are many other possibilities too. In all cases, it is important to note, which context or contexts to bring to bear on the story depends on the audience and how they make sense of the juxtaposition of story and other material in the talmudic *sugya*.

The potential of interpreting stories in multiple contexts—from the immediate literary context, to the broader textual context, to the complete chapter or tractate of Talmud, to the entire Talmud—as well as selecting specific talmudic *sugyot* with which to contextualize the story (for example, interpreting a story about martyrdom in conjunction with other stories and sources about martyrdom from disparate talmudic passages) is part of what makes rabbinic tradition vibrant and meaningful. Different interpreters across the generations generate new readings of talmudic stories by interpreting them in new contexts, in conjunction with different talmudic texts, and also in light of other texts that inform their worldview, implicitly or explicitly. Even the decision to interpret a story on its own terms, independent of its immediate talmudic context, amounts to a choice of context, as such a policy deliberately rejects information from the literary context that may be relevant, and inevitably places the story in another context, drawing on the reader or interpreter's prior information about terms, characters, and motifs that appear in the story. This is why we, as readers, should feel entitled and empowered to interpret talmudic stories anew, joining the interpretive conversation taking place across the centuries by choosing our own textual contexts as well as other contexts—historical, religious, ethical, and spiritual.

# CHAPTER 6
## The Story-Cycle

Most rabbinic stories appear as "stand-alone" sources within the larger flow of the legal discussion of the Talmuds or within the succession of exegetical comments of the collections of midrash. However, there are also examples of series of three or more stories, uninterrupted or almost uninterrupted by other material. A few of these series of stories, also known as "story-cycles," include twenty or thirty stories and comprise a vast quantity of narrative material.

A story-cycle can produce a special experience for the audience by immersing it in a narrative world, an imaginative realm, similar to the way that, when engrossed in a novel, we feel ourselves transported to the place and times of the characters.[1] More importantly, a story-cycle allows the editor or compiler to focus attention on a given theme, or on a few interrelated themes, while varying narrative elements to provide a broader and more complex perspective on the issue. Imagine a single story about a man and his devoted dog that protects him from an attack by a thief. That story communicates certain messages about human-canine relationships, the benefit of a loyal dog, and the dangers that confront us. Now imagine that that story is set within a series of stories about different characters and their various pets (dogs, cats, birds, fish) that make their owners happy in various ways, though sometimes causing problems. A series like this

1 See Eli Yassif, *The Hebrew Folktale*, 209–14.

provides a broader perspective on the issue of owning pets, the advantages and disadvantages, benefits and downsides, and even the nature of relationships between humans and animals or the differences between them. The rabbis did not compose essays or systematic philosophical analyses of issues as did Greek and Roman writers. They did not express themselves in a philosophical idiom. Their way of investigating different aspects of a topic was rather to construct a story-cycle that addresses the diverse sides of an issue in narrative fashion. We in turn, as readers, are offered a more complex window into rabbinic perspectives on the cycle's topics, and are invited to ask, with them, how the stories they relate illuminate their, and perhaps our, religious view of the world.

The following story-cycle about astrology illustrates this phenomenon. This story-cycle appears within a larger talmudic passage that debates the impact of astrology on Jews.[2] As we observed in chapter 1 with the story of "Yosef the Shabbat-honorer," astrology was considered a science in antiquity, so it was extremely difficult for the rabbis to reject it outright. The question was rather the extent and strength of its influence. The Talmud expresses the two sides of the issue with the shorthand expressions "Israel has a *mazal*," יש מזל לישראל, and "Israel has no *mazal*," אין מזל לישראל. The Hebrew word *mazal* refers to the planets and constellations, so these expressions literally translate to "Israel has a planet/constellation" and "Israel has no planet/constellation." The Talmud employs the former expression to refer to the belief that the fate of Jews is determined exclusively by the celestial bodies, that is, that Jews are as subject to astrological influence as gentiles. The latter expression embodies the contrary belief that while astrology does impact the fortune of Jews, they also have free will, such that their sins or righteous deeds also impact the course of their lives. (The deep and long-lasting Jewish belief in astrology is attested by the ubiquitous exclamation *mazal tov,* meaning "congratulations." But the literal meaning is "a good planet/constellation," that is, a benevolent astrological influence or a favorable horoscope.)

2 Much of this analysis is borrowed from my article "Talmudic Astrology." See too Gregg Gardner, "Astrology in the Talmud" and Moshe Simon-Shoshan, "A Doorway of Their Own," 106–13.

**תלמוד בבלי, שבת קנו ע״ב**

[I] [A] ומדשמואל נמי אין מזל לישראל.

[B] דשמואל ואבלט – כי הוו יתבי ואזלי הנך אינשי לאגמא. א״ל אבלט לשמואל: האי גברא אזיל ולא אתי וטריק ליה חיויא ומאית.

[C] א״ל שמואל: אזיל ואתי.

[D] אדיתבי קא עסקי ביה, אזיל ואתא. קם אבלט, שדייה לטוניה, אשכח ביה חיויא דפסיק ושאדי בתרתי גובי.

[E] א״ל שמואל: מה עבדת? א״ל: כל יומא הוינא מרמינן ריפתא בהדי הדדי ואכלינן. והאידנא הוה איכא חד גבן דלא הוה ליה ריפתא בהדיה והוה מכסיף. אמינא לחבראי: אנא קאימנא ומרמינא ליה ריפתא. כי מטאי לגביה שוי נפשאי כמאן דשקלי מיניה, כי היכי דלא ליכסיף. א״ל: מצוה קא עבדת ואתצלת.

[F] נפק שמואל לבי מדרשא ודרש: וצדקה תציל ממות (משלי י:ב, יא:ד). ולא ממיתה משונה אלא אפילו ממיתה עצמה.

[II] [A] ומדר׳ עקיבא נמי אין מזל לישראל.

[B] דר׳ עקיבא הויא ליה ברתא. אמרו ליה כלדאי: ההוא יומא דעיילא לבי גנאנה טריק לה חויא ומתה.

[C] הוה דאיג עלה דמילתא טובא.

[D] ההוא יומא דעיילה, שקלה למכבנתא דעציתה בביזעא. איתרמי לה עיילה בעיינא דחיויא. לצפרא כי קא שקלה ליה, הוה קא סריך ואתי חיויא בתרה.

[E] אמר לה אבוה: מה עבדת? אמרה ליה: בפניא אתא ענייא קרא אבבא. והוו טרידי כולי עלמא בסעודתא וליכא דשמעיה. קמית אנא שקלית ואמרית: הדין דסתאנא דיהביתו לי הבו ניהליה. א״ל: מצוה קא עבדת ואתצלת.

[F] נפק ר׳ עקיבא לבי מדרשא ודרש: וצדקה תציל ממות (משלי י:ב, יא:ד). ולא ממיתה משונה אלא ממיתה עצמה.

[III] [A] ומדרב נחמן בר יצחק נמי אין מזל לישראל.

[B] דאימיה דרב נחמן בר יצחק – אמרו לה כלדאי: בריך גנבא יהא.

[C] לא שבקתיה גלויי רישיה. אמרה ליה: כסי רישך כי היכי דליהוי עלך אימתא דשמיא ובעי רחמי. לא הוה ידע אמאי קאמרה ליה.

[D] יומא חד הוה קא גריס ויתיב תותי דיקלא. נפל גלימא מעילוי רישיה. דלי עייניה. חזייה לדיקלא. אלמיה יצר הרע. סליק פסקיה לקיבורא בשיניה.

**Talmud Bavli, Shabbat 156b**

[I] [A] From [the case of] Shmuel too [we learn that] "Israel has no *mazal*."

[B] For Shmuel and Avlat (a Persian sage)—while they were sitting, certain men were going to the field. Avlat said to Shmuel, "That man will go but not come back, as a snake will bite him and he will die."

[C] Shmuel said to him, "He will go and come back."[3]

[D] While they were sitting and discussing it, he went and came back. Avlat arose, threw off his (the man's) load, and found there a snake that had been cut and thrown into two pieces.

[E] Shmuel said to him, "What did you do?" He said to him, "Every day we throw the bread together [for a common meal] and eat. Today there was one with us who had no bread with him, and he was ashamed. I said to my companions, 'I will get up and throw (=collect) the bread for him.' When I arrived at him, I pretended as if I had taken from him, in order that he not be ashamed." He (Shmuel) said to him, "You did a *mitzvah* and were saved."

[F] Shmuel went out to the study house and expounded, "*Righteousness (tzedakah) saves from death (Proverbs 10:2, 11:4)*. Not [only] from an unusual death but even from death itself."

[II] [A] From [the case of] R. Akiva too [we learn that] "Israel has no *mazal*."

[B] For R. Akiva—he had a daughter. The astrologers (literally "Chaldeans") said to him, "On that day that she enters her wedding canopy, a snake will bite her and she will die."

[C] He worried a great deal about the matter.

---

3 This reading accords with the Munich 95 manuscript and other text witnesses. The standard printing and several manuscripts read: "If he is a Jew, he will go and come back." However, I do not think this variant impacts the meaning of the story.

[D] On that day that she entered [the wedding canopy], she took her wedding crown and stuck it into a crack [in the wall]. It happened for her that it entered the eye of a snake. In the morning, when she took it [from the wall], the snake was adhering [to the wedding crown] and coming out after it.

[E] Her father said to her, "What did you do?" She said to him, "In the evening a poor man came and called at the door [asking for alms]. Everyone was busy with the [wedding] meal, and no one heard him. I got up and took it, and said [to myself], 'This portion [of the wedding meal] that you gave me, I will give to him.'" He said to her, "You did a *mitzvah* and were saved."

[F] R. Akiva went out to the study house and expounded, "*Righteousness (tzedakah) saves from death (Proverbs 10:2, 11:4)*. Not [only] from an unusual death but [even] from death itself."

[III] [A] From [the case of] Rav Naḥman bar Yitzḥak too [we learn that] "Israel has no *mazal*."

[B] For the mother of Rav Naḥman bar Yitzḥak—the astrologers (literally "Chaldeans") said to her, "Your son will be a thief."

[C] She did not allow him to uncover his head. She said to him, "Cover your head in order that the fear of heaven be upon you and pray for mercy." He did not know why she said this to him.

[D] One day he was studying while sitting under [someone else's] date palm. His covering fell from his head. He raised up his eyes. He saw the date palm. The evil inclination overpowered him. He ascended and cut off the date cluster with his teeth.

To analyze the story-cycle as a whole, we must attend to the similarities and differences in language and plot among the three stories in the group, so our first step—as always—must be to understand each story individually. In the first story a Persian sage named Avlat, known from several other talmudic passages, informs Shmuel, one of the leading rabbis, that a certain man will experience a wretched death that same day [I.B]. Based on the introductory line about astrology and on other talmudic sources that present astrology as a Persian or gentile "science," the audience understands the source of Avlat's assertion: he is an astrology expert, and has seen this individual's fate in the celestial bodies. Shmuel rejects Avlat's claim [I.C].[4] Exactly what gives the rabbi this confidence is less clear; apparently he believes all Jews have some good deeds to their credit, or he may be acquainted with the man and know of his virtues. This brief exchange between Avlat and Shmuel pits the two worldviews against each other at the outset and establishes the tension as to which will prevail: Persian sage versus rabbi; astrology versus covenantal theology; determinism versus free will; gentile science versus Jewish wisdom.

The protagonist's return provides unambiguous evidence that Shmuel was correct and Avlat wrong [I.D]. But Avlat knows what he has seen in the stars and suspects that there is more to the matter than meets the eye. He searches the man's backpack and finds the very snake he predicted would kill the man, sliced into two pieces and very dead. The narrative tension now shifts from whether the man would return safely to what happened to allow for his survival, which he recounts in response to Shmuel's query [I.E]. The man had noticed that one among the group who typically pooled their food at lunch had nothing to contribute that particular day and was ashamed to be perceived as a freeloader. To spare his poor colleague embarrassment, he volunteered to collect the contributions from the others, placing their foodstuffs in a basket or bag and pretending to take an offering from the poor worker, too. Shmuel exclaims that the man's performance of this *mitzvah* of preserving the dignity of his fellow worker is what has saved him from the death by snakebite, which otherwise would have killed him.

This account explains why the man was saved but not exactly how. There remains a major narrative gap as to how the snake was cut in half. The medieval talmudic commentator Rashi suggests that the men had sickles or scythes to cut down the stalks in the field they were clearing. While the protagonist took his cutting tool from, or returned it to, his pack, the sharp blade happened to sever a snake that had crawled into it. This may have happened after the lunch break (and immediately after the good deed), when the man withdrew his blade as he set forth to return to work,

---

4 Thus the term for astrologers in the second and third stories is "Chaldeans," because of the strong association between astrology and Chaldea.

or perhaps at the end of the day, when the workers put away their tools to return home.

Now the talmudic storyteller clearly believes in astrology to a certain extent. Had he wanted to reject astrology completely he could have told a story in which the man returns without any incident or danger whatsoever; Avlat, for example, could have searched the pack and found nothing. Here, however, the snake indeed came to strike, as determined by the stars and as read correctly by Avlat. The story demonstrates, more specifically, that "Israel has no *mazal*," meaning that even though astral determinism may be true in part, it does not account for the totality of a Jew's fortune, as righteous deeds can supersede it [I.A].

The story concludes with Shmuel publicizing this lesson by teaching it in the rabbinic house of study, generalizing the moral and also linking it to a biblical verse [I.F]. The man's story exemplifies the Book of Proverbs' promise that "righteousness saves from death," as the verse comes true in the man's salvation. Shmuel clarifies that the "death" mentioned in the verse includes "unnatural death," that is, premature or accidental death (such as death by snakebite), as well as "death itself," that is, extending one's allotted length of life with "bonus" years to live into extreme old age.[5]

In the story-cycle's second story, astrologers make a similar ominous claim concerning R. Akiva's daughter: they have seen in the stars that she will die by snakebite on her wedding day [II.B]. As opposed to Shmuel, R. Akiva does not reject the dire prediction but "worries a great deal" about it [II.C]. The storyteller leaves it to the audience to assess whether this reaction entails fatal resignation, guarded skepticism, persistent low-level anxiety, or some combination of these and other emotions. The maiden is saved when she places her "wedding crown," a tiara or diadem, in a crack in the wall, evidently to keep it safe until the morning, and one of the pins for attaching it to her hair pierces and kills a snake that would have attacked her while she slept [II.D]. This mode of deliverance, though perhaps contrived, creates a powerful irony, as the wedding accoutrements that had marked her for death according to the astrologers instead save her life.[6] R. Akiva understands that this miraculous deliverance must have a

---

5 Shmuel cannot mean that righteousness saves from dying, as all human die eventually.

6 The snake is both the outstanding symbol of death and evil, as per the story of the Garden of Eden, as well as a phallic symbol. The motif of a groom threatened by

cause, and asks her what she did to merit such good fortune. She explains that she selflessly gave her own portion of the wedding banquet to a poor man who had come asking for alms, while everyone else was busy celebrating and failed to notice his presence [II.E]. The story concludes in almost exactly the same way as the previous story, with R. Akiva making the same exclamation as Shmuel ("You did a *mitzvah*...") and also publicly expounding Proverbs 10:2 in the house of study to the same effect [II.F].

In the third story, astrologers foresee an abhorrent future, a life of sin and crime, rather than the unnatural death of the previous two stories [III.B]. The mother attempts to prevent this fate by keeping her son's head covered and constantly admonishing him never to bare it, though she does not disclose the ominous horoscope that motivates her behavior. Presumably she wishes to spare him the anxiety of knowing the miserable destiny that may await him, or perhaps to avoid the potential of turning it into a self-fulfilling prophecy [III.C]. Despite these vigilant efforts, one day the covering falls from his head, the evil inclination overpowers him, and he impulsively climbs a palm and steals the dates growing at the top [III.D]. Although the precise cause-and-effect relationship is not completely clear, the head-covering successfully protected him from such sins, perhaps keeping "the fear of heaven" foremost in his consciousness, as his mother's warning implies, or through some other mystical or talismanic means. Now at first glance it would seem that the astrologers' prognostication comes true, as Rav Naḥman b. Yitzḥak did in fact become a thief at that moment. But since the story is introduced to illustrate that "Israel has no *mazal*" [III.A], it cannot be interpreted in this way. Rather, the story demonstrates "Israel has no *mazal*," that is, the *mitzvot* can mitigate the stars' effect on Jews, because as long as the young Naḥman wore the head-covering, he was impervious to astrological influence. His pious behavior averted the unhappy fate, and only his lapse allowed it to come into effect. Moreover, we also know that this child ultimately grew up to become a sage, the great Rav Naḥman bar Yitzḥak, and therefore despite the apparently real influence on him of the celestial bodies, his mother's intervention worked; despite this one-time event, he did not become a thief for life.

---

a monster or killed on his wedding day is a common folkloristic motif; see Haim Schwarzbaum, "The Hero Predestined to Die."

Having examined each of these three narratives, we can turn our attention to the story-cycle as a whole. We immediately see that the story-cycle is a tightly structured composition. A preliminary line, expressed with the same shorthand phrase, introduces each story as proof of a general perspective on astrology [A]. In the next section of each story, an astrologer (Avlat in [I.B] or astrologers in [II.B, III.B]) makes a dreadful pronouncement about the fate of a Jew. The third sections offer three different reactions by third parties to those predictions [C]. In the fourth sections, the predictions fail to come true [D] (reading the third story as above). The fifth sections (found only in the first two stories) recount the meritorious deed, accounting for how the fate was averted, and a rabbi declares that performing a *mitzvah* brought salvation [E]. In the final sections the rabbi expounds (*darash*) the same lesson based on a biblical verse [F]. Note that the third story lacks parallels to these final two sections due to the different dynamic of the plot: the protagonist does not perform a discrete righteous deed to obviate the dire prediction, as in [E], nor does the fate involve death, so the verse does not apply [F]. (The righteous deed in this story is the continuous wearing of the head-covering, which is part of the mother's reaction to the prediction, recounted in [C]). The structural similarities indicate to the audience that, rather than being three completely independent stories that all deal with astrology but are otherwise unrelated, the stories are all part of a single story-cycle, all connected in one larger composition.

In addition to the parallel structures, the storyteller also connects the stories through shared phrases and narrative elements. The first two stories, for example, include the same threatening prediction that "a snake will bite him/her and he/she will die," while the second and third stories share the phrase "astrologers said to him/her." The righteous acts in the first two stories both involve food. In the first, the protagonist pretends to take food from his colleague who cannot contribute; in the second, the protagonist gives food to a poor person who has none. Head-coverings feature in the second and third story, functioning in almost the opposite ways: in the second story the intentional removal of the head-covering (the wedding crown) ends up preventing the disaster, while in the third story the unintentional removal of the head-covering enables the stars to act on the protagonist. In the first story the man pretended to "take" bread, while in the second the daughter recounts that she "took" the portion she received. So, too, the specific words used to describe that the man stating he will "throw" (מרמינא) the bread [I.E] and that it "happened"

(איתרמי) for R. Akiva's daughter that the wedding crown killed the snake [II.E] derive from the same Aramaic root, ר-מ-י. The first and third stories use the root פ-ס-ק, "cut," in the crucial deed (the snake, the date cluster). All three stories evoke the biblical account of the expulsion from Eden, with the snake in the first two and picking "forbidden" fruit in the third. And the first two stories, as noted above, end in exactly the same way, with the rabbis making the same statement and teaching the same lesson in the study house.

These repeated phrases and words, as well as the shared narrative elements like the common structures, function together to create an integrated and cohesive composition. The compiler of the story-cycle intends the audience to see the three stories as a single unit, and encourages the audience to make comparisons among them. At the same time, the compiler has carefully varied other motifs and elements of the plots to create contrasts. For example, the three stories feature three different reactions in parts [C] to the fate pronounced by the astrologer(s): Shmuel rejects the prediction; R. Akiva worries about it but takes no action; the mother of Rav Naḥman b. Yitzḥak endeavors to obviate it. Attentive reading reveals many more contrasts among all three stories or between two of the three stories. Some of them stand out clearly:

- The protagonists of the stories shift from a man to a woman to a child. The second story tells of a father and daughter; the third of a mother and son.
- The first story features a single, named astrologer (Avlat); the second and third have unnamed and anonymous astrologers.
- All three stories involve sages, but they stand in different relationships to the subject of the astrological forecast: Shmuel is unrelated to the subject; R. Akiva is the father of the subject; Rav Naḥman bar Yitzḥak is the subject himself.

Other contrasts are subtler or more abstract:

- The unfortunate fate in the first two stories is premature and unnatural death, while in the third it is a life of sin and crime. But the type of the premature death predicted shifts from an imminent death that same day in the first story to a death on a specific day (marriage) at some undefined future point in the second.
- The *mitzvot* performed by the protagonists shift from preventing embarrassment to giving charity to keeping one's head covered. The

first two of these are in the category of a "*mitzvah* between human and human" (בין אדם לחבירו) while the third is a "*mitzvah* between a human and God" (בין אדם למקום).

- The astrologers' prediction fails to come true due to inadvertent or chance actions of the protagonist of the first two stories (they did not intend to kill the snakes), as opposed to the constant vigilance of the mother in the third (never leaving her son's head uncovered).

These contrasts among the narrative elements in turn stimulate the audience to consider the theme of astrological influence more broadly, beyond any specific story's particular details, so as to gain a greater understanding of the nature and extent of astrological influence on Jews. If we had been told the first story alone, we might have concluded that only a *mitzvah* to preserve someone's dignity can overcome a pernicious astrological influence. Or that a *mitzvah* can overcome astrological influences that pertain to an unfortunate fate on that same day, but not to a destined event far in the future. Or only those influences that impact men, not women. Likewise, had we heard or read the second story without the others, we might have concluded that giving charity can overcome astrological influences, but other *mitzvot* do not. Or that women can escape their fates, but not men. Or that horoscopes pronounced at birth about the distant future can be averted, but not those celestial influences that impact the present day, as in the first story. Had we only been told the first two stories, we might have concluded that astrological influences causing premature death can be negated, but not those that predict a life of crime or a propensity to sin. Had we received the third story alone, we might have concluded that only rabbis can avoid their fates, or that only *mitzvot* between humans and God can overcome astral powers, but not those *mitzvot* pertaining to relationships among fellow humans.

In offering this varied catalog of relationships between astrology and *mitzvot*, the three stories together thus provide a broader and more general perspective than might be gleaned from any single story or even from two stories in and of themselves. Were the rabbis Greek philosophers like Plato or Aristotle, they would have authored a philosophical tract systematically analyzing the different types of astrology, ways of impacting fates, scope and limitations of astral influences, possibilities and methods of circumventing the forces, and so forth. But the rabbis were not philosophers, and they expressed themselves in a different manner. The story-cycle is designed to address the same questions by bringing the audience into a narrative world that engages different plots, scenarios, encounters, and outcomes. The narratives do not, on the surface, offer systematic or abstract analysis of the issue, but at a deeper level they do provide the audience with an opportunity for similar understandings and insights.

The story-cycle does not completely resolve the tension between astral influences and the standard biblical and rabbinic covenantal theology, in which fate is determined by "reward and punishment," that is, reward for observing the commandments and punishment for sin. Indeed, one of the advantages of addressing an issue through stories, as opposed to a philosophical discourse, is that stories are open to multiple interpretations and can manifest tensions and contradictions without arriving at a complete resolution. To a reader curious about how the rabbinic imagination understands the relationship between fate, or natural science, and the religious worldview that Torah offers us, stories suggest that answers may not be cut and dried—there may be more than one perspective on the significance of the issues that underlie these stories. While few today believe astral determinism to be a type of science (though the presence of horoscopes in newspapers suggests that some aspects of astrology have retained a following), the tension between scientific and theological modes of thought remains relevant. One area where a parallel to this tension between the two worldviews frequently arises is with sickness and health. There is a tension between prayers for healing and petitions for God to remove sickness, recited daily in the weekday liturgy and in special communal prayers on Shabbat (as well as beside hospital beds of the patients), and the medical approach to disease, predicated on the science of viruses, germs, infection, genetics, bodily processes, and suchlike. Understanding sickness as having a divine cause, as punishment for sin and moral failing, as opposed to a scientific-medical explanation, emerges from very different ways of thinking. But in practice many of us live with this tension, perhaps even embrace it, without seeking to resolve it completely. A complex talmudic narrative like this story-cycle gives us both a window into the ways the rabbis grappled with this tension, and a framework for doing so ourselves.

~

Let us take a look at a second example of a story-cycle, a series of stories about charity, which has been an important responsibility of the Jewish community throughout the centuries and to the present day. In this case the story-cycle does not grapple with challenges to Judaism from another worldview, as in the case of astrology, but rather explores different dimensions and complexities of a pillar of Judaism. The following set of four stories is predicated on a *midrash halakhah*, an interpretation of a biblical text:

**דברים טו:ז–ח**

[ז]כי יהיה בך אביון מאחד אחיך באחד שעריך בארצך אשר ה׳ א־להיך נתן לך, לא תאמץ את לבבך ולא תקפץ את ידך מאחיך האביון,

[ח]כי פתח תפתח את ידך לו והעבט תעביטנו **די מחסרו אשר יחסר לו**.

**Deuteronomy 15:7–8**

[7]If there is among you a poor man of your brethren, within any of the gates in your land which YHVH your God is giving you, you shall not harden your heart nor shut your hand from your poor brother,

[8]but you shall open your hand wide to him and willingly lend him **sufficient for his need, whatever he needs**.

This is the New King James Version translation, which sticks close to the Hebrew phrasing and allows us to better understand the rabbinic interpretation. (The NJPS translates 15:8 as, "Rather, you must open your hand and lend him sufficient for whatever he needs.") The commandment to "lend him sufficient for his need, whatever he needs" could be understood in either of two different ways. Does this exhortation indicate the minimum amount of assistance sufficient to maintain a poor person at a basic level of subsistence? In this reading, the verse warns against giving only a token amount of money or food that does not help the poor enough to stave off hunger or emerge from utter penury. This is probably the more straightforward or "contextual" reading of the verse (the *peshat*). But a second reading is also possible: that the verse points to a subjective standard, namely that charity be given to each person sufficient for what they require to feel content—which for some, especially those raised with or accustomed to wealth, may be a considerable amount. The rabbis resolved this dilemma by focusing on the final clause, which appears to be superfluous, as the verse could have ended with "sufficient for his need." They accordingly interpreted the final clause, "whatever he needs" (אשר יחסר לו), as indicating a subjective standard, that the poor must be given whatever they need depending on their individual situations. This understanding appears explicitly in a rabbinic midrash that precedes the stories in the Talmud:[7]

**תלמוד בבלי, כתובות סז ע"ב**

אשר יחסר לו (דברים טו:ח) – אפילו סוס לרכוב עליו ועבד לרוץ לפניו.

**Talmud Bavli, Ketubot 67b**

*Whatever he needs (Deuteronomy 15:8)*—even a horse to ride upon and a servant/slave to run before him.

A horse is a sign of extremely high status, as horses were expensive and required constant care: middle- and lower-class folk might own a donkey or mule but not a horse. Similarly, only the upper classes employed servants or owned slaves. Normally one would not expect that a recipient of alms for their very subsistence be given an expensive horse and the use of a servant. Yet the rabbis recognize that aristocrats used to luxury who lose their fortunes may require some element of the extravagances to which they had been accustomed, in order to make life bearable.

After this midrashic teaching, the Talmud presents the following four stories:

[1] אמרו עליו על הלל הזקן **שלקח לעני בן טובים אחד** סוס לרכוב עליו ועבד לרוץ לפניו. פעם אחת לא מצא עבד לרוץ לפניו ורץ לפניו שלשה מילין.

[2] תנו רבנן: מעשה באנשי גליל העליון **שלקחו לעני בן טובים אחד** מציפורי ליטרא בשר בכל יום...

[3A] **ההוא דאתא לקמיה** דרבי נחמיה. **אמר ליה: במה אתה סועד? א"ל: בבשר** שמן **ויין ישן.**

[3B] רצונך שתגלגל עמי בעדשים? גלגל עמו בעדשים ומת. אמר: אוי לו לזה שהרגו נחמיה...

[4A] **ההוא דאתא לקמיה** דרבא. **אמר לו: במה אתה סועד? אמר לו: בתרנגולת** פטומה **ויין ישן.**

---

7 The teaching also appears in Tosefta Peah 4:10.

[4B] אמר ליה: ולא חיישת לדוחקא דציבורא? א"ל: אטו מדידהו קאכילנא? מדרחמנא קאכילנא. דתנינא: עיני כל אליך ישברו ואתה נותן להם את אכלם בעתו (תהלים קמה:טו). **בעתם** לא נאמר, אלא **בעתו**. מלמד שכל אחד ואחד נותן הקב"ה פרנסתו בעתו.

[4C] אדהכי אתאי אחתיה דרבא, דלא חזיא ליה תליסרי שני, ואתיא ליה תרנגולת פטומה ויין ישן. אמר: מאי דקמאי? א"ל: נענתי לך. קום אכול.

[1] They said about Hillel the Elder that he **purchased for a certain well-born poor man** a horse to ride on and a servant to run before him. Once he did not find a servant to run before him so he ran before him for three miles.

[2] Our sages taught: A story [is told] of the people of the Upper Galilee who **purchased for a certain well-born poor person** from Sepphoris a pound of meat every day…[8]

[3A] **A certain** [poor] **man once came before** R. Neḥemiah [for charity]. **He (R. Neḥemiah) said to him, "What do your meals consist of?" He said to him, "Of** fatty meat **and old wine."**

[3B] [R. Neḥemiah said:] "Will you consent to dine with me on lentils?" He dined with him on lentils and died. He [R. Neḥemiah] said, "Alas for this man whom Neḥemiah has killed."…

[4A] **A certain** [poor] **man once came before** Rava [for charity]. **He said to him, "What do your meals consist of?" He said to him, "Of** fattened chicken **and old wine."**

[4B] He (Rava) said to him, "Do you not consider the burden of the community?" He said, "Do I eat of their [food]? I eat [of the food] of the All-Merciful. For it was taught: *The eyes of all look to You expectantly, and You give them their food in his season (Psalm 145:15)*. It is not said, 'in **their** season' but 'in **his** season.' This teaches that the Holy One, blessed be He, provides for every individual his food in accordance with his own season (=habits)."

8 I have omitted here and after [3B] a brief talmudic clarification about the story.

[4C] Just then Rava's sister arrived, who had not appeared before him for thirteen years, and brought him a fattened chicken and old wine. He (Rava) said, "What is this!?" He said [to the poor man], "I apologize to you. Come and eat."

The four stories divide into two sets of two based on the common phrases, as can be seen from the bolded portions, as well as on the basis of the content. (Compare especially 3A and 4A, which are almost identical, with the exception of the rabbi's name and the type of fatty meat.)

The first story is clearly a narrativization of the *midrash halakhah* that precedes it, generated by the interpretation of the verse as requiring even provision of a horse and servant/slave. That is, the close correlation between the interpretive language of the midrash ("a horse to ride...") and the story's language strongly suggests that the storyteller created a story in which the leading sage Hillel does exactly what the interpretation describes as the extreme case: buy a horse and servant/slave for a formerly wealthy poor man. That the servant/slave's function was to "run before him," to make way for his important master and announce his advent, seems excessive. Yet Hillel not only provided the horse and servant/slave but even played the part himself when none could be found! The absurd lengths to which the great sage went to provide this man his accustomed standard of living makes the didactic point very effectively (albeit not very realistically).

The second story also features "a certain well-born poor" person, an aristocrat who had lost his fortune. Here the community—the people of Upper Galilee—sustain him with an outrageous amount of expensive food, a pound of meat each day, at a time when all but the very upper classes rarely had meat of any kind to eat. This story teaches that the highest quality and most luxurious food must be provided to those poor who were accustomed to eating such delicacies. It complements the story about Hillel, which relates to other comforts.

In the third story, R. Neḥemiah asks a poor man about his typical meals, apparently intending to provide the preferred staple, whether wheat, barley, or other grain. The man, however, replies that he dines daily on "fatty meat and old wine," the diet of the rich [3A]. That the meat is "fatty" and the wine "old" is a nice touch, emphasizing his obscenely sophisticated tastes, as even ordinary meat and new wine would be prohibitively expensive. Ironically, the indigent man's daily fare exceeds that of the rabbi himself, who offers him ordinary and cheap lentils, probably the best food he has available, clearly believing that if lentils are good enough for himself they should suffice for a recipient of alms [3B]. When the man dies after this meal, however, R. Neḥemiah accepts responsibility for the death and laments, "Alas for the man that Neḥemiah killed." This story adds a reason for the ethic of providing the poor "whatever he needs" as modeled in the previous two stories, and a warning that deviating from this standard may be catastrophic.

The final story, the most literarily developed, begins like the third story: a poor man requests alms, the rabbi asks as to his preference, and the man replies with an extravagantly rich diet: fattened chicken meat and old wine. Here the rabbi continues by raising a concern that must be foremost in the audience's mind: Does not the responsibility to provide "whatever he needs" place an unreasonable burden on the community? How is the community to afford such luxuries? Where do all these funds come from? And would not sustaining a former aristocrat at this excessive level come at the cost of providing alms to many others who may simply require basic staples? Rava's pointed question may even be intended to make this individual feel guilty, as if to say: how can you expect the community to pay for such lavish feasts when there are so many other people in need and other worthy causes? But if Rava expected the man to revise his culinary preferences, he must have been sorely disappointed. Instead the man claims that whatever he receives from charity is essentially earmarked for him in the divine economy, and therefore he cannot be charged with depleting community resources [4B]. He argues his case with a midrashic teaching based on a grammatical inconsistency in Psalm 145:15, which praises God for providing food to all creatures. The verse switches from plural to singular, beginning that God "gives them *their* food" and continuing "in *his* season," instead of the expected "in *their* season" (ואתה נותן להם את אכלם בעתו). The switch to the singular indicates that God apportions food for all in accordance with each individual's proclivities or habits, understanding the Hebrew word for "season" or "time" (עת) in this sense. Rava's view that a community has limited resources to be divided among all the poor is incorrect. Rather, God supplies the world with all the food necessary for all humans to have their fill, whether of modest and basic food staples or refined and extravagant delicacies.

As Rava mulls over this claim, his sister unexpectedly shows up bringing a gift of…fattened chickens and old wine [4C]! That she has not visited for thirteen years proves that her appearance is not a coincidence but rather a sign from above. ("Thirteen" is a stock number in talmudic stories that essentially means "a great many" and need not be taken exactly.) Faced with this incontrovertible "evidence" that God indeed supplies each individual "whatever he needs" and provides sustenance "in accordance with his season," Rava apologizes and offers the bounty to the man, evidently the intended recipient. God may work in strange ways, but at least those ways are crystal clear! This story thus raises the obvious problem with the standard of "sufficient for his need, whatever he needs," but parries it with a one-two punch: first, a midrashic teaching that God in fact provides this high level of sustenance, and second, empirical proof in the miraculous advent of Rava's long-lost sister with her chicken.

Taken together, the four stories comprise a story-cycle that explores different aspects of the rabbinic ethic of charity. The first pair of stories sets forth the high standard and applies it to material comforts (horse, servant/slave) and food (a pound of meat). Hillel serves as a role model, not only providing a horse and servant/slave but acting the part himself when necessary. The second pair of stories addresses possible objections to this ethic: the inequity of an indigent man eating better than the rabbi (and perhaps the community members, too), the source of the funds, and the burden imposed on a community to provide sumptuous dinners, with the possible trade-off of not being able to supply cheaper food for other needy individuals. The stories resolve the objections in striking and memorable fashion, with a poor man dropping dead and the serendipitous arrival of the right food at the right time.

Here I have essentially expressed the ideas and themes of the story-cycle in a more conceptual way, translating the narrative elements into abstract ideas. But again, the meaning of the stories and story-cycle as a whole should not be reduced to these formulations. The ideas emerge from the juxtaposition and relationship of the stories within the story-cycle, through the comparisons and contrasts that surface when assessing the stories together. The narrative cycle reflects systematic thinking on this topic, though not expressed in an abstract and philosophical manner.

The questions raised by this story-cycle continue to be relevant today, and it is not clear that we have successfully resolved the issues any more than the talmudic sages. Given the limited resources available to the community or to a particular charitable foundation (or to the wider society for that matter), how ought those resources be distributed? Is it better, for example, to provide jobs and vocational training to make some needy individuals self-sufficient, which could be considered the standard of "whatever he/she needs," even if that investment might reduce contributions to a food pantry, depriving others of basic necessities? Similarly, these considerations can be difficult to negotiate for us as individuals when thinking about giving a certain percentage of our income to charity.

The stories also raise broader moral and theological questions for the audience to ponder. How central a role should faith in God's future beneficence play when apportioning resources? Should we as a community each year distribute all contributions, exhaust food stores and charity bank accounts, trusting in the poor man's response to Rava (as confirmed by the timely arrival of the sister) that God will provide? Should we act this way as individuals too, when thinking either of our own needs or our personal giving? The value of preserving the dignity of every individual and avoiding shame, although not mentioned explicitly, hovers in the background, as the standard of "sufficient for his need" is motivated, in part, to prevent people from feeling ashamed by their poverty.[9] Beyond providing charity for each individual that is sufficient to meet their needs, how do we ensure that their dignity is respected in other aspects of their lives? How can we make sure that others do not feel ashamed, for example, by their lack of education, athletic ability, or disability? The story-cycle does not provide facile answers to these questions, but rather, in offering multiple contrasting narratives, offers a more complex way to address them, helping us think through the factors and trade-offs involved.

---

9 Preventing shame is explicitly mentioned in the Talmud following the story of Mar Ukba that follows shortly after these stories, discussed in the Introduction of this book.

# CHAPTER 7
## Comparative Analysis

COMPARATIVE ANALYSIS, WHICH draws on the multiple contexts in which stories appear, is a useful tool that helps us appreciate both the literary features of a story and the lessons the storyteller wishes to communicate. Many rabbinic stories appear in different versions in disparate rabbinic compilations: the Bavli, for example, may contain one version of a story, while a different version, known as a "parallel" or "literary parallel," appears in the Yerushalmi or a book of midrash. Often these parallel versions resulted from later storytellers reworking an earlier story in light of their own concerns, which differed from those of the original storyteller. The later storytellers may have wished to emphasize a different value, or teach a different lesson, or simply adapt the story to their cultural situation. In some cases we can be reasonably certain that one version of the story was earlier than the other and the later storyteller changed that earlier story, or a version very similar to it. In other cases it is difficult to determine which version was original: both versions may derive from a still earlier version that did not come down to us, and multiple versions may have circulated simultaneously. Comparing two—and sometimes three or four—versions of the story helps us focus on the interests of each storyteller, especially when it seems likely that a later version reworked an earlier one.

One of the stories we discussed in chapter 6, the first of the cycle grappling with the relationship between *mitzvot* and astrology, describes how Avlat, a Persian sage, makes a dire prediction about the fate of a man who sets forth for his daily work. A parallel version of that story appears in the Yerushalmi, which provides us a good opportunity to illustrate the comparative method. Arranging the two versions of the story in parallel columns makes it easier to perceive the similarities and differences between them. However, the first step is to analyze each version independently, as each story has its own literary integrity. Since we analyzed the Bavli version in chapter 6 (pp. 181–90), here we will begin with an analysis of the Yerushalmi story. With that in hand, we can return to our parallel columns and compare the two versions so as to identify what they have in common and where they diverge. The comparisons will enhance our understanding of the Bavli story that emerged from the close reading by illustrating the "way not taken," a possible alternative storyline that the Bavli storytellers did not adopt. Indeed, it seems that the Yerushalmi version is more original, and the Bavli storytellers deliberately introduced changes to teach a different lesson that was important to them.

| תלמוד בבלי, שבת קנו ע"ב | תלמוד ירושלמי, שבת ו:ח (ח ע"ד)[1] |
|---|---|
| [2A] דשמואל ואבלט – כי הוו יתבי ואזלי הנך אינשי לאגמא. א"ל אבלט לשמואל: האי גברא אזיל ולא אתי וטריק ליה חיויא ומאית. | [1A] תרין תלמידין מן דרבי חנינה הוון נפקין מקטוע כיסין. חמתון חדא איסטרולוגוס: אילין תרין מי נפקין ולא חזרין. |
| [2B] א"ל שמואל: אזיל ואתי. | [1B] מי נפקין פגע בהון חד סב. אמר לון: זכון עמי דאית לי תלתא יומין דלא טעמית כלום. והוה עמון חד עיגול. קצון פלגא ויהבינה ליה. אכל וצלי עליהון. אמר לון: תקיים לכון נפשיכון בהדין יומך היך דקיימתון לי נפשי בהדין יומא. |

1 The story is found at Shabbat 6:9 in some printings of the Yerushalmi.

| | |
|---|---|
| [1C] נפקון בשלם וחזרון בשלם. והוון תמן בני אינש דשמעון קליה. אמרין ליה: ולא כן אמרת אילין תרין מי נפקין ולא חזרין? אמר: אי דהכא גברא שקר דאיסתרולוגייא דידיה שקרין. אפילו כן אזלון ופשפשון ואשכחון חכינתה פלגא בהדא מובלא ופלגא בהדא מובלא. | [2C] אדיתבי קא עסקי ביה, אזיל ואתא. קם אבלט, שדייה לטוניה, אשכח ביה חיויא דפסיק ושאדי בתרתי גובי. |
| [1D] אמרו: מה טיבו עבידתכון יומא דין ותניין ליה עובדא. | [2D] א״ל שמואל: מה עבדת? א״ל: כל יומא הוינא מרמינן ריפתא בהדי הדדי ואכלינן. והאידנא הוה איכא חד גבן דלא הוה ליה ריפתא בהדיה והוה מכסיף. אמינא לחבראי: אנא קאימנא ומרמינא ליה ריפתא. כי מטאי לגביה שוי נפשאי כמאן דשקלי מיניה, כי היכי דלא ליכסיף. א״ל: מצוה קא עבדת ואתצלת. |
| [1E] אמר: ומה ההוא גברא יכיל עביד? דאלההון די יהודאי מתפייס בפלגות עיגול. | [2E] נפק שמואל לבי מדרשא ודרש: וצדקה תציל ממות (משלי י:ב, יא:ד). ולא ממיתה משונה אלא אפילו ממיתה עצמה. |

**1. Yerushalmi Shabbat 6:8 (8d)**

[1A] Two students of R. Ḥaninah went out to cut wood. A certain astrologer saw them. He said, "These two will go out but not return."

[1B] When they went out they came upon a certain old man. He said to them, "Give me alms, for it has been three days since I have tasted anything." They had a loaf of bread. They cut it in half and gave it to him. He ate and prayed for them. He said to them, "May your souls be preserved this day just as you have preserved my soul for me this day."

[1C] They went out safely and came back safely. There were some men there who had heard his (the astrologer's) words. They said to him, "Did you not say, 'These two will go out but not return'"? He said, "There is here a man of lies (=me) whose astrology is lies." Even so they went and searched and found a snake, half in this one's load and half in the other's.

**2. Bavli Shabbat 156b**

[2A] For Shmuel and Avlat (a Persian sage)—while they were sitting, certain men were going to the field. Avlat said to Shmuel, "That man will go but not come back, as a snake will bite him and he will die."

[2B] Shmuel said to him, "He will go and come back."

[2C] While they were sitting and discussing it, he went and came back. Avlat arose, threw off his (the man's) load, and found there a snake that had been cut and thrown into two pieces.

| | |
|---|---|
| [1D] They said, "What good deed did you do today?" They told them the deed. | [2D] Shmuel said to him, "What did you do?" He said to him, "Every day we throw the bread together [for a common meal] and eat. Today there was one with us who had no bread with him, and he was ashamed. I said to my companions, 'I will get up and throw (=collect) the bread for him.' When I arrived at him, I pretended as if I had taken from him, in order that he not be ashamed." He (Shmuel) said to him, "You did a *mitzvah* and were saved." |
| [1E] He (the astrologer) said, "What can I do? For the God of the Jews is appeased by half a loaf." | [2E] Shmuel went out to the study house and expounded, "*Righteousness (tzedakah) saves from death (Proverbs 10:2, 11:4)*. Not [only] from an unusual death but even from death itself." |

Let us briefly analyze the Yerushalmi story in the left column before comparing it to the Bavli version we analyzed in chapter 6. Here the students' safe homecoming [1C] demonstrates the untruth of the astrologer's prediction that they would go out but fail to return [1A]. Those who had heard his dire words thereupon call the astrologer on his claim, and he has no choice but to concede that he has spoken falsely and that his entire astrological belief system "is lies" [1C]. Nevertheless, these anonymous onlookers suspect that there is more to the story than that. Maybe they have witnessed this same astrologer's prognostications come true in the past, or they may simply believe so deeply in astrology that they cannot accept that a fate read in the stars should completely fail to transpire. Indeed, upon searching the "loads" carried by the students, the two backpacks or bundles of wood, they find a snake that might well have killed the students, just as the astrologer predicted, severed in two halves distributed evenly between the two loads. They inquire as to what virtuous act the students performed to merit such deliverance [1D], and are told about the bread given to the poor man [1B]. At this point the challenges for the audience are to figure out exactly how the snake was cut and to put together the two elements of the students' account—the encounter with the poor man and the severed serpent—into a coherent whole.

Now from the fact that the two students "went out to cut wood," we know that they had with them an axe or other such sharp cutting tool. This is presumably the same implement with which they cut the loaf of bread in half when solicited by the poor man. The sequence of events now falls into place: First, the students set down their packs to remove the loaf of bread and the axe. Then, while they are giving the bread to the man, receiving his blessing, and perhaps conversing briefly, a snake crawled into one of the packs and then began slithering its long body into the adjacent pack that was set down right next to it. As the students reinserted the remaining half-loaf of bread and axe into their packs, the axe happened to sever the snake in two, such that the head and front part remained in one pack while the bottom half slipped back into the other.

In this way the poor man's prayer comes true according to the measure-for-measure principle: the students' souls were "preserved this day," just as they saved the man's life that day. That the students' lives were saved in one and the same act of saving the man's life creates the ultimate measure-for-measure lesson. Generally the measure-for-measure principle of reward and punishment holds that a good or evil deed is repaid in kind: one who steals will ultimately be the victim of theft, while one who helps carry another's burden will merit that others help carry theirs. But the payback will typically happen at some future time: sooner or later measure-for-measure justice will kick in and punish or reward the agent. In this case, however, the very act of cutting the bread brings about the deliverance there and then. The two halves of the loaf correspond nicely to the two halves of the snake, and the severing of the one to save the man leads swiftly to the severing of the other to save the two students. It is possible to reconstruct the events differently: maybe the snake is cut at the end of the day when the students finish their wood-chopping labor and return the axe to their packs, or when they take a break for lunch, or at some other point. But I think the storyteller intends us to reconstruct the events with this ultimate measure-for-measure principle, which also maximizes the aesthetic quality of the story.

The astrologer—probably consoled that his art was not completely off base, yet annoyed that celestial influences can be superseded—now pronounces the didactic point: the "God of the Jews" can be "appeased" or conciliated by even a trivial amount of charity [1E]. It does not take great acts of piety—years of Torah study, saving many human lives, defending the Jewish people from persecution, or giving away a fortune in charity—to merit that God alter one's fate in the most dramatic way, from death to life. While astrology might impact all human affairs, even a simple and inexpensive *mitzvah* possesses sufficient power to overcome astral influences.

This lesson, I believe, is a powerful embodiment of a core aspect of rabbinic theology and the rabbinic understanding of God as "the Merciful One" (הרחמן/*ha-Raḥaman*). We might think that it is extremely difficult to achieve righteousness or holiness, to attain a status such that God would take note of our deeds. We might think that giving small amounts of charity, and, by extension, carrying out a simple *mitzvah*, do little good in the grand scheme of things, and are outweighed by faults and failings. The story teaches the opposite: "the God of the Jews is appeased by half a loaf." Even small acts of righteousness and piety can have momentous consequences.

At this point we are in position to compare the two stories. It should be clear that, despite the differences, they must be considered two versions of a single story, as evidenced by the same basic plot: an astrologer predicts that a man or men setting out to their work will not return; that work involves cutting trees and foliage; the men perform a *mitzvah*; they return safely; the packs are searched and a snake is found severed in two pieces; the man or men are asked about what they did that day; the *mitzvah* is recounted; a lesson is pronounced. In particular, the shared motif of a snake crawling into a pack or load and inadvertently severed in two is extremely distinctive: it does not appear anywhere else in all of rabbinic literature, or even, to the best of my knowledge, anywhere else in all of world literature.

In light of the strong similarity between the two versions, the differences between them focus our attention on their different lessons, or different areas of importance to the respective storytellers. The main difference between the stories is the nature of the *mitzvah* performed by the heroes. While in the Yerushalmi version the students give charity to the poor man, in the Bavli version the protagonist preserves the dignity of his fellow worker. Thus the storytellers employed this same basic plot pattern in order to teach different messages about the importance of different *mitzvot*. These messages may simply have been the storytellers' personal concerns at the time, though the differences may also point to issues that were most pressing in their respective cultures or be due to a specific crisis that obtained when they told the story. The Yerushalmi storyteller wished to impress his audience with the importance of giving alms, perhaps because he knew many people on the verge of starvation or suffering from extreme poverty, while the Bavli storyteller endeavored to teach that one must go to great lengths to prevent others from experiencing embarrassment, perhaps because to be publicly shamed was a horrific experience in his environment.[2]

Another prominent difference is the role of Shmuel and the setting in the Bavli version within the broader rabbinic world. In the Yerushalmi two rabbinic students perform the *mitzvah* of giving charity, but they do not really take part in the main tension between astrology and the Jewish worldview. Some anonymous people confront the astrologer and search the packs, and the astrologer himself articulates the didactic point at the end. In the Bavli these roles almost switch: here the protagonist is an anonymous man while the rabbi, Shmuel, confronts the astrologer and pronounces the didactic point. Indeed, Shmuel plays a central role throughout the Bavli story: opposing Avlat's pronouncement, inquiring as to the deed, explaining "You did a *mitzvah* and were saved," and then expounding the lesson in the rabbinic study house with a scriptural quotation and midrashic interpretation. This ending connects the narrative to the truth of Torah; the story becomes an exemplification of the eternal teachings of scripture, and Shmuel's teaching provides a more general lesson about the power of "righteousness." In the Yerushalmi the explicit didactic point is limited to almsgiving; the audience may infer that other righteous deeds

---

2 On shame in rabbinic culture, see Rubenstein, *Culture of the Babylonian Talmud*, 67–79.

also counteract baleful astrological influences, but the story makes no such claim. The Bavli story seems to reflect a rabbinic institutional setting, presumably the rabbinic academy where the sages studied, conversed, prayed, spent many of their waking hours, and told these types of stories. The Yerushalmi version is a popular tale that originally may have been told in a synagogue or some other popular setting. The Yerushalmi story is more similar to a folktale with anonymous character types: students, an astrologer, some unidentified people. The only clue as to its setting is the identification of the students with their teacher R. Ḥaninah, but this named rabbi plays no role in the story itself. The storyteller has done the minimum to provide any specificity to the story, which would work equally well without the mention of R. Ḥaninah or with any other rabbi in his place. In the Bavli, by contrast, the named rabbi, Shmuel, is the central character, and we also hear of his conversation-partner and fellow sage, Avlat, in addition to the house of study where he teaches. This story is not a folktale but rather a biographical anecdote about the great Rabbi Shmuel, the subject of many other stories in the Bavli.

The different temporal structures of the two stories offer interesting insight into narrative technique. While the Yerushalmi version proceeds in a straightforward, linear sequence, the Bavli displaces the account of the man's good deed and then relates it as a flashback, as can be seen by comparing sections [1B] and [2B], [1D] and [2D]. In the Yerushalmi the audience knows what the students have done to merit deliverance [1B], although the other characters within the story do not, so the storyteller need not repeat the events and suffices with "They told them the deed" [1D]. In the Bavli neither the audience nor the other characters know of the good deed [2B]. The storyteller tells the story from the viewpoint of Shmuel, who sees the man return but was not privy to his actions that day. Both Shmuel and the audience learn what transpired as the man details his meritorious acts to the rabbi [2D]. This temporal structure creates a puzzle for the audience that is lacking in the Yerushalmi: we initially see the man has returned safely but do not why until he reports the events (though in both stories we must reconstruct how the snake was severed).

These differences in the acting characters, settings, and temporal structure do not impact the fundamental didactic messages, about charity in the Yerushalmi and about preventing humiliation in the Bavli. Rather, comparing and contrasting these aspects of the stories help us appreciate *how* these messages are communicated by the storyteller and received by the audiences. In addition, awareness of these different techniques contributes to our understanding of the aesthetic qualities of rabbinic stories and the narrative art of the storytellers. They shed light on the ways in which the stories work as stories and what makes them effective as didactic literature.

Let me briefly note that comparing the versions also helps us understand how one original story may have developed into two. In this case it appears that the Yerushalmi's version is original, and the Bavli storyteller reworked that story, or a version similar to it. Both meritorious deeds involve food and a poor person, though in almost opposite ways: in the Yerushalmi the students give food to the old man, while in the Bavli the protagonist pretends to take food from his colleague. This scenario in the Bavli is somewhat contrived—a potluck lunch where one worker collects the food from the others. It appears that the Bavli storyteller wished to replace the message about charity with that of preventing embarrassment, so he transformed the good deed but retained the elements of food and a poor person.

Because of this switch in emphasis, the Bavli's version of the story flows less smoothly than the version in the Yerushalmi does. In the Yerushalmi the students take out their cutting implement to cut the bread in half, so we can easily fill the narrative gap of how the snake came to be severed. All the parts of the story fit neatly together: the tool to cut wood; the bread cut in half that both leads to, and corresponds with, the severed snake; and the beautiful measure-for-measure motif that materializes in one and the same act. Because no bread is cut in the Bavli, due to the transformation of giving charity (by cutting the bread) to preserving dignity (by pretending to take food), it is much more difficult to fill in the narrative gap of how the snake was severed, while the omission of the prayer that accompanies the charitable act also entails the loss of the measure-for-measure principle. Thus in his efforts to change the type of the meritorious act, the Bavli storyteller detracted from the narrative art of the story. The Bavli storyteller also made other changes that relate to the Babylonian rabbinic situation, making the great Babylonian sage Shmuel the hero and pitting him against Avlat, a Persian sage known to debate Shmuel in other Bavli passages, and then having Shmuel offer the lesson in the quintessential rabbinic midrashic form in the study house, the main rabbinic institution. These kinds of changes are typical of how later storytellers rework earlier stories: they update aspects of stories that have become dated or are not familiar to their audience, while altering narrative elements to conform to their present circumstances.

Tracing the story's literary development does not necessarily decrease our appreciation of the didactic messages of either story in its own right, and one can profitably compare the two versions without trying to determine priority. At the same time, this approach can provide insights as to why we encounter difficulties understanding elements of a story, as well as how major gaps can develop. In some cases a story does not flow smoothly, or its parts do not cohere as neatly as one might expect, because it has been reworked, adapted, and changed to fit a later storyteller's purposes. Comparing versions also sheds light on the methods of rabbinic storytellers in general and the processes by which they constructed stories to emphasize religious, halakhic, or social lessons that they wanted to teach.

~

Here is another good example of how an analysis that compares versions of a story to each other can help us appreciate what each rabbinic storyteller is trying to teach us and, through that process, ultimately bring larger questions of meaning into view. In this case we have three versions of a story, and each storyteller has a different assessment of the relative weight that rabbis should place upon two important Jewish values: Torah study, on the one hand, and duties to one's wife and family, on the other.[3]

---

3 This discussion draws on Ofra Meir, "Editorial Influence"; Yonah Frankel, *The Aggadic Narrative*, 51–60; and Jeffrey L. Rubenstein, *Culture of the Babylonian Talmud*, 103–12.

| 1. בראשית רבה צה [4] | 2. ויקרא רבה כא:ח [5] | 3. תלמוד בבלי, כתובות סב ע״ב |
|---|---|---|
| | | [3A]<br>רבי חנניה בן חכינאי הוה קאזיל לבי רב בשילהי הלוליה דר״ש בן יוחאי. א״ל: איעכב לי עד דאתי בהדך. לא איעכבא ליה. |
| [1B]<br>חנניה בן חכיניי ור׳ שמעון בן יוחיי הלכו ללמד תורה אצל ר׳ עקיבה בבני ברק ועשו שם שלש עשרה שנה. | [2B]<br>ר׳ חנניה בן חכינאי ור׳ שמעון בן יוחי הלכו ללמוד תורה אצל ר׳ עקיבה בבני ברק. שהו שם שלש עשרה שנה. | [3B]<br>אזל יתיב תרי סרי שני בבי רב. |
| [1C]<br>ר׳ שמעון בן יוחיי הוה משלח כתבין לבייתיה והוה ידע מה בבייתיה. חנניה בן חכיניי לא הוה משלח כתבין לבייתיה ולא הוה ידע מה בבייתיה. | [2C]<br>ר׳ שמעון בן יוחי משלח וידע מה בגו בייתא. ר׳ חנינה בן חכיניי לא הוה שלח וידע מה בגו בייתא. | |
| [1D]<br>שלחה אשתו ואמרה לו: בתך בגרה. בא והשיאה. | [2D]<br>שלחה אשתו ואמרה לו: בתך בגרה. בוא והשיאה. | |
| | [2E]<br>ואפעלפי כן, לא הלך. | |

4 *Midrash Bereishit Rabbah*, ed. J. Theodor and H. Albeck (reprint: Jerusalem, 1965), 1232 (in the Vatican 30 Manuscript).

5 Vayikra Rabbah, ed. M. Margulies, 484–86.

| 1 | 2 | 3 |
|---|---|---|
| [1F]<br>צפה ר׳ עקיבה ברוח הקודש. אמר: כל מי שיש לו בת בוגרת, ילך וישיאה. | [2F]<br>צפה ר׳ עקיבה ברוח הקודש. ואמ׳ להן: כל מי שיש לו בת בוגרת, ילך וישיאה. | |
| | [2G]<br>ידע מהו שמע. קם נסב רשותא ואזל. | |
| | [2H]<br>אזל בעי לה בגו בייתא ואשכחה דפניית לזווית אחרי. | [3H]<br>עד דאתי אישתנו שבילי דמתא, ולא ידע למיזל לביתיה. |
| [1J]<br>מה עבד? אזל למליתה. שמע קלהן דמלוותיה אמרן: בתו שלחכיניי! מליי קולתיך וסוק ליך. | [2J]<br>מה עבד? אזל ויתב ליה על מלויתהון דנשיא. שמע קלהון דטלייא אמרין: בת חכיניי מלאי קולתיך וסוק ליך! | [3J]<br>אזל יתיב אגודא דנהרא. שמע לההיא רביתא דהוו קרו לה: בת חכינאי! בת חכינאי! מלי קולתך, ותא ניזיל. |
| [1K]<br>הוות מהלכה והוא מהלך בתרה עד זמן דעלת לבייתיה. | [2K]<br>מה עשה? היה מהלך אחריה עד שנכנסה לתוך ביתו. | [3K]<br>אמר: שמע מינה האי רביתא דידן. אזל בתרה. |
| | [2L]<br>נכנס אחריה פתאום. | |
| [1M]<br>לא הספיקה ביתו לראותו עד שיצאתה נשמתה. | [2M]<br>לא הספיקה אשתו לראותו עד שיצתה נשמתה. | [3M]<br>הוה יתיבא דביתהו קא נהלה קמחא. דל עינה, חזיתיה, סוי לבה פרח רוחה. |
| [1N]<br>ואית דאמרין חזרת. | [2N]<br>אמ׳ לפניו: רבונו שלעולם! ענייה זו, זו שכרה לאחר שלש עשרה שנה? באותה שעה חזרה נפשה לגופה. | [3N]<br>אמר לפניו: רבש״ע, ענייה זו, זה שכרה? בעא רחמי עלה וחייה. |

| 1. Bereishit Rabbah 95 | 2. Vayikra Rabbah 21:8 | 3. Talmud Bavli, Ketubot 62b |
|---|---|---|
| | | [3A] R. Ḥananiah b. Ḥakhinai was going to the study house at the conclusion of the wedding celebration of R. Shimon b. Yoḥai. He (R. Shimon b. Yoḥai) said to him: “Wait for me until I [am ready to] go with you.” He did not wait. |
| [1B] Ḥananiah b. Ḥakhinai and R. Shimon b. Yoḥai went to study Torah with R. Akiva in Bnei Berak and studied there for thirteen years. | [2B] R. Ḥananiah b. Ḥakhinai and R. Shimon b. Yoḥai went to study Torah with R. Akiva in Bnei Berak. They stayed there for thirteen years. | [3B] He went and sat in the study house for twelve years. |
| [1C] R. Shimon b. Yoḥai would send letters home and he knew what was [going on] in his home. Ḥananiah b. Ḥakhinai did not send letters home and did not know what was going on in his home. | [2C] R. Shimon b. Yoḥai sent [letters] and knew what was [going on] in his home. R. Ḥananiah b. Ḥakhinai did not send [letters] to know what was going on in his home. | |

| | | |
|---|---|---|
| [1D]<br>His (Ḥananiah b. Ḥakhinai's) wife sent to him saying, "Your daughter has grown up. Come and arrange for her marriage." | [2D]<br>His (R. Ḥananiah b. Ḥakhinai's) wife sent to him saying, "Your daughter has grown up. Come and arrange for her marriage." | |
| | [2E]<br>Nevertheless, he did not go. | |
| [1F]<br>By means of the holy spirit, R. Akiva saw. He said: "Whoever has a daughter who has grown up, let him go and arrange for her marriage." | [2F]<br>By means of the holy spirit, R. Akiva saw. He said to them: "Whoever has a daughter who has grown up, let him go and arrange for her marriage." | |
| | [2G]<br>He (R. Ḥananiah b. Ḥakhinai) knew what he heard. He arose and received permission (from R. Akiva to depart) and left. | |
| | [2H]<br>He went and tried [to find] his house and found that it had been moved to another place [within the village]. | [3H]<br>Before he returned the streets of his village had changed, and he did not know how to get to his home. |

| | | |
|---|---|---|
| [1J]<br>What did he (Ḥananiah b. Ḥakhinai) do? He went to the watering trough. He heard the women who were drawing water say: "Daughter of Ḥakhinai! Fill your pitcher and go on up." | [2J]<br>What did he do? He went and sat where the women draw water. He heard the voices of the young women saying, "Daughter of Ḥakhinai! Fill your pitcher and go on up." | [3J]<br>He went and sat on the bank of the river. He heard them saying to a certain girl: "Daughter of Ḥakhinai! Daughter of Ḥakhinai! Fill your pitcher, come and we will go." |
| [1K]<br>She walked and he walked behind her until the time she entered his home. | [2K]<br>What did he do? He was walking after her until she entered his home. | [3K]<br>He thought, "That means this girl is mine!" He followed her [home]. |
| | [2L]<br>He entered after her suddenly. | |
| [1M]<br>His wife had barely seen him when her soul departed. | [2M]<br>His wife had barely seen him when her soul departed. | [3M]<br>His wife was sitting and sifting flour. She raised up her eyes, saw him, her heart leaped and her soul flew away. |
| [1N]<br>And some say that it (the soul) returned. | [2N]<br>He said before Him (God): "Master of the Universe! This poor woman—such is her reward after thirteen years?"<br>At that instant her soul returned to her body. | [3N]<br>He said before Him (God): "Master of the Universe! This poor woman—such is her reward?" He prayed for her and she lived. |

The first, probably earliest, version of the story appears in Bereishit Rabbah, a midrashic compilation on the Book of Genesis, edited about 400 CE. The story divides nicely into two parts: the first set in the house of study [1A–1F], the second in Ḥananiah b. Ḥakhinai's village and home [1G–1N]. The two sages spend "thirteen years" studying Torah with the great R. Akiva in Bnei Berak, apparently far from their unspecified hometowns, as they do not return home during this entire time. As noted in the previous chapter, "thirteen" (also "twelve" in the Bavli's version, 3B) is a stock number in rabbinic sources and essentially means "many years." Granted that travel was much more difficult in antiquity than today, this lengthy absence nevertheless seems excessive. We must be careful, of course, not to anachronistically project our contemporary values upon the rabbis—study of Torah was their greatest value, so the uninterrupted years dedicated to this highest pursuit would have been praiseworthy. Ḥananiah b. Ḥakhinai's main failing, for the storyteller, seems to be not the years away from home per se, but the lack of communication with, and concern for, his family. The contrast between Ḥananiah, who "did not send letters home" and consequently "did not know what was going on in his home," and his colleague R. Shimon b. Yoḥai, who would "send letters home" and accordingly "knew what was [going on] in his home," expresses criticism for Ḥananiah's negligent behavior [1C]. Not only that, but even after his wife summons him to return after his daughter has matured, Ḥananiah tarries and does not leave until his master R. Akiva directs him to go [1F]. The "holy spirit" here is a quasi-prophetic ability some rabbis possess that provides supernatural knowledge; R. Akiva perceived that his student was needed at home, despite not being privy to the letter.

Upon arriving at his village, Ḥananiah b. Ḥakhinai does not proceed directly to his home but rather to the central well or cistern where women procure water [1J]. The storyteller does not tell us exactly why, though we should probably infer that he no longer knows the way—another indication of alienation from his domestic life in contrast to his academic pursuits. Unsurprisingly, he does not recognize his daughter, and only identifies her when he hears other women calling her name. The storyteller deftly has the women refer to her as "Daughter of Ḥakhinai" after her grandfather, not "Daughter of Ḥananiah" after her father, which marks Ḥananiah's absence from home and family in her very identity. Nor does Ḥananiah speak or interact with his daughter but rather trails at some distance behind her—the physical distance another sign of emotional estrangement [1K]. When he enters his home unannounced and unexpected, the shock of seeing her husband in flesh and blood after the long absence proves too much for the wife and she dies [1M]. The concluding attempt to mitigate the catastrophe, that "some say" the wife revived, was probably added later by transmitters who deemed the original story too tragic for their tastes [1N]. Even so, that she either died or almost died due to her husband's insensitivity, in being incommunicado for years and then making a sudden and unexpected entrance to the house, teaches a lesson about proper conduct—at the expense of Ḥananiah, who serves as a negative role model. The story recognizes a conflict between two leading rabbinic values, Torah study and domestic responsibilities, and warns that commitment to the former should not entail neglect of the latter.

The version in Vayikra Rabbah, edited around a century later, about 500 CE, is much the same until the ending. The storyteller expanded the story slightly with a few lines of clarification and embellishment, especially in the first half [2E, 2G, 2H]. He makes explicit that R. Ḥananiah (here provided with the honorific title "Rabbi") refused to heed the summons from his wife [2E] until R. Akiva directed him to depart [2F], which was implied but not actually stated in the Bereishit Rabbah version. The addition that R. Ḥananiah "knew what he heard" also underscores R. Ḥananiah's reluctance to leave: the phrase means that he realized that R. Akiva was speaking specifically to him despite the delicate general formulation ("whoever has a daughter...", [2G]). In the second half the storyteller explains that R. Ḥananiah could not find his way home because his family had moved during his absence [2H]. This explanation departs slightly from the implication of Bereishit Rabbah, namely that he had simply forgotten where he lived, and portrays Ḥananiah in marginally more favorable light: he could not find his way home not on account of forgetting his family, but because his wife had moved in the interim. The added description that R. Ḥananiah "entered after her suddenly" [2L] clarifies that the rabbi's arrival was abrupt, as implied in the version of Bereishit Rabbah.

The ending of the story, however, has been changed much more substantively with the unambiguous happy ending, in stark contrast to the conclusion of the first version, which leaves open the possibility of the finality of her death [2N versus 1N]. R. Ḥananiah's prayer focuses on the wife's patient suffering during the years of his absence and protests the injustice of her fate—and she miraculously revives. We are probably meant to understand that the long years of Torah study and the merit for this devotion are in part responsible for the efficacy of the rabbi's prayer. The reversal of the wife's death, her "reward" for waiting, is thus a function of the husband's reward for Torah study. Moreover, his reference to his wife as "this poor woman" expresses sympathy for her plight, perhaps even a modicum of contrition, suggesting the rabbi is not completely insensitive to the larger picture.

The lesson of the story is accordingly more complex. Certainly one takeaway is the importance of not entering one's house suddenly after a long absence, which seems trivial, but may have been more difficult to orchestrate in antiquity absent modern methods of communication. At least the sage should have kept in touch with letters and communication that would have informed his family of his return. The same contrast between R. Ḥananiah and R. Shimon b. Yoḥai about keeping in touch with home emphasizes this failing, as does the explicit need for R. Akiva to reinforce the summons, and the ironic naming of the daughter after the grandfather. But the optimistic ending and the fact that God answers the rabbi's prayer lessen the criticism and leave the audience with a mixed message, something like: if a student or rabbi pursues the worthy goal of spending long years of study away from home, at least he should try to keep in touch and give advance warning of his return. And insofar as there may be some judgment of R. Ḥananiah's failing in ignoring his wife's feelings and needs, it seems mitigated by the implication that the same scholarship gave him the merit to ask for her revival.

In the third and latest version, that of the Babylonian Talmud, the first part of the story has been altered considerably over against the first two versions, while the ending has been kept pretty much the same as that of Vayikra Rabbah. Here the exposition relates that R. Ḥananiah was so eager to get to the house of study that he would not even wait a few days for his friend and colleague, R. Shimon b. Yoḥai, to accompany him [3A]. A wedding celebration typically lasts seven days, and the story takes place "at the conclusion" of the festivities—perhaps a day or two more to go—yet R. Ḥananiah b. Ḥakhinai will not delay for his newly wedded companion. This opening points both to his enthusiasm and passion for Torah study—he absolutely cannot wait!—and perhaps also his low estimation of marriage and domestic commitments. Another sage might have understood the importance of nuptial celebration both for a groom and a bride, welcomed the opportunity to continue participating in his colleague's party, and certainly tarried a few days more so the two scholars could embark together.

R. Ḥananiah returns home after "twelve" years and cannot find his house because the village has grown and changed in the interim—a slight variation on the second version's explanation that his home had moved elsewhere [3H–3J]. Here too he goes to the place of water drawing, identifies his daughter from the women's talk, and follows her home [3J–3K]. The main difference in the conclusion is that, at this turning point, the storyteller shifts to show us the rabbi's advent through his wife's eyes. She is busy with her domestic labor as usual, sifting the flour to make the daily bread, when she happens to look up—and there stands her husband! Her "heart leaped," or in our idiom "jumped for joy," and she dies of the shock, also to be revived by her husband's prayer. This shift in perspective (or "focalization," to use the technical term) amplifies the audience's sympathy for the wife's plight, as we share her point of view and feel her pain: the drudgery of her routine domestic work to provide meals for her children and the unexpected exhilaration upon perceiving R. Ḥananiah [3M–3N].

Because of the major changes to the first half of the story, the didactic message of the Bavli's version differs considerably from those of the first two versions. There is no contrast between R. Ḥananiah's lack of connection to his home and the appropriate behavior of his colleague, no summons from the wife, and no mention of R. Akiva, let alone a dismissal to return home. In other words, if there is any criticism of R. Ḥananiah in this version, it is extremely subtle. The eagerness to get to the study house is arguably a praiseworthy trait, even if it entails not accompanying his friend on the journey. We do not know exactly why he decides to return home when he does; apparently it is simply a good time to take a break from his studies. His inability to find his way home and his daughter's patronymic are simply functions of the long time away, but not indicative of a failing on his part. The storyteller's sympathy for the wife's solitude through the poignant shift in focus does not necessarily involve disapproval of her husband's conduct. Nor is the collateral damage of his wife's death his responsibility or due to his thoughtlessness. Indeed, the storyteller omits mention of the rabbi entering the house or entering "suddenly" [1K, 2K–2L versus 3K], which avoids even this possible criticism of the sage. The opposite is in fact true: his great merit, presumably on account of the long years of Torah study, heroically revives her [3M]. This storyteller is neither oblivious to the pain caused by the husband's long absence, nor insensitive to the toll on the wife and children: he makes it clear that they have suffered from his absence. At the same time, however, he esteems the great *mitzvah* of Torah study and communicates a more balanced view of the trade-offs involved in dedicating oneself to the rabbinic vocation.

Here we can trace the literary development of these versions with some confidence. The earliest version, that of Bereishit Rabbah, is critical of Ḥananiah b. Ḥakhinai and probably originally ended with the death of his wife, for which he bears the blame. A later storyteller, troubled by criticism of the rabbi and the unjust fate suffered by his wife, tacked on an alternative, happier possibility, adding just three words in the original Aramaic (ואית דאמרין חזרת/ *v'it d'amrin ḥazart*). This happier ending was adopted by the storyteller of the second version, that of Vayikra Rabbah, who added some details but otherwise kept the original story largely intact. This resulted in the disjunction between the story and its ending, the criticism of the rabbi with the fortunate conclusion, producing the mixed message. The storyteller of the Bavli, the third version, altered the first half of the story to conform with the happier ending, eliminating the criticism of the rabbi and offering a more positive lesson about Torah study. This is an instructive example of how stories change and how storytellers rework the stories they received for their own purposes and to communicate their own values. Thus the main factor responsible for the production of multiple versions of a story is the different didactic interests of different storytellers.

However, there is another important consideration involved in the metamorphosis of the story, namely the literary context, a topic discussed in chapter 5. Let us turn now to the context of each of the story's three versions to appreciate this issue.

Bereishit Rabbah, where we find the earliest of our three versions of this story, is a midrashic work organized according to the verses of the Book of Genesis. The story appears in the commentary to Genesis 46:30, where the patriarch Jacob/Israel is reunited with his son Joseph and exclaims: "Now I can die, having seen for myself that you are alive" (ויאמר ישראל אל יוסף אמותה הפעם אחרי ראותי את פניך כי עודך חי). Earlier Joseph had sent his brothers back to Canaan to inform his father that he was alive and to bring Jacob to Egypt (45:25–26). The story of Ḥananiah b. Ḥakhinai and his wife appears as a parallel to the biblical episode, in that both deal with family members who see each other after a long separation.

In the biblical context Jacob's words seem to mean that he can die happy, now that he has witnessed with his own eyes that his favorite son is alive and well. But removed from its context, as is typical of midrash, the words Jacob utters can mean that someone might die upon seeing that a loved one is alive. Indeed, the Hebrew word for "now" (הפעם, *ha-pa'am*) also can mean "this time" or "once" and, by a little stretch, can be understood as "suddenly," such that the verse reads: "I would die suddenly, seeing for myself that you are alive." With this sense the verse can be understood as a warning against Ḥananiah's behavior, as an indictment of his unannounced arrival—as he should have known from Jacob's words that sudden appearances after lengthy absences can result in death. The midrash follows Ḥananiah's story with a tradition about three things that "the Holy One, blessed be He, hates," and then adds a fourth: "and some say also one who enters his house suddenly, and how much the more so [one who enters] the house of his fellow [suddenly]." This is followed by a brief story as illustration:

**בראשית רבה צה**

ר׳ יוחנן כד הווה סלק לבייתיה דר׳ חנינה הווה מכעכע, שכן ישראל אומר ליוסף אמותה הפעם: ראוי הייתי למות באותה הפעם, אילולי ששילחתה ואמרתה לי כי עודך חי (בראשית מו:ל).

**Bereishit Rabbah 95**[6]

R. Yoḥanan—when he would go up to the house of R. Ḥaninah, he would cough, since Israel said to Joseph, *Now I can die*: I could have died at that time, had you not sent and told me *that you are alive (Genesis 46:30).*

R. Yoḥanan wished to alert his colleague that he had arrived, rather than show up suddenly, so he coughed when approaching the house to announce his presence. He learned this from Jacob's words to Joseph—understood in the midrashic way delineated above—that unexpected arrivals can result in death: had Joseph not sent word beforehand but rather appeared suddenly, Jacob would have died from the shock.

Thus, as we think of the wife's distress in terms of Jacob's years of suffering, the midrashic context of the story in connection with Genesis 46:30 emphasizes the long separation and pain caused by the lack of communication. The fact that Joseph sent word to his father that he was alive, preparing him for their meeting, contrasts sharply with Ḥananiah's conduct and contributes to the criticism of the sage. So too does the following tradition castigating those who enter their houses suddenly,

---

6 This passage is found in the Vatican 30 manuscript, in the edition of Theodor-Albeck, (see p. 210 n. 4).

and the story of R. Yoḥanan that illustrates how properly to navigate such situations. This literary context nicely rehearses and reinforces all of the didactic points that emerge from the analysis of the rabbinic story itself.

The second version, that of Vayikra Rabbah, appears in connection with a very different biblical passage, in Leviticus. God first tells Moses to tell Aaron how he is *not* to approach the sanctum (verse 2), and then proceeds to tell Moses the proper ritual with which Aaron *should* enter the shrine:

**ויקרא טז:א–ד**

א וידבר ה׳ אל משה אחרי מות שני בני אהרן בקרבתם לפני ה׳ וימתו.

ב ויאמר ה׳ אל-משה: דבר אל אהרן אחיך ואל יבא בכל עת אל הקדש מבית לפרכת, אל פני הכפרת אשר על הארן, ולא ימות, כי בענן אראה על הכפרת.

ג בזאת יבא אהרן אל הקדש, בפר בן בקר לחטאת ואיל לעלה.

ד כתנת בד קדש ילבש, ומכנסי בד יהיו על בשרו, ובאבנט בד יחגר, ובמצנפת בד יצנף. בגדי קדש הם, ורחץ במים את בשרו ולבשם.

**Leviticus 16:1–4**

1 YHVH said to Moses after the death of the two sons of Aaron who died when they drew too close to the presence of YHVH.

2 YHVH said to Moses: Tell your brother Aaron that he is not to come at all times into the shrine behind the curtain, in front of the cover that is upon the ark, lest he die, for I appear in the cloud over the cover.

3 Thus only should Aaron enter the shrine: with a bull of the herd for a sin offering and a ram for a burnt offering.

4 He shall be dressed in a sacral linen tunic, with linen breeches next to his flesh, and be girt with a linen sash, and he shall wear a linen turban. They are sacral vestments; he shall bathe his body in water and then put them on.

This biblical story thus parallels the story of R. Ḥananiah, in that it conveys that inappropriate entry to a certain place results in death. To avoid such disasters the Bible details the appropriate conduct for entering the shrine. In Vayikra Rabbah, the tradition that precedes the story of R. Ḥananiah is a midrashic dialogue in which God clarifies to Moses that Aaron can indeed enter the shrine "at all times" provided that he follows "this order," namely the ritual prescribed in those next few verses, with two additional rabbinic comments mentioning that Aaron's dress included many bells (see Exodus 28:33–35). After relating the story of R. Ḥananiah, the midrash then quotes the same tradition that appears in Bereishit Rabbah, that some say God hates one who enters one's house suddenly, and then an admonition attributed to Rav not to enter a house or city suddenly. The same story of R. Yoḥanan coughing before entry to his colleague's house follows. Here, however, since this midrash is predicated on the issue of the High Priest's entry into the shrine, the conclusion of the story does not quote Jacob's words to Joseph in Genesis 46:30. Instead the story explains that R. Yoḥanan entered his house by signaling his arrival, because Exodus 28:34–35 instructs the High Priest to wear vestments with bells "so that the sound of it is heard when he goes into the sanctuary before YHVH and when he goes out—that he might not die" (ונשמע קולו בבאו אל הקדש לפני ה׳ ובצאתו ולא ימות).

This context foregrounds R. Ḥananiah's sudden entry to his house and his deviation from proper conduct, as modeled by R. Yoḥanan and spelled out by Rav's admonition. Like the High Priest's entry into God's house, entry to one's own house should be done in the appropriate manner. While this message entails some criticism of R. Ḥananiah, it simultaneously de-emphasizes his years-long lack of communication with his wife and general neglect of his family, focusing instead almost totally on the moment of his return. True, he entered improperly on his return home; but had he done so in the correct way at that moment, then all would have been well, just as God tells Moses that all will be well if Aaron follows the prescribed ritual. We may even be invited to think of his holy pursuit of Torah study in terms of the High Priest's service to God in the Temple. The happy ending to the story fits with the more restrained criticism of R. Ḥananiah brought out in this context. We think of R. Ḥananiah not as insensitively abandoning his wife and completely forgetting his family for many years, but as making a modest mistake in the protocol of returning home. That his prayer protesting his "poor" wife's unjust fate is answered fits this more favorable portrayal of the sage.

The Bavli's version of the story appears in the talmudic commentary to Mishnah Ketubot 5:6, which we discussed in chapter 5 together with the story of Rav Reḥumei. As we saw there, this mishnah rules that students of Torah may leave their homes for up to thirty days without the consent of their wives in order to pursue their studies—an attempt to balance two leading rabbinic values, Torah study and domestic obligations. In the Bavli's commentary on it, a later sage claims that the mishnaic ruling of thirty days represents a minority opinion, and that the majority ruling actually allows rabbis to leave their wives for two or three years without their wives' consent. This extended time may have been due to longer distances required to reach centers of Torah in Babylonia, a region of the vast Persian empire, compared to the smaller contours of Roman Palestine. There follows a story-cycle of seven stories that explores different aspects of this issue of long absences for the sake of Torah study—the dangers, pitfalls, advantages, disadvantages, costs, and benefits—very much in keeping with our discussion of story-cycles in chapter 6. The story of Rav Reḥumei's death upon failing to return home at the designated time is the first story of the story-cycle, and clearly warns sages not to neglect their wives and families. However, other stories in the story-cycle do not unambiguously condemn long absences for the sake of Torah study, but offer a more nuanced or even optimistic perspective on this issue.

Our story of R. Ḥananiah b. Ḥakhinai appears as the third story in this cycle. The substantive change to the first half of the story fits this context nicely, as it emphasizes the appeal of Torah study to the rabbis. R. Ḥananiah is as eager to reach his place of study in this story as Rav Reḥumei, in the earlier story, is reluctant to leave. In this version, R. Ḥananiah is not contrasted with another colleague who sent letters home to know what was going on, as the goal here is not to underscore R. Ḥananiah's failing. Rather the goal is to offer perspectives on the broader tension within rabbinic culture. By placing this story in the context of a larger story-cycle, the compiler draws contrasts among the stories of the cycle more than among characters within an individual story. The disadvantages of spending long years away from home studying Torah include not knowing one's daughter, who has grown up in one's absence, the loneliness experienced by one's wife, and the danger of a sudden arrival. The advantages are the long, uninterrupted years of study and the great merit accrued for this paramount *mitzvah*. The happy ending, with the implication that the rabbi's merit for his Torah study is responsible for counteracting the wife's unjust death, also fits this general context: the mishnah's attempt to balance the two important rabbinic values and the story-cycle manifesting different facets of the issue.

## Tools and Resources for Finding Parallel Versions

How does one find parallel versions to a story in order to explore comparative analysis? Unfortunately, there is no easy or sure-fire method. We lack a comprehensive index of talmudic stories with all their parallel versions—even scholars sometimes have difficulties tracking down parallels of the texts on which they are working.

An internet search for books, scholarly articles, and even popular posts available online will often produce results. Scholars who have analyzed a story will typically discuss the relationship of the story to its parallels, or at least mention whether it has parallels and provide references to where they appear. So scholarly discussions in books, articles, and websites are an excellent and easily accessed resource.

The website and app Sefaria (www.sefaria.org/texts) provides "resources" for many talmudic passages. The resources sometimes include parallels in the Yerushalmi and *midrashim*. Another resource is "sheets," that is, source sheets compiled by Sefaria users, some of which include parallel versions.

For those who read Hebrew there are several additional tools. Among the commentaries printed in the back of most volumes of the standard (Vilna) printing of the Talmud is the Yefeh Einayim by R. Aryeh Leib Yellin (1820–1866). R. Yellin lists parallels to Bavli passages (including stories) in the Yerushalmi and in the midrashic literature. Similarly, the Steinsaltz/Koren Hebrew edition of the Talmud provides references to parallel passages in the Yerushalmi and midrashic literature in the margins of each page of the Bavli. In addition, Bar-Ilan University has provided an online index of parallels to passages in the Yerushalmi that appear in the Bavli and in the Midrash that can be accessed here: https://www2.biu.ac.il/js/tl/yerushalmi/records.html. If you are starting with a story that you know is in the Yerushalmi, its parallels can be found easily. Finally, the critical editions of works of midrash also list all parallels to passages in the midrashic texts that appear in the Talmuds and elsewhere in rabbinic literature. For example, the critical edition of Bereishit Rabbah, edited by H. Albeck and J. Theodor (1903–36; reprinted several times), provides references to parallel passages, including stories, that appear in this midrash. The "traditional" editions of some *midrashim*, such as the standard printing of Midrash Rabbah (known as the Vilna printing), also lists some parallels to midrashic passages, though these lists are not as comprehensive as those of the critical editions.

~

In this chapter, we have expanded our perspective beyond the confines of the talmudic page, venturing into the vast "sea" of rabbinic literature. Many stories appear in multiple versions across different rabbinic compilations, reflecting the fluid nature of storytelling in the oral culture of the sages. These stories were not fixed but were reshaped by different storytellers to suit their own needs, interests, and values. The existence of multiple versions allows for comparative analysis, enabling us to focus on the variations and to appreciate the diverse values, concerns, theologies, and challenges present in different rabbinic cultures and among individual storytellers. This richness of tradition also offers us valuable resources for deriving and teaching different lessons appropriate for different groups of students—students of different ages or intellectual levels, students with different interests or concerns, and students facing different challenges and grappling with different problems. Likewise, the multiple interpretive possibilities of different versions of a story can enrich our religious lives, as one particular version or the nuances that emerge from comparing them may resonate more personally with each of us.

# CONCLUSION

BY WAY OF conclusion I would like to review the literary features presented in the previous chapters by walking us through the reading and study of a story. This exercise will allow us to practice the analysis of a story and the application of a toolbox of methods. This story appears in Menaḥot 44a and concerns the fringes (ציצית/*tzitzit*), the strings attached to the corners of garments that function to recall the commandments:[1]

**תלמוד בבלי, מנחות מד ע"א**

תניא א"ר נתן: אין לך כל מצוה קלה שכתובה בתורה, שאין מתן שכרה בעולם הזה. ולעולם הבא, איני יודע כמה. צא ולמד ממצות ציצית. מעשה באדם אחד שהיה זהיר במצות ציצית. שמע שיש זונה בכרכי הים שנוטלת ד׳ מאות זהובים בשכרה. שיגר לה ארבע מאות זהובים וקבע לה זמן. כשהגיע זמנו, בא וישב על הפתח. נכנסה שפחתה ואמרה לה: אותו אדם ששיגר ליך ד׳ מאות זהובים בא וישב על הפתח. אמרה היא: יכנס. נכנס הציעה לו ז׳ מטות, שש של כסף ואחת של זהב. ובין כל אחת ואחת סולם של כסף, ועליונה של

---

1 A close parallel appears in Midrash Sifrei 115 to Numbers 15:41, ed. H.S. Horovitz (Jerusalem: Wahrmann, 1966), 128–29. The following analysis is indebted to several fine studies on the story, including Warren Zev Harvey, "The Pupil, the Harlot, and Fringe Benefits"; Alon Goshen-Gottstein, "The Commandment of Fringes"; Admiel Kosman, "On the Interpretation of the Story of the Student"; Ido Hevroni, "A Tale of Two Sinners"; Mira Balberg, "Between Heterotopia and Utopia," 199–205; Yosef Marcus, "Tzitzit as a Marker of Identity"; Tali Artman-Partock, "The Tale Type of the Repenting Prostitute."

זהב. עלתה וישבה על גבי עליונה כשהיא ערומה. ואף הוא עלה לישב ערום כנגדה. באו ד׳ ציציותיו וטפחו לו על פניו. נשמט וישב לו על גבי קרקע. ואף היא נשמטה וישבה על גבי קרקע. אמרה לו: גפה של רומי, שאיני מניחתך עד שתאמר לי מה מום ראית בי. אמר לה: העבודה, שלא ראיתי אשה יפה כמותך. אלא מצוה אחת ציונו ה׳ א־להינו וציצית שמה, וכתיב בה: אני ה׳ א־להיכם (במדבר טו:מא) שתי פעמים. אני הוא שעתיד ליפרע. אני הוא שעתיד לשלם שכר. עכשיו נדמו עלי כד׳ עדים. אמרה לו: העבודה, איני מניחתך עד שתאמר לי מה שמך ומה שם עירך ומה שם רבך ומה שם מדרשך שאתה למד בו תורה. כתב ונתן בידה. עמדה וחילקה כל נכסיה, שליש למלכות, ושליש לעניים, ושליש נטלה בידה, חוץ מאותן מצעות, ובאת לבית מדרשו של ר׳ חייא. אמרה לו: רבי! צוה עלי ויעשוני גיורת. אמר לה: בתי! שמא עיניך נתת באחד מן התלמידים. הוציאה כתב מידה ונתנה לו. אמר לה: לכי זכי במקחך. אותן מצעות שהציעה לו באיסור, הציעה לו בהיתר. זה מתן שכרו בעולם הזה. ובעולם הבא, איני יודע כמה!

**Talmud Bavli, Menaḥot 44a**

It was taught: R. Natan says: There is no minor commandment written in the Torah, for which there is no reward (*sekharah*) given in this world. And in the world to come—I don't know how much [is the reward]. Go and learn from the commandment of the fringes. There once was a certain man who was punctilious with the commandment of the fringes. He heard that there was a harlot in the cities by the sea who would take 400 gold coins as her wage (*sekharah*). He sent her 400 gold coins and she set a time for him. When his time arrived, he went and sat at the entrance [of her house]. Her servant-girl entered and said to her, "That man who sent you 400 gold coins arrived and is sitting at the entrance." She said to her, "Let him come in." When he entered she prepared for him seven couches, six of silver and one of gold. There were ladders of silver between all of them, and the top one was of gold. She ascended and sat naked on the top one. He too ascended [in order] to sit naked beside her. His four fringes came and beat him on the face. He withdrew and sat on the ground. She too withdrew and sat on the ground. She said to him, "By the Love-goddess of Rome, I will not leave you be (*maniḥatkha*) until you tell me what blemish you saw in me." He said to her, "By the [Temple] service, I have never seen a woman as beautiful as you. But YHVH our God commanded us one commandment called 'fringes,' and He wrote about it, *I am YHVH your God (Numbers 15:41)* two times. *'I'* am the one who will exact punishment [for violating the commandment]. *'I'* am the one who will provide a reward (*sekhar*) in the future [world]. And now they [the fringes] have appeared to me like four witnesses." She said to him, "By the [Temple] service,[2] I will not leave you be (*maniḥatkha*) until you tell me your name and the name of your city and the name of your master and the name of the school in which you study Torah." He wrote it down and placed it in her hand. She went forth and distributed all of her possessions, one-third to the monarchy, and one-third to the poor, and one-third she took with her, in addition to those beds, and she came to the study house of R. Ḥiyya. She said to him, "My master, instruct [your students] about me that they make me a convert." He said to her, "My daughter! Perhaps you have set your eyes on one of the students." She held out to him the text in her hand and gave it to him. He (R. Ḥiyya) said to her, "Go forth and take possession of your acquisition."[3] Those beds which she prepared for him unlawfully, she prepared for him lawfully. This is the giving of its reward (*sekharo*) in this world. And in the world to come, I don't know how much!

## STRUCTURE

Our first task is to assess the story's structure. As discussed in chapter 1, there is no absolute and single correct structure; the utility of the structure is to allow us to identify the different parts of the story and the relationship among them. If you are working through this exercise along with me, you can copy this text from Sefaria or another online source, and experiment with breaking it up into sections yourself.

A first structural observation is that framing statements bracket the main narrative, which begins with "There once was…" In the

2 The word "By the [Temple] service" (העבודה/*ha-avodah*) does not appear in the Vilna printing but appears in most manuscripts.

3 Some manuscripts and quotations of the passage by medieval commentaries direct this line to the man.

introduction, R. Natan makes a general claim about commandments and their rewards, followed by a charge to "learn from the commandment of the fringes." That is, the commandment of fringes is paradigmatic of all other commandments and demonstrates his claim. The ending also has a concluding thought that reflects back on the story rather than narrating additional events: "This is the giving of its reward..." Here the storyteller asserts that he has proven that initial claim. So we can begin by separating those two sections. I say "storyteller" rather than R. Natan because it is not clear whether R. Natan's words continue with the story itself through to the conclusion or whether they end with "Go and learn…fringes," and subsequently a later storyteller appended the story to this brief tradition.

As we saw in chapter 1 in the story of "Yosef the Shabbat-honorer," shifts in the acting character offer a useful way to identify structural divisions. Our story begins with the man as protagonist: he "heard" of the harlot, "sent" her the payment, "went and sat" at her house. The harlot briefly appears in this section, but only in the background and in order to facilitate the man's progress, setting the time and telling her servant-girl to admit him. The two have not yet met or had direct contact. This is exactly what changes in the second section, as the two characters come together, get ready, ascend to the bed, descend to the floor, and then engage in dialogue. The third section focuses on the harlot alone: she distributes her property, travels to the study house of R. Ḥiyya, and speaks with the rabbi. Indeed, the man drops out of the story completely, and is only mentioned as the object of the ex-harlot's affection. We can therefore make a preliminary division into three sections based on the shift in character: (1) man, (2) man and harlot, (3) harlot. This shift should have implications regarding our interpretation of the story.

The primary structural divisions look like this:

| | | | | |
|---|---|---|---|---|
| תניא א"ר נתן... | [A] | [A] | It was taught: R. Natan says… | Introduction and claim |
| מעשה באדם אחד... | [B] | [B] | There once was a certain man… | Man |
| נכנס הציעה לו ז' מטות... | [C] | [C] | When he entered she prepared… | Man and Harlot |

| | | | | |
|---|---|---|---|---|
| עמדה וחילקה... | [D] | [D] | She went forth and distributed.... | Harlot |
| זה מתן שכרו... | [A'] | [A'] | This is the giving of reward... | Conclusion and proof of claim |

The story thus features the typical tripartite structure discussed in chapter 1, bracketed by an introduction and conclusion.

Within each of the three main parts [B, C, D] we can identify subsections. As we have seen, repetition often functions as a structuring device. Here the most prominent repetition is the three oaths in the middle section [C], all introduced by standard oath formula: "By the..." (that is, "I swear by the..."). The harlot first swears, "By the Love-goddess of Rome, I will not leave you be until you tell me...." and then switches to a rabbinic oath formula: "By the [Temple] service, I will not leave you be until you tell me.... Her second oath follows an oath by the man, "By the [Temple] service, I have never seen a woman as beautiful..." This suggests that [C] be divided into four subsections, the initial tryst followed by the three oaths. And it helps us perceive the beginning of her transformation: she first swears by a Roman goddess, but upon hearing the man swear a Jewish oath, she switches to his formula.

Section [B] and section [D], however, each readily divide into two sections based on their settings. In [B], these are the exposition and preparation for the assignation, which take place in the man's location, and his journey and arrival at the harlot's house, which take place in her domain in the "cities by the sea," and after some time has passed. Section [D] also divides into two primary subsections based on location: first, the harlot's efforts to abandon a life of sin, and second, her journey to the rabbinic school and dialogue with the rabbi, which also takes place at a later time. These pairs of subsections parallel each other: first, the man's plans to sin in [B] parallels her effort to stop sinning in [D], and second, his journey to the harlot's distant home in [B] is echoed by her journey to his study hall in [D]. After the rabbi "blesses" her ("Go forth..."), the final line is a summary of sorts to the story ("Those beds..."), so I would consider it as another subsection in [D]. It does not really belong in the concluding section [A'], as it narrates events within the story, rather than reflecting back upon it, as the concluding section does. Thus one possible structure is as follows:

[A] תניא א״ר נתן: אין לך כל מצוה קלה שכתובה בתורה, שאין מתן **שכרה** בעולם הזה. ולעולם הבא איני יודע כמה. צא ולמד ממצות ציצית.

[B1] מעשה באדם אחד שהיה זהיר במצות ציצית. שמע שיש זונה בכרכי הים שנוטלת ד׳ מאות זהובים **בשכרה**. שיגר לה ארבע מאות זהובים וקבע לה זמן.

[B2] כשהגיע זמנו, בא וישב על הפתח. נכנסה שפחתה ואמרה לה: אותו אדם ששיגר ליך ד׳ מאות זהובים בא וישב על הפתח. אמרה היא: יכנס.

[C1] נכנס הציעה לו ז׳ מטות, שש של כסף ואחת של זהב. ובין כל אחת ואחת סולם של כסף, ועליונה של זהב. עלתה וישבה על גבי עליונה כשהיא ערומה. ואף הוא עלה לישב ערום כנגדה. באו ד׳ ציציותיו וטפחו לו על פניו. נשמט וישב לו ע״ג קרקע. ואף היא נשמטה וישבה ע״ג קרקע.

[C2] אמרה לו: גפה של רומי שאיני **מניחתך** עד שתאמר לי מה מום ראית בי.

[C3] אמר לה: העבודה, שלא ראיתי אשה יפה כמותך. אלא מצוה אחת ציונו ה׳ א-להינו וציצית שמה, וכתיב בה: אני ה׳ א-להיכם (במדבר טו:מא) שתי פעמים. אני הוא שעתיד ליפרע. אני הוא שעתיד לשלם **שכר**. עכשיו נדמו עלי כד׳ עדים.

[C4] אמרה לו: העבודה, איני **מניחתך** עד שתאמר לי מה שמך ומה שם עירך ומה שם רבך ומה שם מדרשך שאתה למד בו תורה. כתב ונתן בידה.

[D1] עמדה וחילקה כל נכסיה שליש למלכות ושליש לעניים ושליש נטלה בידה חוץ מאותן מצעות.

[D2] ובאת לבית מדרשו של ר׳ חייא. אמרה לו: רבי! צוה עלי ויעשוני גיורת. אמר לה: בתי! שמא עיניך נתת באחד מן התלמידים. הוציאה כתב מידה ונתנה לו. אמר לה: לכי זכי במקחך.

[D3] אותן מצעות שהציעה לו באיסור הציעה לו בהיתר.

[A′] זה מתן **שכרו** בעולם הזה. ולעולם הבא איני יודע כמה.

[A] It was taught: R. Natan says: There is no minor commandment written in the Torah, for which there is no **reward** (*sekharah*) given in this world. And in the world to come—I don't know how much [is the reward]. Go and learn from the commandment of the fringes.

[B1] There once was a certain man who was punctilious with the commandment of the fringes. He heard that there was a harlot in the cities by the sea who would take 400 gold coins as her **wage** (*sekharah*). He sent her 400 gold coins and she set a time for him.

[B2] When his time arrived, he went and sat at the entrance [of her house]. Her servant-girl entered and said to her, "That man who sent you 400 gold coins arrived and is sitting at the entrance." She said to her, "Let him come in."

[C1] When he entered she prepared for him seven couches, six of silver and one of gold. There were ladders of silver between all of them, and the top one was of gold. She ascended and sat naked on the top one. He too ascended [in order] to sit naked beside her. His four fringes came and beat him on the face. He withdrew and sat on the ground. She too withdrew and sat on the ground.

[C2] She said to him, "By the Love-goddess of Rome, I will not **leave you be** (*maniḥatkha*) until you tell me what blemish you saw in me."

[C3] He said to her, "By the [Temple] service, I have never seen a woman as beautiful as you. But YHVH our God commanded us one commandment called 'fringes,' and He wrote about it, *I am YHVH your God (Numbers 15:41)* two times. '*I*' am the one who will exact punishment [for violating the commandment]. '*I*' am the one who will provide a **reward** (*sekhar*) in the future [world]. And now they [the fringes] have appeared to me like four witnesses."

[C4] She said to him, "By the [Temple] service, I will not **leave you be** (*maniḥatkha*) until you tell me your name and the name of your city and the name of your master and the name of the school in which you study Torah." He wrote it down and placed it in her hand.

[D1] She went forth and distributed all of her possessions, one-third to the monarchy, and one-third to the poor, and one-third she took with her, in addition to those beds,

[D2] and she came to the study house of R. Ḥiyya. She said to him, "My master, instruct [your students] about me that they make me a convert." He said to her, "My daughter! Perhaps you have set your eyes on one of the students." She held out to him the text in her hand and gave it to him. He (R. Ḥiyya) said to her, "Go forth and take possession of your acquisition."

[D3] Those beds that she prepared for him unlawfully, she prepared for him lawfully.

[A'] This is the giving of its **reward** (*sekharo*) in this world. And in the world to come, I don't know how much!

This structure helps us discern a number of other aspects of the story's dynamic. The focus on location encourages us to understand that there are two journeys made by the protagonists, the one a reversal of the other: the man travels from his home to the harlot's place [B2], followed by the harlot traveling from her domain to the man's school and home [D2]. The reversal, moreover, involves purpose, not only direction: the man journeys to pursue sin, while the harlot journeys to pursue holiness—conversion to the true faith and marriage. If we look to the sections preceding the journeys we note that each mentions money or wealth, [B1] and [D1]. The man amasses his wealth and dispatches it for an illicit purpose, whereas the woman distributes her possessions, some of which go to a holy purpose (charity). When we compare the middle section to these two sections that frame it, we note vertical movement that contrasts with the two travelers' horizontal movements: the ascent to the top of the towering edifice of couches followed by the descent to the ground [C1], where the crucial dialogue takes place [C2–4]. At the center of the story is the man's explanation for his sudden change, which focuses on the scriptural commandment of the fringes [C3], and intersects with the introductory and concluding section.

This is not the only possible structural division. We could include [C3], for example, the man's oath, with the first oath of the harlot [C2], as her two oaths continue with the same verbal repetition "I will not leave you be." Alternatively, the unit with the oaths could be its own section, separate from the failed tryst, which would add another primary section to the five delineated above. The last subsection [D3] could be included with the previous subsection [D2], as it is the (ex-)harlot's response to the rabbi's blessing. And there are other possibilities too. The main goal of identifying the structure, once again, is to allow us to perceive relationships among the parts so as to gain insights into the story's meaning, and different structures will highlight different relationships.

## SYMBOLIC NAMES AND CHARACTERIZATION

This story features only one named character, R. Ḥiyya, and it is not clear why he was chosen, as his name does not seem to have a symbolic meaning, and any other rabbi could have served this role equally. That is, the story would work had the woman come to the study house of R. Akiva or R. Ami or another rabbi. At best, we might suggest that "Ḥiyya" evokes the Hebrew word for "life" (חיים/*ḥayyim*), as well as a common term for "life in the world to come" (חיי העולם הבא/*ḥayyei ha-olam ha-ba*), which the story promises for observing the commandments, both beginning and ending on that note. However, I am not enamored with this explanation, as the term "life in the world to come" does not appear in the story, but only "the world to come," and it may be expecting too much from the audience to make this connection. Alternatively, R. Ḥiyya was among the most prominent sages who lived at the end of the tannaitic period; one later tradition claims: "When Torah was forgotten from Israel, R. Ḥiyya and his sons went up and reestablished it" (Sukkah 20a). Perhaps he was selected simply on that basis, rather than for some more specific connection to this story. Unfortunately, we cannot say much more other than noting that R. Ḥiyya held some special stature in the storyteller's eyes. R. Natan is not a character within the story but responsible for the tradition that precedes the story proper about the great rewards for the commandment of fringes, and perhaps he should be considered the storyteller too, as discussed above.[4]

In other respects the characterization is typical of talmudic stories. The harlot is a stock character and, like other stock characters we have encountered in stories analyzed in the previous chapters—the emperor, a Roman matron, an old man, a *ḥasid*—is identified completely by her profession. That she is a harlot "who would take 400 gold coins as her wage" further characterizes her as an elite, high-class courtesan, the best in the business. What is exceptional in this story is that she turns out to be anything but a stock character, a typical harlot. Instead, she undergoes a development and change of character worthy of a novel. This transformation clues us in to a key aspect of the analysis: that this story is mostly about her, and we should consider her the true heroine.

The man is not named either, but is characterized briefly by the quality salient for the story: "who was punctilious with the commandment of the fringes." This characterization of course underpins the critical and surreal scene where the fringes cause him to desist from sin, which in turn precipitates the major reversal at the story's central turning point. It also makes for an effective opening, as this characterization is immediately followed by the description of his lecherous endeavor, which puzzles and intrigues the audience: how can such a pious individual embark on such a sinful pursuit?

The unnamed servant-girl is also a stock character. She functions primarily to underscore the exceptionally high-class status of the harlot, who has servants to attend to her and her business. The servant-girl also facilitates the delay before the man meets the harlot, which adds to the narrative tension as we, too, wait for the encounter.

## BIBLICAL QUOTATIONS

As we saw in chapter 3, biblical verses often point to a story's concerns and meanings, and the more closely we attend to them the more the story's art becomes clear. In our story, the crux devolves from the man's citation of the biblical verse about the reward for the fringes and his understanding

---

4 The same consideration applies to the parallel tradition in Sifrei 115 to Numbers 15:41 (see p. 227 n. 1). The editors of the Sifrei could have added the story to R. Natan's tradition.

of its implications, so we must explore that verse and the larger biblical passage.

**במדבר טו:לז-מא**

[לז]ויאמר ה׳ אל משה לאמר. [לח]דבר אל בני ישראל ואמרת אלהם ועשו
להם ציצת על כנפי בגדיהם לדרתם, ונתנו על ציצת הכנף פתיל
תכלת. [לט]והיה לכם לציצת, וראיתם אתו וזכרתם את כל מצות ה׳
ועשיתם אתם, ולא תתורו אחרי לבבכם ואחרי עיניכם אשר אתם
זנים אחריהם. [מ]למען תזכרו ועשיתם את כל מצותי והייתם קדשים
לא-להיכם.

[מא]**אני ה׳ א-להיכם**, אשר הוצאתי אתכם מארץ מצרים להיות לכם
לא-להים: **אני ה׳ א-להיכם**.

**Numbers 15:37–41**

[37]YHVH said to Moses as follows. [38]Speak to the Israelite people
and instruct them to make for themselves fringes on the corners
of their garments throughout the ages; let them attach a cord of
blue to the fringe at each corner. [39]That shall be your fringe; look
at it and recall all the commandments of YHVH and observe
them, so that you do not follow your heart and eyes in your
lustful urge. [40]Thus you shall be reminded to observe all My
commandments and to be holy to your God.

[41]**I am YHVH, your God**, who brought you out of the land of
Egypt to be your God: **I am YHVH, your God**.[5]

The man focuses on the repetition of the phrase "I am YHVH, your God" in verse 41. This repetition is problematic according to rabbinic interpretive assumptions. Why does the verse conclude with "I am YHVH, your God" after opening with that very phrase? In fact, even the appearance of the phrase at the beginning of the verse is somewhat problematic, as there does not seem to be any direct relationship between this statement of God's authority, or of the exodus from Egypt, to the preceding verses about putting fringes on garments. Modern scholars might judge the repetition of the phrase "I am YHVH, your God" as a summarizing conclusion to the paragraph, or simply a means to emphasize this idea, and consider the reference to the exodus as the general justification for why the Israelites

5 Based on NJPS, with slight modifications.

should obey God's commandments.[6] Such explanations, however, would not have satisfied the rabbis, who typically understood repeated words to teach additional lessons.

Here, the man explains the two mentions of "I am YHVH, your God" to the harlot in terms of reward and punishment in the next world. This verse follows the commandment of the fringes, he tells her, both to warn of a punishment for violations (the first "I am YHVH, your God" = "I am the One who will exact punishment") and to guarantee a reward for performing the commandment (the second "I am YHVH, your God" = "I am the One who will provide a reward in the future [world]"). For this reason, he cannot go through with the sex act despite the harlot's physical attractions—"never seen a woman as beautiful as you." It is not the beauty of this world, but the "future world," the next world, that concerns him, where rewards and punishments materialize.

Yet there is more to the relationship between the story and the biblical verses than this midrash. We also noted in chapter 3 (pp. 128–34) that some talmudic stories emerge from the interpretation of biblical verses. Here indeed much of the plot is produced through exegesis of the biblical passage. Numbers 15:39, which precedes our verse, explains the function of the fringe to "look at it and recall all the commandments of YHVH and observe them so that you do not follow your heart and eyes in your lustful urge." One can immediately perceive a relationship between the "lustful urge" that motivates the protagonist and the fringes that prevent him from consummating his liaison. The King James Version makes this relationship clearer by translating the verse so as to capture the connotations of the original Hebrew more faithfully: "And it shall be unto you for a fringe, that ye may look upon it, and remember all the commandments of YHVH, and do them; and that ye seek not after your own heart and your own eyes, after which ye use to go a whoring (זונים/*zonim*)." This man did "seek after" his heart and eyes and literally (or literarily) went "a whoring," visiting a whore, זונה/*zonah*. Thus the heart of the story is generated by the literalization of the Bible's figurative language and a dose of surrealism: the fringes prevent the man from consorting with the harlot (= the verse's "go a whoring") by appearing to him as witnesses (= the verse's "look at them and recall") and beating him into submission by reminding him of the reward and punishment promised with the commandment (= "I am

---

6 See, for example, Jacob Milgrom, *The JPS Torah Commentary: Numbers*, 128.

YHVH, your God," two times). The storyteller has combined an explicit midrash on 15:41 with a covert narrativization of 15:39 to construct his tale.

## WORDPLAY

As we saw in chapter 4, wordplay enhances the narrative artistry of rabbinic stories and can be central to their meanings. This story contains a fine wordplay on the word שכר/*sekhar,* which means both "wages" and "reward." In the "introduction," R. Natan's claim centers on the *sekhar* (reward) for the fringes [A], which is followed in the story proper by the exorbitant *sekhar* (wages) the man sends the harlot [B1]. These are the *sekhar* (wages) of this-worldly pleasure, which the man gives, and the harlot receives, for her services. The narrative reversal occurs when the man shifts his attention to the *sekhar* (reward) for the fringes in the world to come [C3]. It is in turn this same *sekhar* that impresses the harlot to the point where she forgoes all this-wordly *sekhar* (wages) for her sinful profession, in favor of that otherworldly *sekhar* (reward) for virtue. The wordplay thus helps focus the audience on the motivation for the heroine's repentance, her resolve to abandon her profession in order to adopt a completely new way of life. It is the man's commitment to spiritual values, transcending the superficial materialism and pleasures of this world, that inspires her to rethink all that she has held true.

The wordplay climaxes in the concluding observation, "this is the giving of reward (*sekhar*) in this world" [A'], which creates a nice complement to the mention of reward in R. Natan's opening. Here we see the deep irony that pervades the story: by forgoing the *sekhar* (wages) the man expended on this-worldly pleasure for the sake of otherworldly *sekhar* (reward), he ultimately ended up enjoying that very this-worldly pleasure by marrying the beautiful and now virtuous (ex-)harlot. This is the reward in both this world and the "world to come" that R. Natan promised.

Another literary feature, though not technically a wordplay, is the motif of special numbers that runs throughout the story and contributes to its literary coherence. We saw examples of this in chapter 1 where the structure had three or seven parts. Here we have four (the four fringes, which appear like four witnesses, and the four hundred gold coins), seven (the seven ladders and couches in the harlot's bedroom), and three (the tripartite distribution of her ill-gotten wealth, the three oaths).

## CONTEXT

Now that we have carefully analyzed all of the literary features of the story itself, on its own terms, we are ready to examine the larger context of the story within the Talmud, as we explored in chapter 5. How does the story's setting within the mixture of halakhic and aggadic discussions in the Talmud and in conjunction with the proximate mishnah contribute to our understanding of it? How, in turn, does the story shed light on the issues discussed in the surrounding talmudic passages?

The story appears in the Talmud's commentary to Mishnah Menaḥot 4:1, spanning Bavli Menaḥot 38a–44a, which begins with a ruling about the blue and white threads of the fringes. There follows a lengthy section of Talmud devoted to other laws about garments and fringes, as well as aggadic traditions about the importance of this commandment. Several of these traditions center on the function of the verse's instruction to "look at it and recall all the commandments of YHVH and observe them" (Numbers 15:39), the same phrase that underlies the story. One of these traditions in fact states:

**תלמוד בבלי, מנחות מג ע"ב**

וראיתם אותו וזכרתם את כל מצות ה' (במדבר טו:לט).
שקולה מצוה זו כנגד כל המצות כולן.

**Talmud Bavli, Menaḥot 43b**

*Look upon it and remember all the commandments of YHVH (Numbers 15:39).*

[This teaches that] this *mitzvah* (fringes) is equal to all the *mitzvot* [of the Torah].

Our story follows a little later in the text, after the close of this discussion.

The context therefore underscores the importance of the commandment of the fringes as well as its distinctiveness: the fringes remind the wearer of all the other commandments, and so—allowing for hyperbole in the expression—wearing them is "equal to all the commandments." It is that life dedicated to the commandments and their reward that impresses the harlot and thus stands very much at the forefront of the message. In turn, the story helps us better understand the surprising exaggeration of this tradition: why would this one commandment of fringes be equal to all the other commandments? Because, as in the story, it has the power to change lives dramatically and turn them from sin to piety.

The words "come forth and enjoy your acquisition" (לכי זכי במקח), with which R. Ḥiyya sanctions the conversion and marriage, are also illuminated by the talmudic context. This phrase is essentially a technical legal term that appears in several other talmudic passages. It is therefore part of the larger talmudic context, though not the immediate literary context. These technical legal terms may be difficult to access for those not familiar with the Talmud, though those who read Hebrew and Aramaic can often find parallels through searches in talmudic dictionaries and concordances. Elsewhere in the Talmud this phrase appears in cases where the groom has raised questions about his bride's virginity and the rabbi resolves the issue such that the marriage can proceed.[7] Here, by contrast, the rabbi raises questions about the propriety of the conversion and marriage, and the woman resolves them to his satisfaction: although she has indeed "set her eyes" on R. Ḥiyya's student, her conversion is sincere and the marriage may proceed. That this phrase, spoken to potential grooms, generally functions to mitigate a claim that the bride has engaged in pre-marital sex and lacks the tokens of virginity is brilliant storytelling technique, as the charge would undoubtedly be true in this case. Yet by using the familiar phrase the rabbi counterfactually recognizes her purity, as if her spiritual rebirth has produced a physical rebirth as well.

## Reading a Talmudic Story

We are now in a position to put these insights together and to read the entire story. R. Natan's claim provides an engaging, even perplexing introduction to the story. The Torah routinely promises rewards for observing the commandments in general, though rarely promises rewards for individual commandments. Moreover, the rabbis tended to understand those rewards—and the punishments for violating commandments—as materializing in the world to come. An oft-quoted rabbinic tradition states: "There is no reward in this world for observing

---

7 Ketubot 10a–b.

the commandments."[8] What then can R. Natan mean by asserting that even minor commandments confer reward in this world? Second, the rabbi presents the commandment of the fringes as paradigmatic of this claim, but, as noted above, the biblical source of the commandment says nothing explicit about a reward. Initially, and until the story clarifies what R. Natan means, the audience will be intrigued as to his surprising assertion and how to derive it from the commandment of fringes.

More puzzling, as also noted above, is the exposition of the story proper of a man "punctilious with the commandment of fringes" yet willing to spend a tremendous sum of money, and to travel a considerable distance, to consort with a harlot [B1]. This man's punctiliousness is not limited to his religious devotions but extends to his sinful pursuits as well: he amasses the requisite funds, arranges that they be sent abroad (not an easy prospect in antiquity), receives in return a designated date, and makes his preparations for the voyage. This is not a case of a man suddenly overcome by desire for someone on whom he has impulsively "set his eyes," who cannot resist an impulsive visit to the local brothel—but rather a calculated and premeditated venture for no purpose other than sin. What kind of a reward will this lustful adventurer receive?

Beyond the intriguing opening, the story divides into the three parts delineated above: the man's pursuit of the harlot [B1–B2], the encounter [C1–C4], and the harlot's pursuit of the man [D1–3]. He pursues her for sin and illicit sex, while she pursues him for conversion and marriage. The man travels a great distance horizontally from his home to the harlot's residence: the "cities by the sea" in rabbinic sources connotes a distant and even alien place, similar to the "faraway land" of fairy tales. ("A long time ago in a land far, far away....") At the harlot's abode he ascends, vertically, seven ladders to arrive at the golden couch at the top. The horizontal and vertical movements emphasize the magnitude and exoticism of the journey, as does the seemingly unnecessary detail of the servant-girl who relays news of his arrival to her mistress. This minor interlude enhances the anticipation and excitement: after a lengthy and presumably arduous voyage the man arrives—but must now wait before he lays his eyes (and other body parts) on the object of his quest. After his failure to consummate the sex act, they both invert the vertical ascent by descending immediately to the ground [C1]. This rapid and precipitous descent symbolizes a fall

---

8 Kiddushin 39b and parallels.

to the depths of sin. Both characters then independently retrace the horizontal journey back to his home town and study house: first the man, and sometime later, the woman.

At the center of the story is the surreal beating the protagonist receives from the four fringes of his garment [C1]. Some interpreters suggest that all this happens only in a vision or in his imagination. But the beating is described in the standard narrative voice, and the Talmud is replete with other miraculous and supernatural events, as we have repeatedly seen. While the protagonist may be imagining the fringes as witnesses testifying about his sin in court, as implied by the simile and personification ("appeared to me *like* four witnesses"), the beating, at least in the fantastic and fictional world of the storyteller, actually takes place. Now there is something heroic in overcoming the temptation to sin, even if assisted by one's fringes, having come so far and so close to the goal. As a famous rabbinic adage puts it: "Who is a hero (גבור/*gibbor*)? He who overcomes his inclination" (Mishnah Avot 4:1).[9] Yet this episode portrays the man in a comic way: he sits on a golden couch, naked but for the four-cornered, fringed undershirt, with the most expensive courtesan in the world—and then cannot go through with "that act," the storyteller's delicate euphemism. His scrupulous observance of the commandment of the fringes, ostensibly high praise in the exposition, makes him ridiculous when attempting to consort with a harlot in her opulent den of iniquity.

After the man's sudden and unexpected withdrawal, the narrative focus shifts such that the harlot becomes the protagonist, demanding to know why the man desisted, soliciting his personal information, distributing her wealth, journeying to his abode, converting, and marrying him. If the man is a comic hero, this woman is a true heroine, exchanging her life of (extremely lucrative) sin, her affluence and splendor, for God and Torah.[10] What prompts this radical reversal in her way of life, in everything she is and does, this remarkable repentance? She has never been rejected before, and cannot fathom why this otherwise unimpressive client wrapped in a fringed garment resists her charms. She entertains the possibility that he has noticed a "blemish," perhaps a skin lesion or rash or bruise that she overlooked in her ablutions and preparations, which disgusted him and squelched all desire [D1]. To her, superficial appearances and externalities

9 Quoted in connection with the story and this context by Harvey, "The Pupil," 261.

10 Harvey makes this point nicely.

like the showy silver and gold furnishings are most important. But upon hearing his explanation she resolves to upend her life and everything she has known.

His explanation, as discussed above, presents the interpretation of the biblical passage about fringes in terms of a reward. And as noted, this passage is the very source that generated the basic contours of the story. This moment, too, is the pivot of the story, the shift in focus from the man's sin to the harlot's reform, which is adumbrated in the shift in the formulation of her oaths. She initially swears by the "Love-goddess of Rome," invoking her pagan deity to adjure the man to explain his abrupt halting of their proceedings [C2]. Certainly of all the gods and goddesses by which to swear, the love-goddess seems to fit this context! Upon hearing the man swear by the "[Temple] service," a classic Jewish formulation, she then emulates his oath to learn more about him [C3–C4]; here is the function of the verbal repetition in the oaths observed above. The parallel phrasing of the oaths—"By the Love-goddess of Rome, I will not leave you be" and "By the [Temple] service I will not leave you be"—underscores the change in her perspective. This marks the beginning of her spiritual journey to conversion, as she abandons her previous custom and adopts that of the new faith. The cold and hard ground on which she now sits contrasts with the luxurious and sumptuous golden couch, symbolizing the shift to the renouncement of her former way of life for a new one. Herein lies the significance of the wordplay on שכר/*sekhar* as wages/reward, which captures the shift in the harlot's life and worldview, as she trades the *sekhar* of her profession for the *sekhar* of the commandments.

She continues in her new path by donating one-third of her money to the poor, another narrative reversal from the accumulation of wealth through sin to the distribution of wealth through virtuous acts. That she pays "the monarchy," that is, the Roman government or local Roman officials, suggests that she has connections in high places, and evidently has provided services to influential magistrates. This datum adds another dimension to her elegant and splendiferous image, which has been constructed through her pricey fee, her reputation extending to distant lands, the gold and silver furnishings, and the maidservant who attends to her clients. She is both wealthy and connected, consorting with the powerful and aristocratic upper class who can afford the 400 gold coins she charges. There may also be the implication that she is "paying off" government officials, who may otherwise have sought to prevent her from absconding, either because they wish to continue to enjoy her charms, or, if they know her designs, because they object to her desertion to another people and faith. If so, then her choice is even more worthy of admiration, as it requires considerable courage and risks reprisal.

With the remaining third of her resources, she retraces her client's journey, traveling from "the cities by the sea" to the Land of Israel, to R. Ḥiyya's house of study, and requests the great sage convert her to Judaism. This movement completes the narrative reversal by which she abandons her house of prostitution for the house of study, replacing the house of sin with the house of Torah. The sage is cautious, questioning her motives, namely whether she lusts after a particular young man she has observed attending the school and is thus driven by carnal, rather than spiritual, concerns. This suspicion is particularly ironic given that the man had sought the woman for precisely that purpose, whereas her motives are completely pure. When she shows him the text, presumably also explaining how she came to possess it, recounting their (mis)adventure and her resolve to change her entire way of life, R. Ḥiyya immediately understands. She has indeed "set her eyes" on one of the students, but not for the unacceptable purpose that R. Ḥiyya suspected.[11] This woman desires not the man as much as his spiritual commitments, and also the anticipated divine rewards that ultimately motivated him, for which he resisted her this-worldly beauty.

The rabbi's response, "come forth and enjoy your acquisition" (לכי זכי במקחך), shows that R. Ḥiyya recognizes her sincerity and will facilitate the union through conversion and marriage. As we have noted, the deployment of this phrase, used elsewhere in the Talmud to confirm the bride's virginity, is particularly effective in underscoring the extent of her abandonment of her previous life and commitment to a new path. The rabbi essentially enhances her spiritual rebirth with a physical rebirth, communicating that she has made herself a new woman, body and soul, worthy of marriage to a rabbinical student.

This leads to the final reversal of the man marrying the (repentant) harlot, in the end consummating the relationship he had relinquished with the marital "acquisition" whom he had initially paid to acquire. Contributing to the reversal, she even brings the third of her wealth and the beds[12] that she retained of her property as a type of dowry. As

11 "Set eyes upon" is a phrase often used for sin or illicit purposes. See above, p. 166–7.

12 It is possible that "beddings" are meant, but the meaning is the same.

the story concludes: "Those beds that she prepared for him unlawfully, she prepared for him lawfully" [D3]. This happy ending may even be the continuation of the narrativization of the biblical passage, which envisions the result of the fringes, "Thus you (plural) shall be reminded to observe all commandments and to be holy (קדושים/*kedoshim*) to your God" (Numbers 15:40), perhaps playing on the rabbinic term for betrothal, קי־ דושין/*kiddushin*, from the same root. The couple ends up leading a pious life together, observing the commandments in the holiness of marriage.

In the conclusion, the storyteller brings to a climax the tension between this-worldly and other-worldly reward with a final rhetorical flourish [A′]. He capitalizes on the ironic reversal by which the man's other-worldly focus unexpectedly produces this-worldly recompense, and now adduces it as further evidence for that reward in the world to come. The argument is a type of "a fortiori" or "how much the more so" argument (קל וחומר/*kal va-ḥomer*): if observing the commandments produces a wonderful reward in this world (which is not necessarily promised, according to rabbinic theology), how much the more so should it produce an even more wonderful reward in the world to come (where such rewards are guaranteed): "I don't know how much," the storyteller confesses. But he obviously believes that it is a lot!

There are great rewards for studying talmudic stories in this world. And in the world to come, I don't know how much!

# APPENDIX
## Guide to the Main Works of Rabbinic Literature

### *Mishnah*

The earliest rabbinic work, the Mishnah is primarily a compendium of legal traditions attributed to sages who lived before 200 CE. According to rabbinic tradition, Rabbi Yehudah HaNasi (also known as Rabbi Judah the Prince or Judah the Patriarch) edited the Mishnah by selecting rabbinic traditions and organizing them topically. Although the Mishnah bears some affinity to a law code, it also includes scriptural interpretations, wisdom sayings, and a few stories. The term "mishnah" comes from the Hebrew verbal root ש-נ-י/*sh-n-y*, which means "to repeat," and refers to the process of orally repeating traditions in order to memorize them. The Mishnah contains six major divisions or orders, which in turn are divided into sixty-three smaller books known as tractates. Thus "Mishnah Shabbat 6:4" refers to the Mishnah, tractate Shabbat, chapter 6, paragraph 4.

### *Tosefta*

The Tosefta, meaning "supplement," is a companion to the Mishnah. It follows the Mishnah's structure, comprising the same six orders and sixty-three tractates. It too contains traditions attributed to sages who lived prior to 200 CE. Many traditions not included in the Mishnah were collected in the Tosefta. Some toseftan traditions appear to be variants of those found in the Mishnah, while others comment upon, complement, or supplement the Mishnah's rulings. The Tosefta is about 1.5 times the size of the Mishnah and was edited during the third century CE.

## *Tannaitic Midrashim*

The term "midrash" (from the root ש-ר-ד/*d-r-sh,* "search," hence also "interpret") refers both to individual scriptural interpretations (a midrash on Exodus 2:3) and to compilations of scriptural interpretations (books of midrash). The *tannaim* (singular, *tanna*) are the rabbis who lived prior to 200 CE, whose traditions are contained in the Mishnah and Tosefta. Tannaitic *midrashim* are those volumes of midrash containing the scriptural interpretations attributed to the *tannaim,* although the editing of these compilations took place somewhat later. There are seven extant tannaitic *midrashim,* which comment on substantial portions of Exodus, Leviticus, Numbers, and Deuteronomy. The most important and well known are the Mekhilta of R. Yishmael on Exodus, the Sifra on Leviticus, and the Sifrei on Numbers and Deuteronomy. The tannaitic *midrashim* include interpretations of both the legal and narrative portions of these biblical books.

## *Amoraic Midrashim*

The *amoraim* (singular, *amora*) are the rabbis who lived from 200 to 450 CE, whose traditions are contained in the Talmuds and in later midrashic compilations. As opposed to the tannaitic *midrashim,* which include a great deal of legal exegesis, the amoraic *midrashim* comment almost exclusively on the narrative portions of the biblical books. Many amoraic *midrashim* originated as sermons preached to audiences in synagogues. These works were edited in the Land of Israel in the fifth and sixth centuries CE. In this book I draw on the early amoraic *midrashim* Bereishit Rabbah and Vayikra Rabbah.

## *Yerushalmi*

The Yerushalmi or Jerusalem Talmud (also known as the Palestinian Talmud) is the exposition to the Mishnah produced by the sages who lived in the Land of Israel from 200 to 400 CE. *Talmud*, which means "study, instruction, teaching," follows the Mishnah's structure and primarily consists of explanations and discussions of its rulings. However, the Yerushalmi also includes biblical interpretation (midrash), records of court cases, stories, and sayings. Like the Mishnah and Tosefta, the Yerushalmi is divided into orders and tractates. Thus "Yerushalmi Peah 8:9 (21b)" designates the Yerushalmi's commentary to the mishnaic tractate Peah, chapter 8, paragraph 9, found on folio 21, column b in the first edition (Venice, 1523). There is Yerushalmi to thirty-nine of the Mishnah's sixty-three tractates.

## *Bavli*

The Bavli or Babylonian Talmud (or simply "the Talmud") is the great commentary on the Mishnah produced by the rabbinic sages of Babylonia from 200 to 700 CE. The Bavli, too, contains a variety of materials, including scriptural interpretations, records of court cases, folklore, liturgical texts, and stories. Jewish communities in the Middle Ages considered the Bavli to be the authoritative source of Jewish law and made study of the Bavli the cornerstone of the rabbinic curriculum. Consequently, the stories of the Bavli are generally among the best-known stories of rabbinic tradition. The Bavli, too, follows the order of the Mishnah, but is simply referred to by the folio number of the standard printed edition, for example, "Bavli Shabbat 34a." There is Bavli to thirty-six of the Mishnah's tractates.

# BIBLIOGRAPHY

Artman-Partock, Tali. "The Tale Type of the Repenting Prostitute: Between Rabbis and Church Fathers." *AJS Review* 42 (2018): 1–20.

Balberg, Mira. "Between Heterotopia and Utopia: Two Talmudic Journeys to Prostitutes." *Jerusalem Studies in Hebrew Literature* 22 (2008): 191–214 (Hebrew).

Bar-Asher Siegal, Michal. *Early Christian Monastic Literature and the Babylonian Talmud.* Cambridge: Cambridge University Press, 2013.

__________. *Jewish-Christian Dialogues on Scripture in Late Antiquity: Heretic Narratives of the Babylonian Talmud.* Cambridge: Cambridge University Press, 2019.

Barnes, T. D. "Christians and the Theater." In *Roman Theater and Society: E. Togo Salmon Papers I*, edited by William J. Slater, 161–80. Ann Arbor: University of Michigan Press, 1996.

Blackburn, Simon. *Ethics: A Very Short Introduction.* Oxford: Oxford University Press, 2001.

Boyarin, Daniel. *Intertextuality and the Reading of Midrash.* Indiana: Indiana University Press, 1990.

__________. *Carnal Israel: Reading Sex in Talmudic Culture.* Berkeley: University of California Press, 1993.

_________. "Homotopia: The Feminized Jewish Man and the Lives of Women in Late Antiquity." *differences: A Journal of Feminist Cultural Studies* 7 (1995): 41–81.

Calderon, Ruth. *A Bride for One Night: Talmud Tales*. Translated by Ilana Kurshan. Lincoln: University of Nebraska Press and Jewish Publication Society, 2014.

Cohen, Norman. "Structural Analysis of a Talmudic Story: Joseph-Who-Honors-The-Sabbaths." *Jewish Quarterly Review* 72 (1982): 161–77.

Cohen, Shaye J. D. "The Conversion of Antoninus." In *The Talmud Yerushalmi and Graeco-Roman Culture I*, edited by Peter Schäfer, 141–71. Tübingen: Mohr-Siebeck, 1998.

Doran, Robert. "The Martyr: A Synoptic of the Mother and Her Seven Sons." In *Ideal Figures in Ancient Judaism: Profiles and Paradigms*, edited by J. J. Collins and G. W. Nickelsburg, 189–221. Chico: CA: Scholars Press, 1980.

Faust, Shmuel. *Agadata: Stories of Talmudic Drama*. Tel Aviv: Dvir, 2011. (Hebrew)

Feintuch, Yonatan. "'Anonymous *Hasid'* Stories in Halakhic *Sugyot* in the Babylonian Talmud." *Journal of Jewish Studies* 43 (2012): 238–47.

_________. "The Aggada About R. Assi and His Mother." https://www.etzion.org.il/en/talmud/studies-gemara/midrash-and-aggada/aggada-about-r-assi-and-his-mother (2015).

_________. "The Talmudic Chassid and the Stone-Clearer, and Chassidic Tales (1)." https://www.etzion.org.il/en/talmud/studies-gemara/midrash-and-aggada/sippur-hachasid-vehamesakel-1 (12/2023).

Fisch, Menachem. "Bossy Matrons and Forced Marriages: Talmudic Confrontationalism and Its Philosophical Significance." *Open Philosophy* 3 (2020): 335–48.

Fonrobert, Charlotte Elisheva. "When Rabbis Weep: On Reading Gender in Talmudic Aggadah." *Nashim* 4 (2001): 56–83.

_________. "Plato in Rabbi Shimeon Bar Yohai's Cave (B. Shabbat 33B–34A): The Talmudic Inversion of Plato's Politics of Philosophy." *AJS Review* 31 (2007): 277–96.

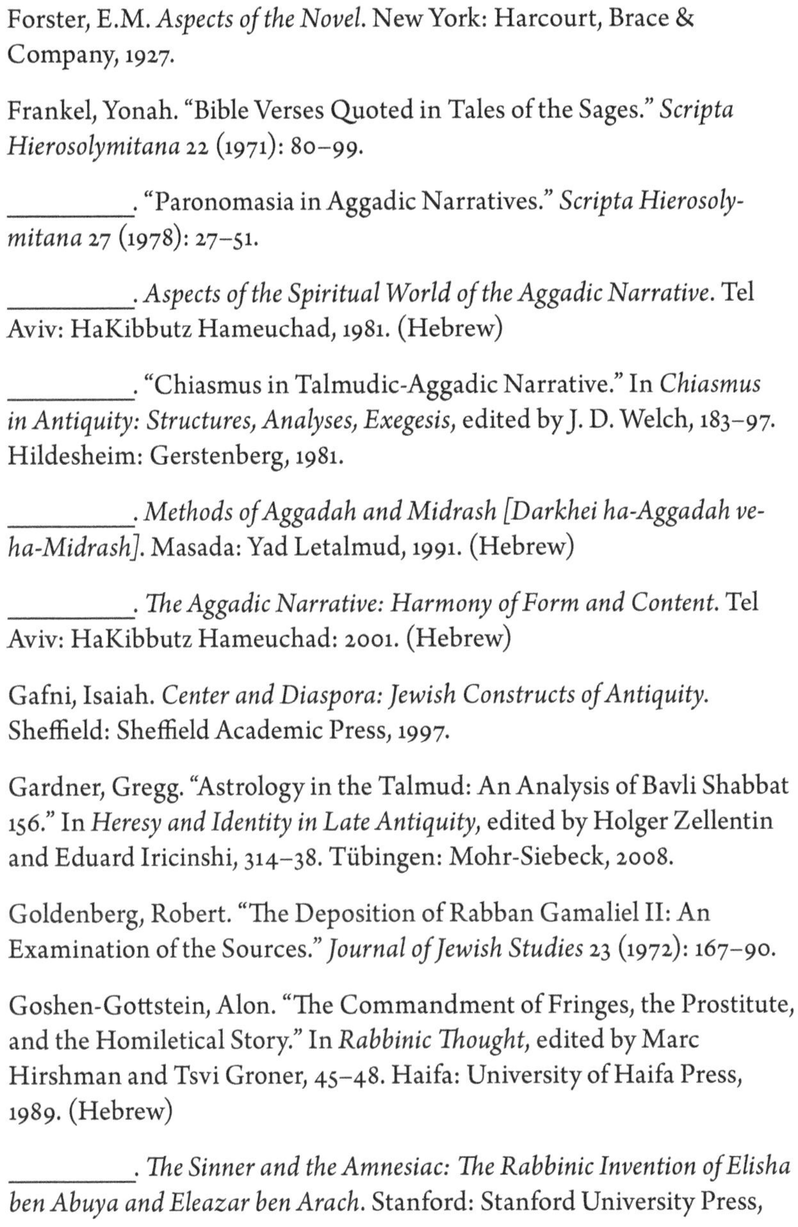


Forster, E.M. *Aspects of the Novel.* New York: Harcourt, Brace & Company, 1927.

Frankel, Yonah. "Bible Verses Quoted in Tales of the Sages." *Scripta Hierosolymitana* 22 (1971): 80–99.

_________. "Paronomasia in Aggadic Narratives." *Scripta Hierosolymitana* 27 (1978): 27–51.

_________. *Aspects of the Spiritual World of the Aggadic Narrative.* Tel Aviv: HaKibbutz Hameuchad, 1981. (Hebrew)

_________. "Chiasmus in Talmudic-Aggadic Narrative." In *Chiasmus in Antiquity: Structures, Analyses, Exegesis,* edited by J. D. Welch, 183–97. Hildesheim: Gerstenberg, 1981.

_________. *Methods of Aggadah and Midrash [Darkhei ha-Aggadah veha-Midrash].* Masada: Yad Letalmud, 1991. (Hebrew)

_________. *The Aggadic Narrative: Harmony of Form and Content.* Tel Aviv: HaKibbutz Hameuchad: 2001. (Hebrew)

Gafni, Isaiah. *Center and Diaspora: Jewish Constructs of Antiquity.* Sheffield: Sheffield Academic Press, 1997.

Gardner, Gregg. "Astrology in the Talmud: An Analysis of Bavli Shabbat 156." In *Heresy and Identity in Late Antiquity,* edited by Holger Zellentin and Eduard Iricinshi, 314–38. Tübingen: Mohr-Siebeck, 2008.

Goldenberg, Robert. "The Deposition of Rabban Gamaliel II: An Examination of the Sources." *Journal of Jewish Studies* 23 (1972): 167–90.

Goshen-Gottstein, Alon. "The Commandment of Fringes, the Prostitute, and the Homiletical Story." In *Rabbinic Thought,* edited by Marc Hirshman and Tsvi Groner, 45–48. Haifa: University of Haifa Press, 1989. (Hebrew)

_________. *The Sinner and the Amnesiac: The Rabbinic Invention of Elisha ben Abuya and Eleazar ben Arach.* Stanford: Stanford University Press, 2000.

Gray, Alyssa M. "The Power Conferred by Distance from Power: Redaction and Meaning in b. AZ 10a–11a." In *Creation and Composition: The Contribution of the Bavli Redactors (Stammaim) to the Aggada*, edited by Jeffrey L. Rubenstein, 23–70. Tübingen: Mohr-Siebeck, 2005.

Halbertal, Moshe. "Discipleship in Rabbinic Literature." In *Swimming Against the Current: Reimagining Jewish Tradition in the Twenty-First Century. Essays in Honor of Chaim Seidler-Feller*, edited by Shaul Seidler-Feller and David N. Myers, 67–94. Boston: Academic Studies Press, 2020.

Halevi, A. A. *Gates of Aggadah*. Tel Aviv: Devir, 1982. (Hebrew)

Hamel, Debra. *Trying Neaira: The True Story of a Courtesan's Scandalous Life in Ancient Greece*. New Haven: Yale University Press, 2003.

Harvey, Warren Zev. "The Pupil, the Harlot, and Fringe Benefits." *Prooftexts* 6 (1986): 259–64.

Hasan-Rokem, Galit. "An Almost Invisible Presence: Multilingual Puns in Rabbinic Literature." In *The Cambridge Companion to the Talmud and Rabbinic Literature*, edited by C. E. Fonrobert and M. S. Jaffee, 222–40. Cambridge: Cambridge University Press, 2007.

Hayes, Christine. "The 'Other' in Rabbinic Literature." In *The Cambridge Companion to the Talmud and Rabbinic Literature*, edited by C. E. Fonrobert and M. S. Jaffee, 243–69. Cambridge: Cambridge University Press, 2007.

Held, Shai. *Judaism Is About Love: Recovering the Heart of Jewish Life*. New York: Farrar, Straus and Giroux, 2024.

Herman, Geoffrey. *A Prince Without a Kingdom: The Exilarch in the Sasanian Era*. Tübingen: Mohr-Siebeck, 2012.

_________. "Insurrection in the Academy: The Babylonian Talmud and the Paikuli Inscription." *Zion* 79 (2014): 377–407. (Hebrew)

Hevroni, Ido. "A Tale of Two Sinners." *AzureOnline* 33 (2008): 93–112.

Ilan, Tal. "Matrona and Rabbi Jose: An Alternative Interpretation." *Journal for the Study of Judaism* 25 (1994): 18–51.

Jacobs, Martin. "Theatres and Performances as Reflected in the Talmud Yerushalmi." In *The Talmud Yerushalmi and Graeco-Roman Culture I*, edited by P. Schäfer, 341–44. Tübingen: Mohr-Siebeck, 1998.

Jacobson, Howard. "Ketiah Bar Shalom." *AJS Review* 6 (1981): 39–42.

Jospe, Raphael. "Hillel's Rule." *Jewish Quarterly Review* 81 (1990): 45–57.

Kehily, Mary Jane and Anoop Nayak. "'Lads and Laughter': Humour and the Production of Heterosexual Hierarchies." *Gender & Education* 9 (1997): 69–88.

Kiperwasser, Reuven. "Wives of Commoners and the Masculinity of the Rabbis: Jokes, Serious Matters, and Migrating Traditions." *Journal for the Study of Judaism* 48 (2017): 418–45.

_________. "What Is Hidden in the Small Box? Narratives of Late Antique Roman Palestine in Dialogue." *AJS Review* 45 (2021): 76–94.

Kosman, Admiel. "A Talmudic Detective." *Sifrut Aggadah* 2 (2004): 132–35. (Hebrew)

_________. "'Internal Homeland' and 'External Homeland': A Literary and Psychoanalytical Study of the Narrative of R. Assi and His Aged Mother." *Hebrew Studies* 46 (2005): 269–77.

_________. "On the Interpretation of the Story of the Student, the Harlot, and the Fringes." *Moed* 16 (2007): 61–74. (Hebrew)

_________. "R. Simeon ben Eleazar and the Offended Man: The Ugliness of a Haughty Scholar." *European Judaism* 40 (2007): 116–25.

_________. "The Woman's Spiritual Place in the Talmudic Story: A Reading of the Narrative of Mar Ukba and His Wife." In *Gender and Dialogue in the Rabbinic Prism*, translated by E. Levin, 29–62. Berlin: De Gruyter, 2007.

_________. "On the Use of the Protagonist's Name as a Literary Tool in the Talmudic Story in Gendered Contexts," in *Ve'eleh shemot: meḥkarim be'otsar hashemot hayehudiyim*. Volume 4, edited by A. Demsky, 51–80. Ramat Gan: Bar-Ilan University Press, 2011. (Hebrew)

Lieberman, Saul. *Greek in Jewish Palestine.* New York: Jewish Theological Seminary, 1942.

Lorberbaum, Yair. *Disempowered King: Monarchy in Classical Jewish Literature.* New York: Continuum, 2011.

Manekin-Bamberger, Avigail. "The Vow-Curse in Ancient Jewish Texts." *Harvard Theological Review* 112 (2019): 340–57.

Marcus, Yosef. "Tzitzit as a Marker of Identity: Analyzing the Story of the Fringe-Wearer and the Harlot in its Broader Literary Context." *Netuim* 19 (2014): 107–20. (Hebrew)

Meir, Ofra. "Editorial Influence on the Worldview of Aggadic Narrative." *Tura* 3 (1994): 74–83. (Hebrew)

__________. "The Historical Contribution of the Aggadot of the Sages in Light of the Aggadot of Rabbi and Antoninos." *Mahanayim* 7 (1994): 8–25. (Hebrew)

__________. *Rabbi Judah the Patriarch: Palestinian and Babylonian Portrait of a Leader.* Tel- Aviv: HaKibbutz Hameuchad, 1999. (Hebrew)

Meshel, Naphtali S. "Measure for Measure." *Jewish Quarterly Review* 114 (2024): 1–8.

Milgrom, Jacob. *The JPS Torah Commentary: Numbers.* Philadelphia: Jewish Publication Society, 1990.

Nadler, Jennifer. "Mar Ukba in the Fiery Furnace: A Meditation on the Tragedy of the Norm." *Law and Literature* 19 (2007): 1–13.

Newman, Hillel I. "Closing the Circle: Yonah Fraenkel, the Talmudic Story, and Rabbinic History." In *How Should Rabbinic Literature Be Read in the Modern World?*, edited by Matthew Kraus, 105–36. Piscataway, NJ: Gorgias Press, 2006.

Oppenheimer, Aharon. "The Attempt of Hananiah, Son of Rabbi Joshua's Brother, to Intercalate the Year in Babylonia." In *The Talmud Yerushalmi and Graeco-Roman Culture II*, edited by Peter Schäfer, 255–64. Tübingen: J. C. B. Mohr-Siebeck, 2000.

Rieser, Louis. *The Hillel Narratives: What the Tales of the First Rabbi Can Teach Us About Our Judaism*. Teaneck, NJ: Ben Yehudah Press, 2009.

Rovner, Jay. "Rav Assi Had This Old Mother': The Structure, Meaning, and Formation of a Talmudic Story." In *Creation and Composition: The Contribution of the Bavli Redactors (Stammaim) to the Aggada*, edited by Jeffrey L. Rubenstein, 101–24. Tübingen: Mohr-Siebeck, 2005.

_________. "Structure and Ideology in the Aher Narrative (bHag 15a and b)." *Jewish Studies, an Internet Journal* 10 (2012): 1–73.

Rubenstein, Jeffrey L. "Elisha ben Abuya: Torah and the Sinful Sage." *Journal of Jewish Thought and Philosophy* 7 (1998): 141–222.

_________. *Talmudic Stories: Narrative Art, Composition, and Culture*. Baltimore: Johns Hopkins University Press, 1999.

_________. *The Culture of the Babylonian Talmud*. Baltimore: Johns Hopkins University Press, 2003.

_________. *Creation and Composition: The Contribution of the Bavli Redactors (Stammaim) to the Aggada*. Edited by Jeffrey. L. Rubenstein. Tübingen: Mohr-Siebeck, 2005.

_________. "Talmudic Astrology: Bavli Šabbat 156a–b." *Hebrew Union College Annual* 78 (2007): 109–48.

_________. *Stories of the Babylonian Talmud*. Baltimore: Johns Hopkins University Press, 2010.

_________. *The Land of Truth: Talmud Tales, Timeless Teachings*. Nebraska: Jewish Publication Society and University of Nebraska Press, 2018.

_________. "The Story-Cycles of the Bavli: Part 1." In *Studies in Rabbinic Narratives: Volume 1*, edited by Jeffrey L. Rubenstein. Providence: Brown Judaic Studies, 2021: 227–80.

Schwartz, Daniel R. "2 Maccabees." In *Outside the Bible: Ancient Jewish Writings Related to Scripture*, edited by L. Feldman, J. Kugel, and L. Schiffman, 2854–56. Lincoln: University of Nebraska Press and Philadelphia: Jewish Publication Society, 2013.

Schwarzbaum, Haim. "The Hero Predestined to Die on His Wedding Day (AT 934B)." *Folklore Research Center Studies* 4 (1974): 223–35.

Shapira, Hayyim. "The Deposition of Rabban Gamaliel—Between History and Legend." *Zion* 64 (1999): 5–38. (Hebrew)

Shinan, Avigdor. "'Difficult as the Parting of the Red Sea', or What Has the Institution of Marriage To Do with the Parting of the Red Sea?" In *The Parting of the Red Sea*, edited by Avigdor Shinan and Yair Zakovitch, 23–37. Jerusalem: The Presidents Study Group on the Bible and the Sources of Judaism, 1997. (Hebrew)

Simon-Shoshan, Moshe. "A Doorway of Their Own: Female Ethos in Dialogue in the Talmuds." *Nashim* 35 (2019): 97–127.

Sokoloff, Michael. *A Dictionary of Jewish Palestinian Aramaic of the Byzantine Period*. Ramat Gan: Bar-Ilan University Press, 1990.

Sperling, David. "Aramaic Spousal Misunderstanding." *Journal of the American Oritental Society* 115 (1995): 205–9.

Spooner, W. A. "The Golden Rule." In *Encyclopedia of Religion and Ethics*, edited by James Hastings, 6:310–12. New York: Charles Scribner's Sons, 1914.

Stanzak, Steve. "Manipulating Play Frames: The Yo Momma Joke Cycle on YouTube." *Children's Folklore Review* 34 (2012): 7–32.

Stein, Dina. "The Untamable Shrew: Language and Women as Institutional Markers." *Jerusalem Studies in Hebrew Literature* 22 (2008): 243–61.

__________. "Linguistic Liaisons: Wives and Vows in the Babylonian Talmud (BT Nedarim 66a–b)." *Nashim* 35 (2019): 176–83.

Steinberg, Milton. *As a Driven Leaf*. New York: Behrman House, 1939.

Steinmetz, Devora. "Must the Patriarch Know 'Uqtzin? The Nasi as Scholar in Babylonian Aggada." *AJS Review* 23 (1998): 163–89.

Telushkin, Joseph. *Hillel: If Not Now, When?* New York: Nextbook, 2010.

Tropper, Amram. "On Condition That You Teach Me the Entire Torah While I Stand on One Foot: The Inception of a Story." In *Between Babylonia and the Land of Israel: Studies in Honor of Isaiah M. Gafni*, edited by Geoffrey Herman et al., 267–86. Jerusalem: Zalman Shazar Center, 2016. (Hebrew)

Valler, Shulamith. *Woman and Womenhood in the Stories of the Babylonian Talmud*. Translated by Betty Rozen. Atlanta: Scholars Press, 1999.

Wasserman, Mira Beth. *Jews, Gentiles, and Other Animals*. Philadelphia: University of Pennsylvania Press, 2017.

Weiss, Haim and Shira Stav. *The Return of the Missing Father: A New Reading of a Chain of Stories from the Babylonian Talmud*. Translated by Batya Stein. Philadelphia: University of Pennsylvania Press, 2022.

Weiss, Zeev. "Theatres, Hippodromes, Amphitheatres, and Performances." In *The Oxford Handbook of Jewish Daily Life in Roman Palestine*, edited by C. Hezser, 629. New York: Oxford University Press, 2010: 623–40.

Wojczuk, Tana. "How Shakespeare Paperbacks Made Me Want To Be a Writer," *New York Times Sunday Magazine* (June 7, 2020): 16.

Yassif, Eli. *The Hebrew Folktale: History, Genre, Meaning*. Translated by Jacqueline S. Teitelbaum. Bloomington: Indiana University Press, 1999.

Zeller, Tom. "These Artful Dodgers Doth Protest Too Much." In "Week in Review," *New York Times* (April 15, 2001): 5.

Ziolkowski, Jan. "Avatars of Ugliness in Medieval Literature." *The Modern Language Review* 79 (1984): 1–20.

Zuckier, Shlomo. "Cutting a Peace: A Holistic Analysis of the Ketiah bar Shalom Story," in *Studies in Rabbinic Narratives: Volume 2*, edited by Jeffrey L. Rubenstein, 243–64. Providence: Brown Judaic Studies, 2025.

# SOURCE INDEX

www.ingramcontent.com/pod-product-compliance
Ingram Content Group UK Ltd.
Pitfield, Milton Keynes, MK11 3LW, UK
UKHW041635190726
13854UKWH00006B/2511

9 781946 611109